Successful School Leadership

ALSO AVAILABLE FROM BLOOMSBURY

An Intellectual History of School Leadership Practice and Research, by Helen Gunter

Educational Leadership for a More Sustainable World, by Mike Bottery

Education in the Balance, by Raphael Wilkins

Leading Schools in Challenging Circumstances, by Philip Smith and Les Bell

Sustainable School Transformation, edited by David Crossley

Successful School Leadership

International Perspectives

EDITED BY
PETROS PASHIARDIS
AND OLOF JOHANSSON

Bloomsbury Academic
An imprint of Bloomsbury Publishing Plc

BLOOMSBURY
LONDON · OXFORD · NEW YORK · NEW DELHI · SYDNEY

Bloomsbury Academic

An imprint of Bloomsbury Publishing Plc

50 Bedford Square	1385 Broadway
London	New York
WC1B 3DP	NY 10018
UK	USA

www.bloomsbury.com

BLOOMSBURY and the Diana logo are trademarks of Bloomsbury Publishing Plc

First published 2016

British Library Cataloguing-in-Publication Data
A catalogue record for this book is available from the British Library.

ISBN:	HB:	978-1-4725-8637-7
	PB:	978-1-4725-8636-0
	ePDF:	978-1-4725-8639-1
	ePub:	978-1-4725-8638-4

Library of Congress Cataloging-in-Publication Data

Typeset by RefineCatch Limited, Bungay, Suffolk
Printed and bound in India

Contents

List of Contributors

Helene Ärlestig is an associate professor at the Centre for Principal Development, Umeå University, Sweden. Her research interest concerns organizational communication, pedagogical leadership and principals' role and work. She is involved in several international comparative studies about principals' leadership, for example the International Successful School Principal Project and International School Leadership Development Network. Ärlestig is convener for network 26 Educational Leadership in the European Educational Research Association. She is deputy director at the Centre for Principal Development at Umeå University. The Centre runs the National Principal Program which is compulsory for all newly appointed principals in Sweden. She teaches leadership at the National Principal Program as well as courses about quality assurance. Ärlestig has a background as a principal in compulsory schools.

Stefan Brauckmann is Professor of quality development and quality assurance in education at the Institute of Instructional and School Development (IUS) of the Alpen-Adria-University Klagenfurt, Austria. For more than ten years he was a research scientist at the Center for Research on Educational Governance of the German Institute for International Educational Research (DIPF) in Berlin. Dr Brauckmann participated as a researcher in several international comparative studies. His main academic fields and interests lie within framework conditions in the education system as well as the different governing mechanisms in educational administration which affect the development of quality assurance in education. He has published in international book series and peer-reviewed journals, and has given keynote presentations at international symposia and congresses. Furthermore, he was a visiting scholar at: the Institute PACE (Policy Analysis for California Education) of UC Berkeley, USA; and Stanford University, USA; the Open University of Cyprus; the University of Stellenbosch, South Africa; and the University of Umeå, Sweden. Brauckmann has also acted as a consultant on a large-scale school leadership needs assessment study on behalf of the Commonwealth Secretariat.

Yan Ni Annie Cheng is an assistant professor of the Department of Education Policy and Leadership and a research fellow of the Asia Pacific Centre for

Leadership and Change at the Hong Kong Institute of Education, Hong Kong. She has participated in the newly appointed principal programme since 2013. Her research interests cover various aspects in the fields of educational leadership and teacher education, including beginning principal leadership, social justice leadership and teacher leadership. She teaches a range of undergraduate and postgraduate courses.

Simon Clarke is professor and deputy dean in the Faculty of Education at The University of Western Australia, Australia, where he teaches, supervises and researches in the substantive field of educational leadership and management.

Lawrie Drysdale is a senior lecturer in educational leadership at the Graduate School of Education, The University of Melbourne, Australia. He has a background in teaching, human resource development, lecturing and research. His career spans over forty years in education. He coordinates postgraduate courses in educational management and teaches subjects in leadership, human resource management, marketing, school effectiveness and improvement. His research interests are in marketing in education, and successful school leadership, and he is a member of the International Successful School Principalship Project. Lawrie has written extensively in both academic and professional journals and is a member of the Australian Council for Educational Leaders. He was made a Fellow of the Victorian Branch in 1996, a National Fellow in 2012, and in 2014 was the recipient of the Hedley Beare Educator of the Year award.

Candido Alberto Gomes is professor of education at the Postgraduate Program in Education, Brasília Catholic University, Brazil, and was formerly legislative adviser at the Federal Senate and the National Constituent Assembly. He holds a masters degree in sociology and a PhD in education from the University of California, Los Angeles, USA. He is author of over 250 academic publications in many countries of the world, particularly on educational policies, education and work and educational financing.

David Gurr is an associate professor in educational leadership within the Melbourne Graduate School of Education at The University of Melbourne, Australia, and has a thirty-five-year background in secondary teaching, educational psychology, school supervision and research in educational leadership. He is a founding member of the International Successful School Principalship Project and the International School Leadership Development Network. He has more than 100 publications and has presented at more than 100 international conferences. David has been the vice-president of the Australian Council for Educational Leaders and past editor of *Hot Topics*, *Monograph* and *Leading and Managing*. He has received several honours from ACEL, including being awarded the National Presidential Citation in 2004, a national fellowship in 2006, the Hedley Beare Educator of the Year award in 2012 and the Gold Medal in 2014.

Philip Hallinger is a professor of educational management at Chulalongkorn University in Bangkok, Thailand. In 2014 he was awarded the Roald F. Campbell Lifetime Achievement Award for Distinguished Service in Educational Administration from the University Council for Educational Administration (USA) and the Excellence in Research Award from the American Educational Research Association. His research interests are in leadership effects, school improvement and leadership development.

Jan Heystek is currently the research professor for education leadership and management at the North-West University at Potchefstroom, South Africa, and was formerly an academic at the University of Pretoria and Stellenbosch University, South Africa. He works within the field of education, specifically with a focus on leadership, management and governance in schools and in the broader education system. The main focus of his work is about school leadership development and the relationship between the different role players to implement and enable quality education for all learners in developing and diverse contexts. Two books have been published under his editorship, *Human Resource Management in Education* and *People Leadership in Education*, along with numerous chapters in international books. Five doctoral and twenty-seven masters degree students have completed their research under his leadership and he has authored or co-authored more than thirty articles and presented numerous papers at national and international conferences.

Disraeli M. Hutton is a lecturer in the School of Education, Faculty of Humanities and Education, at the University of the West Indies at Mona, Jamaica. He holds a PhD in educational administration and supervision in higher education and a masters degree in supervisory management and training and development. His work experience spans both the private and the public sector, including teaching in the public school system for many years. Disraeli also taught at the College of Arts, Science and Technology, Jamaica (now the University of Technology, Jamaica), and he is a lecturer in the Human Resource Development programme currently being offered by the Department of Sociology, Psychology and Social Work, University of the West Indies, Jamaica. He also worked at Jamalco as the training director and at the HEART Trust/National Training Agency as chief technical director. He has done consultancy work with various government and private entities in the areas of training and education, programme design and implementation and production system evaluation, among others.

Stephen L. Jacobson is distinguished professor at the State University of New York at Buffalo USA, and the coordinator of educational administration programmes for the Graduate School of Education at the State University of New York, USA. He has also served as the associate dean for academic affairs and as chair of the Department of Educational Leadership and Policy. His current research interests include the reform of school leadership preparation and practice, and successful principal leadership in high-poverty schools. His 2011 book (co-edited with Rose Ylimaki), *U.S. and Cross-national Policies, Practices, and Preparation: Implications for successful instructional leadership, organizational learning, and culturally responsive practices*, addresses this research. He is past president of the University Council for Educational Administration and the Association for Education Finance and Policy. He is currently lead editor of the Taylor & Francis journal, *Leadership and Policy in Schools*, and co-editor of the Springer book series, *Policy Implications of Research in Education*.

Olof Johansson is professor of political science and director of the Centre for Principal Development at Umeå University, Sweden and an executive member on the board of governors of the Consortium for the Study of Leadership and Ethics in Education (CSLEE), a program center of the University Council for Educational Administration (UCEA) based at the University of Virginia (USA). In 2010 he received the Donald J. Willower Centre for the Study of Leadership and Ethics Award of Excellence in Research. His research interests are school leadership, principal training, school governance, school effectiveness, school improvement and values and ethics in relation to school leadership. He is working on four large research projects which all have international counterparts: The International Successful School Principalship Project; Structure, Culture, Leadership: Prerequisites for Successful Schools?; National Policy meets Local Implementation Structures and European Policy Network on School Leadership. In 2014/15 he was the principal researcher for the government of Sweden in relation to 'Principals' working conditions and pedagogical leadership'.

Wowek S. Kearney is associate professor of educational leadership at Texas A&M, San Antonio, USA. He has experience as a school administrator and has led regional consortiums of campus and central office administrators from across South Central Texas. He has research interests in the areas of principal influence, change orientations, school culture and climate, and the confluence of administration, ethics, and emotionally intelligent leadership. His work has been published in the *International Journal of Educational Management*, the *Journal of School Public Relations*, and *Educational Management Administration and Leadership*.

Tai Hoi Theodore Lee is a lecturer in the Department of Education Policy and Leadership at the Hong Kong Institute of Education, Hong Kong. He completed his PhD at the University of Waikato, New Zealand. His research interests include teacher leadership, teacher professional development and assessment in learning.

Magali de Fátima Evangelista Machado is an instructor at the Postgraduate Program in Education at Brasília Catholic University, Brazil, where she earned a masters and a PhD degree in education. She has extensive experience as a basic education teacher at the State Secretariat of Education, Federal District. Besides several academic articles, her first book, jointly published by Líber and the UNESCO Chair of Youth, Education and Society, focuses on successful schools for underprivileged students.

Raj Mestry is professor in the Department of Education Leadership and Management at the University of Johannesburg, South Africa. He serves on the executive of the Education Association of South Africa.

Paul Miller is reader in education at Brunel University London, UK. Prior to that he was professor of educational leadership and management in the School of Graduate Studies, Research and Entrepreneurship at the University of Technology, Jamaica. He is a director in the Institute for Educational Administration and Leadership-Jamaica (IEAL-J) and a member of the Board of the Commonwealth Council for Educational Administration and Management (CCEAM). Paul has an evolving research profile in the area of comparative school leadership practices.

Elizabeth T. Murakami is a professor and director of programmes in educational leadership in the College of Education and Human Development at Texas A&M, San Antonio, USA. She earned her masters and doctorate at Michigan State University. Before becoming a professor, she worked in American international schools for fourteen years. Her research focuses on successful school leadership and social justice at national and international levels, including research on leadership dynamics and identity, gender, race and the academic success of Latin populations from P-20 to advanced professions in education. She has published in journals such as the *Journal of School Leadership*, *Educational Management Administration and Leadership* (EMAL), the *Journal of School Administration*, *Academe*, the *Journal of Studies in Higher Education* and the *International Journal of Qualitative Studies in Education*. Her latest co-edited book focuses on a social justice leadership agenda for P-20 professionals and is entitled *Educational Leaders Encouraging the Intellectual and Professional Capacity of Others: a social justice agenda*.

Georgia Pashiardi is a principal in a public elementary school in Cyprus. She graduated from the University of Texas at Austin, USA, and holds a diploma in teaching, a BSc in education, and a Masters degree with a major in elementary and special education. In March 2000 she received her doctorate in school pedagogy and leadership from the Faculty of Philosophy (Department of Education) at the Aristotle University in Thessaloniki, Greece. Her research interests lie in the areas of pedagogical leadership, teaching methodology, effective schools, organization and management of the classroom, and school climate. She participates and presents her research work at international conferences on a regular basis. She is the author of a book on school climate and her articles have been published in refereed international journals.

Petros Pashiardis is a professor of educational leadership at the Open University of Cyprus. He has worked and lectured in many countries including Great Britain, India, New Zealand, Greece, Germany, South Africa and the United States. At various periods he was invited to be a visiting associate research scientist at the Texas A&M University. He has also been a visiting professor at the University of Pretoria in South Africa, and a visiting scholar at the University of Stellenbosch, South Africa, as well as a visiting professor at the Centre for Principal Development, Umeå University, Sweden. He is also an external examiner for doctoral dissertations for universities in Australia, England, India and South Africa. For the period 2004–8, Professor Pashiardis was president of the Commonwealth Council for Educational Administration and Management (CCEAM). During his travels as president of the CCEAM, he collaborated extensively with CSOs in the areas of school leadership and educational policy, training school leaders and creating school leadership organizations in various countries around the Commonwealth in an effort to contribute towards the attainment of the Millenium Development Goals (MDGs), as they relate to improving equality of opportunity for education for all. In 2008 he co-edited the *International Handbook on the Preparation and Development of School Leaders*, together with Jacky Lumby and Gary Crow, published by Routledge, Taylor & Francis. In 2014 his new book, *Modeling School Leadership Across Europe: In Search of New Frontiers*, was published by Springer Publications. His research interests are in leadership effects on student achievement and school improvement, and leadership development, as well as teacher and school principal evaluation.

Elson Szeto is an assistant professor in the Department of Education Policy and Leadership and a research fellow of the Asia Pacific Centre for Leadership and Change at the Hong Kong Institute of Education, Hong Kong. He has a dual research focus on educational leadership and higher education teaching and learning. Recently, he has been working with researchers from over twenty countries on school leadership development through international collaboration. Elson has coordinated principal preparation programmes at the Institute. He also teaches undergraduate and postgraduate courses.

Alexandre Ventura was formerly Portuguese Deputy Minister of Education and is now a professor at the University of Aveiro, Portugal, a researcher and a prolific writer, credited with a wide range of publications. He is a versatile speaker on educational issues and has given many public lectures and presented papers at a large number of seminars and conferences in twenty countries. He has strong international interests and connections and is an international consultant on educational issues.

Allan David Walker is Joseph Lau Chair professor of international educational leadership, dean of the Faculty of Education and Human Development, and director of the Asia Pacific Centre for Leadership and Change at the Hong Kong Institute of Education, Hong Kong. Allan has published extensively on educational administration and leadership, and leadership development and learning. His work also explores the relationship between culture and leadership. Allan serves on the editorial boards of the top-ranked journals and has published over 300 books and articles with international publishers and in the world's most prestigious academic journals. He is co-editor of the *Journal of Educational Administration*. His recent research focuses on expanding knowledge of school leadership in Chinese and other Asian societies and disseminating this internationally. Allan has acted as a consultant/adviser on large-scale research and development activities in more than fifteen countries. He has also won more than twenty-five competitive research and development grants.

Helen Wildy is professor and dean of the Faculty of Education at The University of Western Australia, Australia. She researches and publishes extensively in the field of educational leadership and school improvement.

INTRODUCTION

What Is Successful and Effective School Leadership?

Petros Pashiardis and Olof Johansson

Introductory comments

School leadership issues are becoming increasingly debated and explored in an international and comparative context, due to the changing context of education. Currently, school leadership has been gaining growing attention from educational policy makers, as research evidence indicates that the principal's role is crucial for improving students' academic achievement (e.g. Hoy, 2012; Kythreotis et al., 2010; Marzano et al., 2005; Nihlfors & Johansson, 2013; Pashiardis, 2014). As a result, the various stakeholders have increased their expectations from school leaders demanding, for instance, higher academic results and performance standards. However, despite the changing roles and higher expectations of school leaders, it seems that most receive little formal or structured preparation for the job. One example of a country with extended in-service training of principals is Sweden. The Swedish training on the job goes on for three years and must be finished before the principal's fourth year in the position. There is a wide agreement about the need to have school leaders who exhibit the capacity to improve the quality of teaching and learning that takes place in their schools, thus creating what has come to be known in the literature as 'successful and effective school leaders' (Brauckmann & Pashiardis, 2011; Merchant et al., 2012). Thus, during recent years, many countries have come to realize the importance of investing in school leadership support systems. Policy makers in Europe, North America and Australasia have launched programmes designed to support leadership development in education.

At the same time, school leaders' roles and responsibilities are being reconceptualized. School leaders are not limited to bureaucratic functions, as used to be the case, but on the contrary they have an increasing repertoire of roles and responsibilities, such as being the pedagogical or the entrepreneurial leader of the school, or taking charge of creating the necessary vision and structures for the school to improve in a safe environment (Moos et al., 2011). However, the international community of school leadership researchers has been using the terms 'successful' and 'effective' interchangeably and with not much agreement as to what these two terms really mean in a particular context.

Actually, what successful and effective mean seems to depend on the degree and level of (1) centralization/decentralization of the educational system of a specific country as well as on (2) the accountability and evaluation mechanisms in place and (3) the ability of parents to choose schools for their children (Brauckmann & Pashiardis, 2011; Hoy, 2012).

Thus, since the terms successful and effective are used interchangeably in the international literature, a core purpose of this book is to define and provide substance and content for these two terms from an international/regional perspective, as they have been developed in the various continents and regions of the world for which the authors are writing about. Therefore, as there is no universally accepted definition of what constitutes successful and effective, we will look at this issue from an international/comparative perspective.

In essence, the effort in this book is to provide various points of view from around the world of what constitutes successful and effective schools and leaders and not to begin with a 'homogenized' idea of what these two terms mean. Moreover, we will not try to discover a universally accepted definition of these terms, as they still mean different things to different researchers and practitioners. Actually, we are hopeful that the differences in perspectives and indeed definitions of these concepts will enrich the book, as this is a major purpose of it and this chapter in particular.

More specifically, we realize that successful and effective school leadership is enormously varied in its conceptual foundations depending on where researchers and practitioners live and work, as well as where they are receiving their epistemological influences from. Thus, in this introductory chapter we are tackling the necessity for this book; that is, the necessity for us to comprehend the richness of the current literature on successful and effective school leadership and to use it as a guiding framework for both the local development of leaders into successful careers and for mutually supporting the development of school systems throughout the globe, to become successful and effective educational systems. Therefore, the main purpose of this chapter is to examine perspectives of success and effectiveness from a historical and critical point of view in order to provide a brief current synthesis of the literature from a critical and international-comparative perspective. The need for indigenous views on what constitutes successful and effective is central as well, since the issue of what constitutes successful and effective school leadership is increasingly becoming a global debate. To begin with, we should state at the outset that we consider the term 'successful' as a more inclusive term, a kind of an umbrella term, which includes effectiveness as well. However, this does not mean that the term 'successful' is a substitute for effective.

In essence, is successful about putting the right systems and structures in place and improving on them, so that we can get the necessary results that are required (that is, being effective)? In sum, is successful more about *processes* for good results and effective more about results? Additionally, most of the time we also see a connection in the literature between affective and efficient use of resources in order to get the best possible results, which is another aspect of the distinction between successful and effective.

Successful school leaders and successful schools: a brief historical account

A successful school is one that can facilitate mobility in a society. In effect, through the school everybody gets a chance to develop irrespective of the social class they come from; the '*social class ceiling*' can be broken within a successful school. This is done through the creation of the processes and putting the systems in place, thus creating something like a springboard from where everybody can jump onto educational processes that might lead to success for the individual and all fellow students.

This is one of the reasons why, in the Swedish education system, for instance, lunch (and in some schools breakfast) is provided for free to all students in all schools so that there is an equal treatment of all and so that society can guarantee that all students have their physical needs taken care of, as a necessary prerequisite for being able to participate in the educational process on an equal footing. To make that possible, even books and writing materials are provided for free. Further, the argument is that if everybody gets a free lunch and breakfast, nobody can know whether only the poor and needy get it, and in this way we do not jeopardize the dignity of any student. In contrast, in Cyprus, only the needy get breakfast and sometimes lunch. This makes it easier for students to be discriminated against, and to not be treated on an equal footing by their peers. Because of this probability, there are many instances where school principals in Cyprus provide free breakfast to needy students 'covertly', so that these students are not identified by their peers in their school, in order to avoid possible issues of discrimination.

Thus, another important issue for the delimitation of what is successful and what is effective is how resources are distributed at the school level. Perhaps, in order to be successful and effective for all its students, a school needs to redistribute its monies and other resources *unevenly* among the various subsets of the student body, and this kind of distribution may cause some unrest among parents. In more concrete terms, what if the school decides to provide more resources to the more needy children, and then the parents of middle- and upper-class students are unhappy and do not agree with this redistribution? What if they believe that their children are being treated unfairly and do not get what they deserve as taxpayers? These parents need to accept their school's policy; otherwise, there will be unrest and dissatisfaction within a group of parents. In short, Aristotle's dictum is very useful here: the greatest inequality is the equalization of unequals. That is, treating unequal entities as equal produces injustices.

It is interesting to note that more and more of the middle/upper class in Sweden are sending their children to private/independent schools because (probably) they do not like the redistribution as described above which is happening in the public schools in more visible and tangible ways, and they believe that there is a certain injustice being inflicted upon their children. But it could also be a sign of mistrust. Parents mistrust the schools to have the capacity to create success in the public school environment. In short, we need to ask ourselves, what is the threshold at which parents and society at large will accept some income and resource redistribution and when will they say, 'Enough is enough, and I don't accept this policy any more'? Therefore, defining these issues of context and resource redistribution as well as finding out the minimally acceptable threshold are important elements in the effort to critically examine the concepts of successful and effective schools; or one could say that the acceptance of high redistribution is linked to success. We can have a high redistribution policy for schoolchildren from lower social classes as long as we can show success for all.

Effective school leaders and effective schools: a brief historical account

School effectiveness research

In the field of educational research, the tradition of school effectiveness research (SER) has been expanding in the last forty to fifty years. The first phase of SER began in the early 1970s, mainly in the USA, as a reaction to the pessimistic findings of the congressionally mandated study which was carried out by Harvard Professor James Coleman and his colleagues, known as the Coleman Report (Coleman et al., 1966). The original title of this report was *Equality of Educational Opportunity*. Coleman was interested in the educational opportunities that were available to different racial and ethnic groups in the schools of America. The research was massive and analysed the results of standardized tests on ability and achievement for 645,000 students all over the USA. The research results were used to relate school resources to student achievement. The main (and disappointing for the schools) conclusion was that schools do not really make a difference in students' achievement. Based on this result, which was indeed disheartening for schools, schooling, teachers and school leaders, researchers began an effort to find out if there are indeed schools that are effective with their students irrespective of where they come from, their socioeconomic status (SES) or even against the odds. Some schools were indeed found to do just that: they were effective with student achievement irrespective of the students' socioeconomic background and in spite of the context from which they came. This is a very interesting result and one that tells us that the expectations that are put on schoolchildren by teachers are of central importance when it comes to raising standards of teaching and students' outcomes.

Researchers began to look deeply into what these schools were doing that made them effective with all their students. Therefore, the initial phase of SER was mostly involved with case study schools which were examined in order to find out the correlates of their effectiveness. Several important factors were found to be in place in these schools, such as high expectations from students and teachers; excellent school leadership; excellent teachers who cared about the impact they were having on their students; a climate conducive to teaching and learning; and very strong ties with the parents and the community of the schools.

However, researchers wanted to find out if these effective correlates existed in other schools and if larger numbers of teachers and school leaders shared them as well. Thus, the second phase of the SER studies began in the mid-1980s. This was the era when researchers attempted to utilize new statistical techniques that took into consideration the hierarchical structure of educational systems, such as multi-level and multivariate models making it possible for all of the main school effectiveness variables to be included in the equations and the various models that were constructed. During this phase of SER as well as the first phase, the emphasis was mostly on procedural grounds, i.e. what were the processes utilized which made these schools so effective in their results? The pure interest on mainly results, outcomes and student achievement was indeed intensified later on during the 1990s and likewise into the current era.

Effective school leadership

One of the main school effectiveness variables researched in the literature is, of course, school leadership. Several researchers investigated the relationship between school leadership and student achievement through various models, such as the direct model, the reciprocal model and the indirect model (Kythreotis et al., 2010; Hallinger & Heck, 1998). The topic is still very much the favourite object of investigation in many parts of the world. A recent attempt to explore school leadership effectiveness and its effects on student achievement is provided in a book by Pashiardis, published by Springer Publications in 2014. In this book, an in-depth description of the EU-funded LISA (Leadership Improvement for Student Achievement) project is provided, where the main aim was to explore how leadership styles, as conceptualized in the complex dynamism of the Pashiardis-Brauckmann Holistic Leadership Framework, directly or indirectly affect student achievement at the lower secondary level of education in seven European countries. In its methodological design the study utilized a mixture of research methods and collaborative action research shared by practising school leaders and researchers. As Pashiardis and Brauckmann (2008) claim, the quantitative analyses stemming from confirmatory factor analysis and structural equation models (SEMs) identified five robust underlying dimensions of effective leadership styles across the seven participating European countries, namely England, Germany, Hungary, Italy, Norway, Slovenia and the Netherlands. After the completion of the research on the various components of the Pashiardis-Brauckmann Holistic Leadership Framework, they began putting it together so as to begin creating a *leadership cocktail mix*. It should be remembered that in this project, *leadership* was treated as a multi-level and multidimensional construct which may affect school and student variables but is also likely to be influenced by contextual variables (Pashiardis, 2014).

The centrepiece of the framework became the *leadership radius* which is the action area of the school leader, as the central figure within the school. This action area is manifested when school leaders perform their duties through five main styles of leadership as follows: (1) instructional style, (2) structuring style, (3) participative style, (4) entrepreneurial style and (5) personnel development style. Each leadership style consists of specific behaviours and practices which are likely to be exhibited by school principals. However, it is stressed that the leadership styles exist and are operationalized not just as they are perceived to be exercised by school leaders themselves, but also as they are perceived by teachers and other types of personnel working at the school, as well as students, parents and other stakeholders (both internal and external to the school). Thus, the exercised styles or the 'styles-in-use' are as perceived by the school leaders as well by other employees at the school. These styles constitute the main vehicle through which school leaders operate and exhibit their public behaviour. The five leadership styles are not discrete, but rather there is a degree of overlap among them, and thus 'hybrid' styles begin to emerge as well (Pashiardis, 2014).

Indeed, these preliminary results constitute enrichment in the grounding of more hypotheses and theoretical ideas as well as professional development for both school principals and researchers in the area of effective school leadership. However, it is further stressed that the future of the study of school leadership and its effects on student achievement is not simply more complex statistical analyses and large international studies. The way forward for the years to come is to advance through a study of the unique characteristics of the context of each educational system, its history, culture and local needs.

Therefore, it is increasingly acknowledged that school leaders do not operate in a vacuum. On the contrary, their actions greatly depend on their perceptions of the particular context in which they operate (Bredeson et al., 2011). Moreover, school leaders' actions are influenced by context and, at the same time, they try to influence context to their benefit. In essence, what we are arguing here is that the quest for leadership effectiveness can be better conducted at the local level, but with a global view. On the local level, effectiveness often means keeping to the budget and success is more linked to having a good climate in the school and parents that are appreciative of the school. The concrete everyday realization of school leadership has to take the context into account, as leadership is always context-specific. In general, leadership is dependent on and limited by the context. One underestimated factor here is the governing chain from national to local policy. In Sweden we can see that the local school owner is too friendly and exercises too little control in their leadership of the individual schools (Holmgren et al., 2013). It is a reciprocal relationship which seems to operate rather like osmosis (Pashiardis, 2014). It should be stressed that, by context, we really mean the 'immediate' surroundings of the school, as perceived by school leaders and not some remote national context which oftentimes leaves them 'unaffected'. More specifically, the main interest lies in examining the leaders' perceptions of their context and how this interplay produces the best leadership cocktail mix of effective leadership behaviours and practices for school success for all children. For example, is it 20 per cent of the instructional style and 50 per cent of the participative style that a leader has to adopt in order to be most effective within a particular context? And then, which specific behaviours and practices make up these percentages for each style (Pashiardis, 2014)?

Thus, school leaders need to be able to understand the complexity of the system and the complexity of the self. They need to be familiar with the potential 'stumbling blocks' that may exist (both within the self and within the context) and how these obstacles can become challenges that they will need to overcome. School leadership must shape the school and its context so that the teachers who work there can then ideally be more effective in supporting their pupils in order to achieve better learning outcomes. Thus, the quest for effective school leaders and effective schools continued into the modern era by trying to find out both the processes and the desired outcomes in order to have effective schools, but primarily the focus in SER is still on achieving the end results for all students.

Effective schools

Even the definition of what constitutes an effective school became the product of the degree to which the objectives of the school were achieved and the extent to which targeted problems were resolved. The term effectiveness, as used in our context, is determined without reference to costs, but, at the same time, effective leaders do not waste their resources on unattainable goals. They set realistic goals and prioritize them in order to achieve them. At the same time, when one strives for effectiveness, the processes or the means through which one achieves this are not considered as important as long as one can achieve one's goals. The mission is to achieve the targets as set by the school. Moreover, the definition of an effective school during the current era has acquired some new content in that an effective school is the school which can prove that in its classes there is *quality* and *equality*. The definition of *quality* is that the school has good results, or the best possible results, for its students at a minimally acceptable level; the educational system decides what results are important (academic, citizenship, affective, a combination of these, etc.) and the minimally acceptable level that these are considered good enough in a particular country/society. *Equality* means that the various academic achievements are equitably distributed among the various subsets of the student population of the school. That is, the school teaches and educates its students irrespective of their SES and/or where they come from or which family they belong to or their ethnic and religious background.

Another important issue in this debate is the direction of movement of the successful and effective continuum, which started from the macro, and increasingly has been moving towards the micro level. Thus, as the research on these issues began in the 1970s, 1980s and part of the 1990s, there was an attempt to *decompose* the big picture and move into the individual players of what constitutes successful and effective schools in the late 1990s and in the current era. Thus the direction of this movement has been in the way indicated by the arrows:

Context ——→ School ——→ Class ——→ Student ——→

During the examination of the factors that make up successful and effective schools, researchers began looking at the context of the school (at the national as well as the local level), and thus describing the factors that would make it more successful from a contextual point of view (especially SES context variables, as influenced by the Coleman Report). Then, the focus and interest shifted to the school factors. Which are those school factors that can create an effective and successful school? After this, the researchers began to look more into the classroom where the most important aspects of the teaching and learning processes take place. Finally, the individual student became the object of research in order to find out how we can best influence a student in order to become an effective learner. Through the renewed interest in the student, this new angle shifted again to the characteristics of the individual student as well as the student's family and their background. The authors believe that the reverse process is beginning to take shape during our era, but more on this in a later section of this chapter.

Context as the bridge between success and effectiveness

The importance of context was highlighted earlier in this chapter. Moreover, during the discussions and explorations about successful and effective schools, the issue of what is more important, process or products/outcomes, came up constantly. That is, the main questions with which researchers have been concerned are: Are process and product equally important? How are they associated with success and effectiveness? Is context, then, the bridge between process and product? The notion here is that even if one focuses on the product (which is the current tendency in SER), process is important and even more so is context. At the same time, we need to think and examine these two notions (process-product) from the students' perspective: What if their individual (home) context is NOT conducive to learning? What if they do not have a private room/office in their house to complete their homework? Then, should homework be completed at school where all students have the same opportunities and an environment which is conducive to learning? Should we not give homework to students because perhaps their home environment and their parents cannot really help them grow academically, in the same ways as other parents and homes who can? So context (not just from the school's point of view, but from the student's point of view as well) is very important in terms of how we define successful and effective schools.

By studying context then, are we really striving to close the gap between processes and product? What is context for each individual student? Can schools make up for the deficiencies of a student's individual context? Is that not the whole essence of successful and effective schools? Following on from this, are schools able to fill in for the deficiencies of society at large and make up for some of the socioeconomic backgrounds from which students come? Is this possible (realistic and fair for schools to take on their shoulders) or are schools getting themselves into a trap which really is 'mission impossible' and will only result in their being blamed for all the ills of society? So, depending on the context (its current state) one can talk more of successful or more of effective.

Successful and effective schools: do they mean the same thing to different people?

From the above discussion, we return to the following questions once more: What is success? Is it related to effectiveness? Is effectiveness better measured as related to academic results or is it better to use other criteria? Does 'success' deal more with procedural issues and is effectiveness more related to the end result? Would this 'division of labour' be fairer and more justified if we were to stress the fact that a successful school is one that institutionalizes the right processes in order to achieve desired objectives and thus become effective?

Going a step further, could the notion of equality (as described earlier) be tied to a successful school (i.e. it is more of a process towards a goal), and the notion of quality (a minimally acceptable achievement for all) be tied to an effective school? That is, could we say that a school is effective because it has quality results at (at least) a minimum acceptable level (however they are measured) for a number of its students (how many students? All? Only a part of the student body?)? And if along the way the processes to achieve these results are equitable and they lead to fair treatment of all students, does this make it a successful school? On the other hand, could we say that an effective school is the one that produces better results which are evenly distributed to its sub-populations? That is, the school is effective with its student population irr   ive of their SES, gender, ethnic/immigrant background, etc.?

‑tioned previously, historically, SER started by closely examining ‑hrough which a school was trying to educate its students. Now, is more towards the *products* (results), and therefore there is en the two 'Ps' of this movement on a continuum. The will probably reach equilibrium between these two ‑nd product.

Discussion and concluding comments

Finally, an important theme that we need to come to terms with is the probability that the issues of quality and equality are conflicting as goals to be achieved. That is, the more one strives for quality, the less equality there will be and the more one strives for equality the less quality there will be. If this is true, what should schools strive for? Are we not successful in public education because we are striving to achieve antithetical or contradictory and conflicting goals? How much of each of the two concepts should a society achieve in order to be balanced in the provision of education opportunities to its citizenry? The answer is of course that we should strive for quality but at the same time understand that equality does not mean equal for all. Equality can *never* mean the same for all because we as individuals have different needs. Effective redistribution is the key to equality for all and also to success for all students.

Moreover, currently, the focus of research interest on successful and effective schools is being reversed. As previously mentioned, during the preceding decades, the movement was towards a decomposition of the whole or the 'big picture' to the individual element or cell (the student). Currently, we are moving away from the student and back into the classroom, and then back into the school, and from the school we are moving towards the national educational policy context in order to reconstruct the big picture and start the recomposing process of what constitutes an effective and successful school and classroom and in what kind of environment.

The effort has been to shift the blame about whose fault it is when students, schools and educational systems are not successful. Thus, what was presented before is probably a process of shifting the blame as follows:

Context ⟶ School ⟶ Class ⟶ Student

Meaning shifting the blame to:

Politicians ◄— Principals ◄— Teachers ◄— Parents/students

Thus, societies and other stakeholders have blamed parents and students for the failures of the education system. The process is now beginning its reverse course: the parents/students have begun to shift the blame for less quality of education and poor student achievement to teachers. The teachers will then shift the blame to the school leadership, that is the principals and the rest of the management team, and the school leadership will begin again the process of blaming the politicians and the structures they impose on the schools, with less funding and more stringent accountability processes which make it an impossible task to educate the children. In sum, due to shrinkir resources, politicians and education systems and societies are a⁻'

more with less. The race to the bottom is an unequal one and the blame is shifted towards politicians. Perhaps this will mean a paradigm shift in order to find more equitable and redistributive ways of enhancing educational success and effectiveness.

It is increasingly obvious that more research concerning the needs of educational leaders within a specific cultural context is definitely necessary in order to prepare successful and effective school leaders. This kind of research, as Brauckmann and Pashiardis (2011) suggest, should be intensive, diagnostic and developmental in nature, in order to predict the needs of, and develop new approaches to, successful and effective educational leadership. This is what we hope will be achieved through this book and the various chapters from different continents and areas around the world. Such a book should be valuable, as:

> there is no single model of leadership that could be easily transferred across different school-level and system-level contexts. The specific contexts in which schools operate may limit a school leader's room for manoeuvring, or provide opportunities for different types of leadership. Depending on the school contexts in which they work, school leaders face very different sets of challenges.

> OECD, 2008: 20

Approaches to school leadership policy need to be based on careful consideration of the contexts in which schools operate. It should be borne in mind that policy initiatives that work well in one country cannot necessarily be transferred across national borders. But the so-called 'governing chain' from national politics down to the school level must be worked on more intensively. Today we see very high aspirations set in school laws but the resources provided are not adjusted to the aspirations, which makes it very difficult for principals and teachers (Johansson, 2015). Moreover, *depending on the country's stage of development as well as on the education system's phase of evolution in the different contextual domains, different definitions of success and effectiveness will be applicable.* At the same time, a regrouping of c⌐ ⌐ntries and regions around the world can tell us more about the existing ⌐isting contextual balance of the education system (is the quality of ⌐onal governance cocktail mix constraining or liberating school ⌐gards to their development? What does the best mix probably ⌐ver, based on this comparative analysis, we will probably be ⌐xtent to which contextual regulations are reflected in the ⌐ogical and non-pedagogical actors of the education

PART ONE

Developing Successful and Effective School Leadership

1

African Perspectives

Jan Heystek

Introduction

South Africa is a developing country and a young all-inclusive democracy. The country is a member of the BRICS community with Brazil, Russia, India and China, as well as a member of the G20 economic forum. However, according to Statistics South Africa (2014) the country has an unemployment rate of at least 25 per cent. Such diverse contextual challenges are also typical of the principal leadership in South Africa. It is therefore important that the education system must provide sufficiently qualified and employable workers to sustain the country's position as an important role player in the global economy.

Successful schools are schools where there is a learning community that pays attention to both the child and the teacher as human being; it is these schools that achieve academic success (Pashiardis & Heystek, 2007). Quality education with quality educational leadership is therefore an essential requirement for future development. According to Handford and Leithwood (2013), principals are entrusted with improving the quality of education, which in the South African context also implies educating employable citizens in a society striving to become a democratic one offering equal opportunities. According to Bush (2009) and Mulford and Silins (2011), successful and effective school leaders are equated with successful schools, which leads to the conclusion that the development of school leaders is important.

This chapter will focus on South Africa because there is sufficient literature available, while there is limited literature available for the rest of Africa with regard to leadership development (Asuga & Eacott, 2012; Chapman et al., 2010). Currently, no leadership qualification is required before a teacher can become a principal in a South African school. Despite this non-requirement, different universities have started offering education leadership programmes (a Further Diploma in Education Leadership – FDE, and later an Advanced Diploma in Education Leadership – ACE) for educators at any level in the system. In 2006 the National Department of Education (referred to henceforth as the Department) accepted a new revised ACE as an acceptable qualification in preparation for principalship, although it was and still is not an official requirement in order to become a principal. This chapter will mainly provide an overview of the ACE as a principal development programme.

The official vision of the ACE programme that is acknowledged by the Department is to develop a corps of educational leaders who apply critical understanding, values, knowledge and skills to school leadership and management in line with the vision of democratic transformation (South Africa Department of Education, 2008). The pronounced expectation is that this programme must be a quick fix for the problems in education. These problems include, for instance, the underperformance of schools as noted by the national departmental representative at the launch of the programme at the University of Stellenbosch in 2006 where I was present. Although the 'noble' goals for school leadership emphasize equality and democracy, the reality, according to Huber (2004a), is that leadership development is one of the international driving forces from governments and the emphasis is on the principal's responsibility to lead schools to achieve academic results. Mncube and Harber (2010) indicate that the National Minister of Education interprets quality education according to values such as accountability, standards and testing, which is an indication of the strong emphasis of the academic results obtained in the school-leaving examination. Principal development programmes must therefore empower principals to account for the full process, starting with the provision of textbooks. All of this is expected to culminate in an improvement of the pass rate in the school-leaving examination.

Historical perspective on South African educational context

Most principals in South Africa work in impoverished circumstances, specifically with regard to infrastructure in schools. There is, for example, not enough (or any) running water, sanitation or ablution facilities, a lack of access to electricity and the internet, along with communities having poor socioeconomic circumstances, high unemployment, as well as low literacy levels among parents in many communities (Bush & Oduro, 2006), but there are also a small number of schools, about 5 per cent, with very good facilities and good socioeconomic circumstances. This demographic diversity of South

Africa emphasizes the complexity of having a one-size-fits-all leadership development programme for school principals. A large percentage of the South African population are not sufficiently functionally literate to meet the requirements of reading and drafting policies. Only 40.3 per cent of people older than 20 have completed primary education, and another 30.8 per cent have completed some secondary education. The literacy rate in some of the countries where there is some literature about education leadership development is as follows: in Kenya about 82 per cent of youth between 15–24 are literate (Kenya, 2014); Tanzania has a 74 per cent literacy rate for youth between 15–24 (Tanzania, 2014); with Uganda (Uganda, 2014) on 87 per cent and Ghana (Ghana, 2014) with 86 per cent literacy rate for their youth.

In 2013 statistics from the South Africa Department of Basic Education (2014) indicated there were 12,489,648 learners in public and independent schools in South Africa attending 25,720 schools and served by 425,023 educators. There is a large number of underperforming schools in South Africa. Heystek and Terhoven (2015) state that the majority of these previously disadvantaged schools are situated in townships established for people of colour during apartheid in South Africa and are categorized as underperforming schools (Hoadley et al., 2009; Moloi, 2010). These underperforming schools have achieved a pass rate of less than 60 per cent (South Africa Department of Basic Education, 2011a, 2013) in the national school-leaving examination. The matriculation results have improved since 2008, although this may not necessarily be an overall improvement in the quality of education for all children. The matriculation pass rate has increased, but there is still a dropout rate of 42 per cent for a group of children moving from grade 1 to 12 as a cohort (South Africa Department of Basic Education, 2011b).

Principals' leadership development in South Africa

The general approach in leadership development in South Africa is an attempt to merge the western developed leadership and management theories with the South African and broader African philosophy of Ubuntu (Bush, 2007). The Ubuntu philosophy holds that the group is more important than the individual – a communal societal approach, with a strong emphasis on the humanity of people and interaction. This seems to link to shared leadership or participative leadership, as well as social learning theories. A leader embracing the Ubuntu philosophy and way of life may therefore be rather a servant leader than an autocratic leader (Lessem and Nussbuam, 1996). Although these theories are included in the leadership curricula, it is not necessary because it is aligned with the Ubuntu philosophy, although the theories are rather copies of the theories developed in the western world.

Bush and Oduro (2006) indicate that in most African countries, including South Africa, there are currently no requirements for any leadership development before a person can be appointed as a principal. The basic minimum requirements of a four-year teacher qualification are acceptable to be appointed as a principal. In spite of this non-requirement, there are already more than twenty-five years of education management and leadership academic programmes at an undergraduate as well as honours level (the first postgraduate level) at universities. This undergraduate programme was supported by specific tailor-made leadership and management programmes, namely a Further Diploma in Education (FDE) Leadership, which has been replaced by an Advanced Diploma in Education (ACE) Leadership. Teachers, heads of departments, deputy principals and principals could register for any of the above-mentioned programmes since they are academic programmes at universities and no selection criteria linked to management and leadership experience are required. Academic criteria are the only applicable criteria. More than 90 per cent of the students in the FDE and ACE programmes were teachers from the pre-apartheid dispensation who were labelled as black, coloured or Indian students.

In 2006 the National Department of Basic Education (DBE) (formerly the Department of Education) drove the development and implementation of the Advanced Certificate in Education (leadership) in collaboration with the universities in South Africa. The Department provided significant funding for this programme, paying accommodation as well as travel and subsistence for the students of the programme. The Department of Education (2008) explained that the ACE is an attempt to create an academic programme to serve as preparation for principalship and to strengthen the professional role of principals. The principals receive directed and self-directed learning in teams and clusters, site-based learning (dependent on the content) and a variety of learning strategies – i.e. lectures, practice and research portfolios, among others. The ACE will be replaced by an Advanced Certificate in 2016.

The official curriculum developed for the ACE programme by the Department included ICT and language competency, contextual leadership, governance, leading people, financial management and teaching and learning. Possible electives were subject or phase area management, mentorship, as well as assessment. Higher education institutions can supplement the fundamental and core modules with one or more elective modules that respond to particular national/provincial/regional needs, for example HIV/AIDS and gender issues.

Scott (2010), as well as Bush et al. (2011) and Kiggundu and Moorosi (2012) wrote in detail about the ACE; they provided empirical perspectives on the potential influence of the leadership development programme. The aim of the larger research project was to carry out a comprehensive evaluation of the first pilot cohort of participants to inform the development of the ACE course and to advise the Minister of Basic Education about the suitability and sustainability of the qualification for its intended purpose, namely to improve school leadership and management (the official report is included in South Africa Department of Basic Education, 2009).

At this stage it is only Bush et al. (2011) who have attempted to make a link between leadership development and the academic achievement of learners. Their survey evidence shows that most respondents (75 per cent) claim that their school is 'improving'. This was self-reported evidence and the criteria for improvement were not clear. The criteria were broadly based on the development of the ACE programme; hence the questions were about whether the ACE programme had helped to improve a school. There is anecdotal evidence that the ACE programme specifically, but also the honours programme, have had a positive influence on students (principals, heads of departments and teachers). However, the secondary school case studies show that only 12 per cent of schools have shown clear improvements in matric results, while performance has declined slightly in 38 per cent of schools and fallen significantly in 50 per cent of them. It is not possible to reach firm conclusions on such limited data, but it is clear that the ACE programme has not led to short-term gains in matric results at the case study schools. However, this finding should be set against the national data, which show that overall matric results declined between 2006 and 2008 (2006: 66.5 per cent; 2007: 65.2 per cent; 2008: 62.57 per cent), while the percentage of matriculants passing the final school-leaving examination rose to 78.2 in 2013 (South Africa Department of Basic Education, 2013). The composition of learners was offered as a reason for the decline in some cases, but the research team also found examples of poor management. These data suggest that the initial effects of the ACE programme on learner achievement were, at best, neutral, although there was also evidence of principals beginning to implement their leadership learning.

Piggot-Irvine et al. (2013) make an important comment with regard to leadership development in South Africa. Their research confirms the Matthew Goniwe School for Leadership and Governance's research finding that principals spend a great deal of time attending to the educational/curriculum leadership role (greater than any other country), but that the academic results of schools do not reflect the time spent on this task. This self-reported evidence seems to be misrepresenting their own abilities and knowledge, as reported by Bush et al. (2011) about the positive influence of the ACE on the academic achievement of learners in their schools. Hoadley et al. (2009) show that only 17 per cent of the 142 principals in their South African study identified curriculum leadership as their main task. The self-reported, high number of principals who reported that they are highly involved with instructional leadership on a frequent basis is also consistent with the findings of Bush et al. (2011), who found that most principals have a weak grasp of instructional leadership.

Leadership development issues addressed in research not directly linked to the ACE programme in South Africa

Moorosi (2012) indicated that mentorship can be an advantage during the development of principals. Conditional factors in the South African context are gender sensitive and racial sensitive. Mentorship is a complex interpersonal relationship and in an official programme like the ACE, where students are spread over a large area, it is difficult to make personal preferences and interpersonal relationships a key driver for the match between mentor and mentee. In these official mentorship programmes, the mentoring has become a high cost component of the programme, but still most mentees reported a positive experience from the process. Programme presenters must be sensitive to include more female mentors, because most teachers and many principals, specifically in primary schools, are female. The potential racial tension must also be considered when mentors are selected to ensure an open, positive attitude from the mentor's side towards all mentees under his or her mentorship. In spite of the emphasis in the ACE programme that women must have at least equal opportunity and numbers in the programme, *City Press* (2013) reports that the National Minister stated that there are only 8,210 female principals and 14,337 male principals appointed in permanent posts in South Africa. This is a cause for concern, particularly because women constitute the majority in society and in the education sector in particular.

There are many other education leadership development projects that are not directly linked to the ACE programme. These also inform the potential improvement of the official leadership programmes. Wood and Govender (2013) worked with an action research approach that emphasizes the community of practice (COP) for the development. They emphasize that the participants were invited to attend, but they made sure that they were willing to participate and that they were not forced by their principals to do so. Many principals were not interested and sent their deputy principals and heads of departments, but they did not feel they were forced to participate. The learning principles of openness, motivation and a positive attitude were important for their development. Another important principle in this project for leadership development was that the aims were not to improve examination or test scores. The aims were to improve reading, specifically the love of reading, and to regenerate the moral values of the community. This is an important emphasis, because the leaders did not put themselves under pressure to measure quantitatively if the results were better. It was a broader aim, but it may have, and most probability will have, positive examination and test results. Naidoo (2011), in a similar vein, indicates in her research that another possibility within leadership practice communities is that principals may use their knowledge for their own development. This form of development can be conducted as part of an official programme such as the ACE programme, as well as the self-initiated activities between principals in any part of the country.

Network learning is also linked to peer support and collaborative and constructivist learning. Kiggundua and Moorosi (2012) also found that networks can foster improved learning, improved programme completion rates and improved academic performance among school faculty. Visiting other schools, particularly those in similar contexts, appears to provide powerful potential for leadership learning, and inter-school networks are powerful tools for school development.

Grant (2014) emphasizes that groups of educational leaders (in her research it is education management students) can be more successful when they are working in collaboration with research a specific issue. Although her research was with students (teachers and principals in an official university programme similar to most principal development programmes in South Africa) it is also possible to use this method for any group of school leaders. Research must also not be seen as only a method for students in an official academic programme. Research in its essence implies asking the right questions and using the most appropriate methods to get an answer, rather than to talk about the problem with no specific method or strategy in mind.

Jooste (2008) and Thom (2014) emphasize specific issues that need attention in education leadership development. Thom conducted his research in private schools, while Jooste worked in a rural area in public schools. The five most important competencies identified by the fifty principals in Thom's survey were: stress management, conflict resolution, financial management, performance management and customer relationship management. It has become clear through the survey and interviews that there are big 'gaps' in the business leadership competencies of the education managers, so we can safely assume that their past education, training and development have lacked efficacy in these specific areas. Most of the education managers chose a course (usually a few days long and with regional schools) as the most appropriate continuous professional development (CPD) method for most of the competencies. A national conference is expensive, but can be held occasionally, especially with top management, as the business managers suggested. A seminar for a few hours with individual schools can be used for specific competencies that are lacking in particular school education management teams. Personal reading, coaching and mentoring can be ongoing.

Jooste's (2008) research emphasizes what is expected from principals in rural areas. Development has to focus on, among other things, taking responsibility to ensure a sound culture of lifelong learning and teaching, with a strong vision, mission and objectives for the school. Principals must establish and manage structures, ensure effective, efficient and economical utilization of resources and fulfil the monitoring (control) function. Above all, principals must be humanitarians, ensure interaction between the school and the community and influence tradition and culture.

Current approaches to successful and effective school leadership development

According to Bolden and Kirk (2009) and Eacott and Asuga (2014), it is important to understand African leadership in the context of Africa but also to realize that leaders in Africa also function in a global world. The limited scope of education leadership development in a few African countries does not signify any real specific focus and similar problems occur in most countries in Africa.

Many policy changes do not anticipate the preparedness of principals before the policies are implemented – for example, in Uganda where universal secondary education was introduced (Chapman et al., 2010). Preparedness has to do with the applicable knowledge, experience and skills, but also the attitude which is needed to bring about change.

Leadership for Learning (LfL), a programme of school leadership developed at the University of Cambridge for Ghana over a period of ten years in conjunction with an international group of researchers and practitioners, is an example of private or external small-scale involvement in leadership development in Africa. The emphasis is not so much on outcomes and standards but rather on the interest and sustainable learning of the participants (Jull et al., 2014). Conclusion: small-scale initiatives seem to be the most relevant current development opportunities for principals in Africa. In concurrence with DeJaeghere et al. (2009), a more structured and planned system for all principals must be a short- to medium-term vision for African countries. In spite of critique about formal and structured one-size-fits-all development programmes, these can provide a starting point for the large-scale sustainable development of quality education. Along with these large-scale programmes there will always be a need for smaller tailor-made programmes.

Kitavi and Van Der Westhuizen (1997), with their research in Kenya, already indicated many years before what Asuga and Eacott (2012) further indicated:

that after appointment, principals are expected to undergo an induction programme but due to a range of issues, mostly to do with the geographical isolation of many schools, this induction never takes place. This means that many principals are left with little more than a trial and error approach to improving their performance. These findings are consistent with the argument that principal programmes are poorly aligned to the self-perceived needs of participants. The notion of 'self-perceived' is important here. There is a common-sense argument that aspiring school leaders do not necessarily know what it is that they need to know, or they place higher value on learning less important information as a result of not being in the role. Principals' preparation and development is mainly school-based, along with with some in-service courses such as seminars and workshops. School-based learning helps the principals to understand their specific contexts and the application of what has been learned. Onguko et al. (2012) confirmed this in their qualitative research and found a similar trend in the rest of Africa. Their research in Dar es Salaam indicated that leadership preparation in Tanzania is not structured consistently. The principals' preparation consists of the learning they garnered by working closely with previous headteachers, and from accredited certificate or non-credit-bearing programmes at universities and informal professional development offered on the job. However, it was clear that preparing for the headship was up to individuals and not part of a district or national programme for aspiring headteachers.

There are similar problems and initiatives in South Africa. Moyo (2004) focused on the possibility of change in the school and community as a focus for a leadership development programme for all players in an academic programme at a university. He indicated that there can be unique and specific development of educational leadership programmes, as indicated in the programme at the University of Fort Hare. They combined the development of the principals with all the role-players, including the school governing body (SGB) and the community members, in one cohort and received positive feedback from the participants. In this development programme there was a difference in opinion about the academic approach and the more skills- and development-orientated approach in one programme. This balance seems to be a familiar issue when universities are involved in development programmes for principals and educational role-players. The challenge in relation to the purpose of programmes also expands to the assessment of a given programme to see if it has achieved its goals. Academic knowledge and development targets for schools and communities must be assessed differently, and in this regard the programme plan must also address assessment as an integral part of the programme's development.

Although the decentralized accountability makes it appear that principals have more power, leadership development, specifically in areas where it is compulsory or demanded (e.g. France and Ontario), and even where it is optional (e.g. England and Australia) became a very prescriptive type of training (Heystek, 2007; Huber, 2004b). The ACE leadership programme took a centralized approach, but since each university had more or less its own autonomy to deliver the programme according to its own interpretation, the potential value of a centralized programme has been lost. A very structured programme may be construed as a negative aspect, but in a diverse society with many schools underperforming, a more centralized approach may be valuable, and could ensure that all principals achieve the same level. Another centralization attempt from the Department was the publication of the draft of the Standards for Principalship (South Africa Department of Basic Education, 2014). This document, although still vague, determines standards and the indication is that principal development programmes will be demanded or encouraged so that they can be used as a main criterion to provide centralized quality for all principals. If this is achieved, it may address the problem that diversity poses in cases where principals have had limited exposure to all kinds of schools; which may lead to the possibility that any principal may be appointable at any school in the country.

According to Amagoh (2009), to be successful, organizations must be willing to invest in building leadership capabilities at all levels. This leadership development on all levels must become part of the organization's normal working process; it must be institutionalized to be effective in the longer term. The long-term success of leadership development initiatives depends on an organizational culture that considers the development of future leaders as a long-term strategic priority.

Conclusion

Leadership development in Africa must be contextualized not only within the communal philosophy but also within the structural and sociocultural context (LEAD-Link 2009). Although these sentiments are expressed, the research indicates that the format and curriculum in education in Africa does not really consider this sentiment as indicated in this chapter. The challenge for development is that Africa is part of the global world and is challenged to achieve world competitive academic results given the socioeconomic circumstances in the continent. There is, for example, 'Standards for Principalship' which is a typical international one-size-fits-all approach but which has the potential consequence that contextually determined development needs may be sacrificed. Hoadley, Christie and Ward (2009) found that none of the individual-level factors, especially those concerned with the principals' pedagogical expertise and 'connection to the classroom', emerged as significant factors to improve the quality or standards of examination results. Their study suggests the importance of a broader, institutional view of instructional leadership that emphasizes teacher cultures and school organization, rather than focusing only on individual teacher and manager behaviours that influence student learning. Heystek (2014) refers to the same issues because principals feel that factors other than instructional knowledge, such as the attitude of teachers and external influences like teachers unions, have a more important influence on academic performance in schools. Wood and Govender (2013) also claim that there may be other goals and that not only examination results can be linked to leadership development. These research results indicate that although leadership development may have a positive influence on the individual, it should be translated to the local context and specifically to the demand for improved examination results.

Teaching or developing leaders is not a simple matter of putting a few modules or activities together (Lumby et al., 2008; Snook et al., 2012). It requires in-depth critical reflection about the why and the how of the training of principals, deputy principals and heads of department. Lumby, in Young et al. (2009), refers specifically to a narcissistic approach in the research of education leadership development. In spite of this restriction, there is sufficient evidence that leadership is important and can make a difference in quality education for more children.

The following problems with principal development programmes in Africa are identified when also considering international trends:

- A university programme, for example in Kenya or the ACE programme in South Africa, is more academically orientated than a workshop for leadership. As Scott (2010) critically indicates, the practical application of the programme is lacking since it is content-driven and there is not sufficient assessment of the implementation in schools.

- Financial as well as geographical constraints are important to develop principal development programmes – for example, the mentoring programme in the ACE makes the programme very expensive and it therefore may not be sustainable for the DBE to continue with the programme in the shorter to medium term. A more appropriate approach, rather than a full two-year academic programme, may be shorter official programmes, but there is evidence from Kenya that the distance between schools and the centres where short courses are presented prevents the implementation of these programmes.

Some recommendations for the development of educational leaders in Africa are the following:

- Official development programmes are important to ensure that all principals are at least aware of what is expected from a principal to lead a school to world competitive quality education standards.

- These generic programmes, specifically if presented by universities, cannot prepare principals for every change and every new policy. It may be expected that these programmes may provide principals with the skills and attitudes to embrace change and to be open to it, and to see change as an opportunity, but not actually to be fully equipped for every change.

- Short courses must support and be part of leadership programmes as indicated by the example in Uganda with the introduction of universal secondary education. These short courses must not only be informative but must allow the principals to gain new skills, knowledge and values if needed.

- Initiatives from non-governmental organizations must be encouraged. Although these programmes may only reach smaller numbers of schools, they are an important starting point to initiate change and inspire people to improve themselves. These smaller programmes can lead to an expansion effect to motivate other individuals who are not part of the programme to join or to begin to develop a programme of their own.

Professional development must be an internally driven need and not an external or compulsory departmental requirement. This is particularly important in Africa with restrictive financial and geographical challenges. National departments of education can emphasize self-development and provide support for individual's and small groups to take the initiative for development and not wait for the national or local authorities to initiate development opportunities.

2

South Asian Perspectives

Tai Hoi Theodore Lee, Allan David Walker and Philip Hallinger

School leaders have a significant influence on school improvement and student performance (Hallinger, 2011b; Hallinger & Heck, 1996; Leithwood et al., 2006). Successful school leaders set organizational direction, and work purposefully and ethically to influence instructional and human activity in their schools through 'connecting, disconnecting and in some cases reconnecting pathways', different school constituents, curriculum, pedagogy and policy (Leithwood et al., 2006; Walker, 2012: 1). Successful leaders remain responsive to complex environmental demands and balance the need for change with those of stability and security. Although effective school leaders tend to draw on the same basic set of leadership practices (Leithwood et al., 2008), how they enact these influences is in turn influenced by the context within which they work (Walker & Ko, 2011).

How leaders have been socialized and trained, the communities and cultural contexts within which they work, and the policy frameworks regulating their schools all influence how they conceptualize and enact leadership (Walker, 2004, 2007; Walker & Qian, 2011). Through looking at the contexts within which school leaders work and the challenges they increasingly encounter, we can construct a more complete understanding of how and why leadership is practised in different contexts. This chapter will outline the policy contexts and trends within which school leaders in Southeast Asia work. It then pulls together a number of what we see as the dominant trends around school leadership in Southeast and East Asia, and discusses the key challenges facing principals as they work to become more effective and successful in their schools. The identification of trends and challenges across such a large, diverse and rapidly changing region is a risky business, but we hold that these issues are at the heart of the further development of successful leadership.

For example, the absence of a solid database in the area makes it difficult to identify beyond quite broad speculation what appears to be working well in schools, and what needs further thought and development.

Education reform

Over the last few decades, Southeast Asian societies have been undergoing intensive educational reform. For example, reforms in Hong Kong have sought to overhaul the entire school system after 1997 (Education Commission, 1996; Lam, 2003), the Malaysia Education Blueprint stipulates comprehensive reform at all levels (Ministry of Education Malaysia, 2013) while education reforms in China aim to develop a more inclusive system with high expectations of student performance (OECD, 2011). However, especially in China, despite the positive stated intentions of many reforms, the educational community remains sceptical of their real effect in schools (Walker & Qian, 2012). School leaders in the region, however, often find it difficult to adjust to the changes of role expectations from such reforms.

Although travelling at different speeds, the education reforms influencing the region appear remarkably similar (Cheng & Tam, 2007; Walker et al., 2007). The waves of education reform flowing across the region are inevitably changing the role of school leaders as they place enormous demands on the skills, knowledge and abilities required to lead successful schools (Hallinger, 2003b; Mok, 2007; Walker et al., 2012). Reform agendas drive new visions for education, and, in some countries and regions, expansion, education restructuring and the quest for quality education. For example, reforms have marked a shift to decentralization and school-based management (SBM) which requires principals to share power with multiple stakeholders (Hallinger, 2011a; Lin, 2003; Walker, 2003). On the other hand, the education reforms often focus on increased accountability and quality assurance (Walker et al., 2007). For example, teachers in Korea, Japan and Taiwan face annual reviews of their performance, and Hong Kong teachers are required to account in quantitative terms (hours) for professional development undertaken. Apart from managerial responsibilities for overall school management, school leaders must also perform other roles, such as developing the school-based curriculum, using information technology, leading teacher professional development, improving instructional practices and aligning student achievement with reform intentions. The number of new responsibilities means that school leaders face a raft of new expectations, which, if not managed effectively, create negative effects on their work (Walker & Ko, 2011; Walker & Qian, 2012).

Since the government or a single authority usually centrally administers education reforms in Southeast Asia, prescribed and piecemeal educational reform agendas appear common in the region. These national policies usually have great impact on the direction of reform and change (Hallinger & Bryant, 2013b): strong central governments tend to have more control over education across different aspects of school operation (Hussein, 2014); school leaders act more or less as policy implementers (Tang et al., 2014); and demands around centralized implementation can lessen the involvement, flexibility and effectiveness of reforms (Hallinger, 2001; Hallinger et al., 2000; Walker & Hallinger, 2013). This comment from Walker and Qian (2011: 456) on the development of principalship in China, also reflects the challenging circumstances of school leaders in Southeast Asia:

> Successful principals did not seem to differentiate their educative and political roles. In their accounts, these roles appeared so tangled yet similarly aims at separating them were impractical. The principals were pragmatic in a very real sense. They accepted the system as it stood, and rather than trying openly to challenge it, successful principals learned to mediate and work within the system for the benefit of their schools and students, and themselves.

Influence of culture and tradition

The education context in the region can also be considered through the lens of indigenous cultures. Southeast Asian societies are characterized by traditional and hierarchical cultures that differ in a number of ways from western societies. As education reforms administered in Southeast Asia are based mainly on the theories and knowledge imported from western societies, they risk downplaying the differences between local cultural characteristics (Lam, 2003). Although borrowed policies are interpreted as a move to stimulate local education development, they often carry values which can clash with the traditional values that guide societal behaviour. This 'cultural mismatch' can reduce the effectiveness of policy as it drives practice. For example, the western conceptual base of *sushijiaoyu* education in China has not transferred smoothly into Chinese schools because the ideologies underpinning the reform clash with traditional embedded practices (Walker et al., 2012). As Hallinger and Bryant (2013b: 415) suggest, 'where educational changes conflict with fundamental cultural values, the process is likely to encounter even greater resistance and require a longer time frame for implementation'.

School leaders in Southeast Asia often find themselves facing dilemmas as they attempt to successfully translate imported education initiatives into effective practice in their quite different cultural contexts and traditions. They struggle to filter out irrelevant and inappropriate reform elements in order to 'retain the values of their communities while macerating the benefits reform brings to the educative process' (Walker & Hallinger, 2007: 270). Until we have more knowledge about ways to effectively adapt globalized reforms to local contexts, leader effectiveness may be an unsteady business (Hallinger, 2011b).

School leaders' perceptions of leadership are influenced by societal and cultural traditions (Hallinger et al., 2005; Walker, 2003; Walker & Hallinger, 2007). Research shows that the conflict of different cultural values may affect the ways that school leaders implement education reforms and unnecessarily complicate leadership practices across the region (Hallinger, 2001; Lee & Hallinger, 2012; Walker & Chen, 2007). This is not to say that there are no generic leadership practices which describe successful leadership across contexts, but the enactment of these practices may be very different. Because of differences between foreign ideologies that underpin education reforms and traditional values that drive their behaviours, school leaders can experience high levels of dissonance around fundamental changes to the school environment (Hallinger et al., 2005). This often results in a struggle between preserving the valued traditions while, at the same time, responding to externally driven reform agendas (Hallinger et al., 2005). Furthermore, school leaders do not necessarily have autonomy when dealing with these issues. High power distance breeds a cultural tendency for compliance. Because of the high power distance common across the region, school leaders are less likely to question authority (Hallinger, 2001). They need to be tactful and pragmatic in order to negotiate the application of reforms but, at the same time, they need to be careful not to offend their superiors' authority (Qian & Walker, 2011). This often means they work in an environment rife with tension, dilemmas, compromises and trade-offs (Cheng & Walker, 2008; Day & Leithwood, 2007; Qian & Walker, 2011).

School leadership is a representation of the sociopolitical contexts of a society. Societal contexts represent accepted patterns and norms that influence leaders' decision making (Walker et al., 2012). School leaders must therefore be sensitive to the challenges which emerge from societal contexts, as these may create both constraints and opportunities for schools (Lee et al., 2012; Walker et al., 2012). Schools in the region were traditionally concerned, almost exclusively, with what happened within the defined boundaries of their school. As a result, they had considerable power to decide what happened in the school (Hallinger et al., 2000; Walker & Qian, 2006). Recent reforms have challenged this orthodoxy. School leaders can no longer work simply 'within' their schools and must be more sensitive and responsive to what external stakeholders expect (Lee et al., 2012).

Common trends around the principalship in Southeast Asia

In short, education reforms implemented throughout Southeast Asia over the past twenty years have sought simultaneously to restructure education systems and reshape the modal teaching and learning methods employed by schools in order to produce more active, capable and independent learners (Fry & Bi, 2013; Hallinger, 2010). In Thailand, for example, this was noted by the Secretary General of Thailand's Office of Basic Education Commission (OBEC) ten years after passage of the National Education Act: 'The reforms undertaken at the national level cannot be accomplished without active involvement and leadership from our school principals. Without skilful leadership and active support from the principal, how can teachers hope to make these changes in curriculum and teaching? But our principals need motivation as well as more skills to lead these changes in their schools' (Varavarn, 2008).

Various scholars have sought to assess the impact of education reforms on schools and classrooms during the past twenty years in Southeast Asia (e.g. Cheng & Walker, 2008; Dimmock & Walker, 1998; Fry & Bi, 2013; Hallinger, 2010). Consistent with studies conducted in other countries, progress has been slower than expected by policy reformers. For example, in a recently published evaluation of Thailand's progress in reform implementation, the authors concluded:

> We interpret our results as largely consistent with these [other] empirical studies of education reform implementation in Thailand. Our findings similarly suggest evidence of progress, but a lack of deep penetration of the reforms in a large percentage of schools. Thus, all three studies describe the pattern of implementation as variable across teachers, and partial or surface in the nature of impact. In sum, we conclude that the picture of reform progress offered here is one of slow progress with a record of mixed success.
>
> Hallinger & Lee, 2011: 155–6

A number of policy trends especially relevant to school principals appear to cut across these societies.

Principals in Asia have been slow to don the garb of instructional leaders

The 'genetic code' of Southeast Asian principals as 'government officials' appears a significant factor in understanding change, or lack of change, in the principals' role and behaviour during the reform era. This has shaped their role orientation to an extent that has maintained the centrality of managerial and political approaches even in the face of centrally directed reforms that call for more active instructional leadership (e.g. Ministry of Education Malaysia, 2013). We note that Southeast Asian societies have no historical orientation towards leadership as an *instrumental* activity. Instead, Southeast Asian conceptions of leadership emphasize the leader as a 'figurehead'.

An analysis of trends across Southeast Asian societies highlights the cultural gap faced in Asian societies when they borrow policies and practices from western societies (Dimmock & Walker, 2005; Walker & Dimmock, 2002). Value differences underpinning imported innovations can slow the process of reform adoption (Hallinger, 2010; Walker et al., 2012). Incorporating instructional leadership into the practice of Thai principals, for example, involves not only the development of capacity (e.g. knowledge and skills), but also a more fundamental change in normative expectations and role identity. Although we assert that the latter represents the more significant challenge, neither has been addressed adequately to date (Hallinger, 2004).

Principals in the region remain in large part government officials and guardians of tradition

In Southeast Asian countries the traditional identity of principals as government officers continues to exert a powerful influence on principals' beliefs and practices, often skewing these towards the managerial and the political. Southeast Asian principals have traditionally been situated in local communities as key representatives and guardians of the national culture and system policies (Hallinger, 2004). Indeed, prior to the late 1990s, terms such as 'instructional leadership' and 'leadership for learning' did not even have translated equivalents in Asian languages.

Values around current reform often clash with existing norms and challenge principals

Recent reforms often convey a new set of institutional expectations. These are not only different, but often clash with the existing role expectations of Southeast Asian school principals. For example, the managerial and political dimensions of the principal's role are traditionally highly weighted in Thailand (Hallinger & Lee, 2013). In this 'post-reform era' principals in most of these countries (Vietnam as an exception) are expected to actively lead teaching and learning development to an extent that simply did not exist in the past. For the first time in the Southeast Asian context, leadership among principals has taken on an explicitly instrumental aspect.

The clash of values changes the traditional place of the principal and confuses them about how to effectively enact their roles

The concurrent implementation of 'school-based management' resulted in new expectations for principals to involve a broader variety of stakeholders in formal decision-making in their schools (Walker & Ko, 2011). This was a major change as well, since the Southeast Asian principal traditionally acted as a unitary leader. This meant that not only are principals now expected to lead more actively, but for the first time their leadership is open to broader scrutiny (Lee et al., 2012). Empirical evidence suggests that although principals have evinced acceptance of these changes, many remain uncertain about how to enact these new roles effectively (e.g. Cheng & Walker, 2008).

There is a disconnection between the reforms themselves which challenges their implementation at the school level

Although Southeast Asian countries have invested considerable resources in supporting specific education reforms, there is a lack of systemic integration. For example, training is typically provided on a project-by-project basis, in the absence of an overarching framework or curriculum. Too seldom are the supporting mechanisms required to bring about change in practice evident (e.g. ongoing development and coaching). Our observations would suggest that changing the focus of the work of school principals in Southeast Asia depends on a concerted effort to reshape the human resource systems embedded in the region's Ministries of Education. In some settings (e.g. Singapore), this type of change has been reasonably successful. In others (e.g. Thailand, Vietnam), much additional investment will be required in order to support change in the capacity of school-level leaders.

High power distance is an important factor in strategies implemented around reform implementation

The top-down approach to change utilized in Southeast Asia is certainly not unique as a strategy for large-scale system reform (Hallinger, 2010). However, the way leaders and schools across the region respond to this may differ in character and expression. The large power distance that characterizes the cultures of Southeast Asia creates respect for authority and a passive receptivity to change, at least at a surface level (Hallinger et al., 2005; Walker, 2004; Walker & Qian, 2012). The high value placed on education, as well as a strong cultural belief in the central role of educational attainment for social mobility, further strengthens societal receptivity to educational reform.

Principal resistance to change is culturally grounded and often hidden

Receptivity to change does not necessarily translate into higher engagement or real changes in practices at the school and classroom levels. Cultural norms of power distance as well as collectivism (Hampden-Turner & Trompenaars, 1997; Hofstede, 1983, 1991; Holmes & Tangtongtavy, 1996) create tendencies to avoid public dissent and maintain group harmony. Thus, although resistance tends to be passive, it can be even stronger than in societies in which questions are openly asked. The fact that dissent remains hidden may also result in a longer process of mutual adaptation (Walker & Qian, 2012). There appears to be a process of consensus-building that over time modifies the top-down proposals for change. However, this seems to occur only *after* the change has stalled due to lack of local understanding and support.

Principals still tend to lead by 'telling'

McLaughlin (1990) earlier observed that: 'You can't mandate what matters to people.' Large power distance breeds a cultural tendency for Southeast Asian leaders to lead by fiat and to focus more on 'telling' staff the tasks to be accomplished with relatively little two-way communication. This was the case even in Singapore which was an exception to the trend in several other respects. Reliance on 'telling people to change' reflects the tendency to give greater weight to formal authority (i.e. large power distance) and to accept top-down commandments, at least in terms of surface compliance. However, implicit in this strategy is the limitation of constant application of pressure (Walker & Wang, 2011). There is a shared cultural assumption that leading change entails establishing orders – which will be followed – and applying pressure in special cases where it is needed. Even twenty years ago it made sense for a few smart decision makers at the top of the education ministries across Southeast Asia to make system-wide decisions and pass these along through the principals to the schools. This is, however, an impractical approach to leading change today, when the pace of change is simply too rapid for a few smart decision makers to keep up.

In summary, cultural norms such as power distance and collectivism are not in and of themselves obstacles to change. If the *interest* of relevant social groups in collectivist societies can be engaged, the groups can provide even greater momentum for change than might be the case in individualistic societies. However, the reverse is also true. Failure to tap into the interests of the relevant stakeholder groups will create an even higher degree of resistance. Even though the resistance may be passive, it will be difficult to overcome.

Challenges for the principalship in Southeast Asia

When put together, the pressures and trends described above produce an environment of excitement, uncertainty, confusion and paradox. As they face often contradictory demands, many principals struggle to find their place and make sense of their new roles (Chu & Cravens, 2012). On the one hand, they are expected to retain their traditional role as 'stabilizer' in the school and uphold tradition. On the other hand, they are being increasingly called upon to change, reform and redefine their schools. In the midst of such demands, principals are also pushed to reshape their own place and power in relation to parents and teachers. On a more positive note, at the same time as reforms such as decentralization threaten the traditional role and comfort of principals, they also expose unheralded opportunities to change schools and improve the range of student outcomes.

As reforms continue to evolve, Southeast Asian principals face a number of challenges. A first challenge, to the extent to which the principal's role will actually change, is the degree of fit between reform components and the societal culture and context within which they are implemented. With increasing globalization, education stakeholders in Asian countries are increasingly exposed to values, knowledge and skills that were heretofore unavailable. As the social and cultural influence of globalization continues, the influence on education policy and the principalship is indisputable. However, theories, policies and practices implemented in specific social settings may not be valid and applicable in other social-political-cultural contexts. This is because societal cultures, along with local economic, political and religious conditions, act as mediators and filters to policies and practices imported from overseas (Dimmock & Walker, 2000; Hallinger, 2004, 2010).

It is customary to recognize three stages in the policy process – formulation, adoption and implementation. The role of the principal is pre-eminent at the implementation stage. It is relatively easy to formulate and adopt policies from elsewhere but the real test of their suitability and efficacy comes at the implementation level. If the policy formulation and adoption stages fail to act as effective filters and mediators, the policy may meet its first real opposition at the school and principalship level. When reform policies aimed at reshaping the role of the principal fail to adequately account for cultural and contextual conditions it becomes unlikely that the role will be genuinely transformed.

Reforms in these Southeast Asian countries have, to varying degrees, advocated a change in principals' leadership style, from an authoritarian to a more collaborative, participative approach. There is an obvious attempt to disperse some of the power and authority exercised by upper levels of the education bureaucracy to principals and for them to develop more collaborative leadership styles, a trend in vogue in many western societies (Cheng and Wong, 1996; Thang, 2013). Broad involvement, or shared leadership, in schools is a new concept to both principals and teachers in Southeast Asia, and in some cases may be incongruent with existing cultural values and norms (Cheung, 2000).

For example, studies have found that the ways in which Southeast Asian principals perceive, manage and solve dilemmas are profoundly influenced by entrenched values that highlight the importance of relational/organizational harmony (Hallinger, 2004; Thang, 2013; Walker & Dimmock, 2000). If decentralizing reforms overtly clash with such values, or are implemented too quickly, it becomes more difficult for principals to meaningfully adopt new ways of working. For example, many reforms targeting the principalship demand deep and rapid participation which may well contradict the high power distance prevalent in many Southeast Asian countries and cities (such as Hong Kong, China and Malaysia) and so minimize the chances of real change in the role of the principal.

A second challenge to the meaningful reshaping of the principalship in Southeast Asia is the preparation and professional support provided to new principals (Cheung & Walker, 2006; Hallinger, 2003a). The extent to which this occurs varies widely across countries. Singapore and Hong Kong appear to provide considerably systematic support to new principals. In recent years, Malaysia has also developed new selection criteria and provides relevant professional development for prospective principals (Ministry of Education Malaysia, 2014).

It remains important for principals to have access to meaningful professional development. For such development to become relevant and offer any chance of real change it should be developed in concert with principals themselves and be adequately resourced and rewarded by Departments and Ministries of Education. It should also be linked closely to the reforms principals are expected to implement and shaped to form a coherent programme rather than the piecemeal, fragmented attempts that comprise the norm (Chu & Cravens, 2012).

A third challenge is related to the degree to which decentralization and other reforms have or have not been implemented and whether the depth of the reforms is either too extensive or too narrow to encourage a meaningful reshaping of the principalship. For principals to reshape their role in line with the demands of decentralization reforms it may not be enough to implement piecemeal reforms which, for example, force principals to share power with teachers but give them no say over the teachers hired.

On the other hand, some commentators might claim that reforming the role of the principal in Southeast Asia has gone too far. The effect of too many reforms, and reforms that appear to run in assorted directions, is that they further confuse principals by presenting them with more contradiction, incoherence and conflict (Cheng & Walker, 2008; Hallinger, 2010; Hallinger & Lee, 2011, 2013; Walker & Qian, 2012). Reforms that appear to lack connection are unlikely to encourage a meaningful reshaping of the principalship. An overly demanding and incoherent reform environment can also lead to a situation where potential leaders simply do not want to be school principals. Multiple reforms, especially if they lack coherence, may retard the reshaping of the role of the principal – after all, it is not easy to reshape your role if you are unsure what the role is meant to be.

Emerging from this assessment of challenges for policy and practice is the corollary observation concerning the relative weaknesses of the Southeast Asian knowledge base in educational leadership and management (Hallinger & Bryant, 2013a). Given the pattern of research performance portrayed earlier in this chapter, we assert the need for more focused efforts in regional cooperation and collaboration. We further suggest that effective strategies for accelerating the development of a regional knowledge base should be grounded in capacity building, making local knowledge from the region's societies accessible to each other as well as to international scholars, and cross-national coordination of research through collaborative structures.

Capacity building strategies should include instrumental activities as well as those that can shape more productive research cultures in universities over time. This has implications for faculty selection, evaluation and reward, course load assignments, inter-institutional research collaboration, faculty mentoring and provision of advanced training to faculty at all levels. This is not to imply that capacity building needs to be based in universities. For example, in Hong Kong much principal preparation is built around peer mentoring and support structures, and these have long operated in Singapore (Walker & Stott, 1993; Walker et al., 2008). However, in some systems, such as Thailand and Vietnam, the capacity of universities themselves to offer worthwhile training is restricted. Perhaps the key constraint that impacts institutions in these countries, with respect to this leverage point for improvement, is the lack of senior faculty capable of modelling expectations, sharing knowledge and mentoring junior faculty. This implies the need for regional universities intent on the development of research productivity to reach out beyond their local area for faculty recruitment. It also suggests the importance of forming regional and international alliances that can connect local faculty members with productive researchers on a continuous basis.

There is also an urgent need to conduct systematic reviews of research in those countries in which there may be a 'hidden literature' in educational leadership and management. We have reason to believe that a substantial number of research papers have been written in indigenous languages in these countries. This assertion is supported by a recent review of research on the principalship in China conducted by Walker et al. (2012). This review uncovered a large Chinese language literature that is largely inaccessible to an international audience. We suggest that similar 'hidden literatures' worthy of exploration may exist in other Asian countries.

The goal of these reviews should be to examine both indigenous language and English language literature from masters and doctoral theses as well as domestic and international journals. Scholars undertaking these reviews should not only synthesize substantive findings, but also assess the methodological quality of the 'national literature'. As these reviews are published internationally, the field will begin to develop a richer understanding of both the diversity and commonality that characterize the practice of educational leadership and management globally. Hopefully, these reviews would also inform policy makers. Hallinger and Bryant's (2013a) review of the East Asian literature yielded a number of conclusions that appear salient to analysis of educational leadership in Southeast Asia.

The overall volume of knowledge production from East Asia between 2000 and 2011 was quite low, less than 6 per cent of total output in the relevant journals. This represented a mean of 15.3 articles published per year from the region during the twelve-year period.

- Although there was a discernible increase in the annual rate of publication over the course of the twelve-year period, we treat the increase as relatively unimportant given the small volume attained even during the latter period.

- Our map of the publication terrain across the seventeen societies found a very uneven distribution with respect to contributions to the regional knowledge base. We identified Hong Kong as a 'peak' with extremely high productivity at one end, and most of the societies located in a long, low 'valley' with few or no contributions at the other end. This means that we have little or no knowledge of policy and practice in most of the countries in the region!

● Analyses of contributions by universities mirrored the societal pattern with one useful elaboration. A substantial majority of the publications not only came from a few societies, but from a small number of universities within them.

● Citation analyses performed on the body of articles in this corpus were highly consistent with these trends, and reinforced a picture of limited impact (Hallinger & Bryant, 2013a).

In summary, school leaders in Southeast Asia are facing challenges in the change of roles and responsibilities in leadership in the era of education reforms. They have to deal with the resistances created from societal and cultural aspects, and the struggles of defining and making sense of new roles of leadership. Local knowledge in leadership development must be accumulated to inform the progress of change in response to the challenges that inhibit school leadership advancement.

Looking forward

In light of the above, we wish to close by noting a number of relevant research questions that emerge from this consideration of the changing principalship in Southeast Asia. By addressing these and similar questions, scholars can expand the knowledge base of the Southeast Asian principalship and play a worthwhile role in the field both locally and internationally.

● How do Southeast Asian principals manage changes modelled on western education systems?

● What practices and beliefs have Southeast Asian principals inherited from traditional Southeast Asian education systems? How do traditional beliefs either clash or cohere with the demands of modern reforms?

● How do Southeast Asian principals balance change and stability?

● How do Southeast Asian principals understand, interpret and implement major reform initiatives such as the promotion of instructional leadership and how do patterns of practice vary across the region?

● What is the nature of the human resource management frameworks and systems that guide school leadership in Southeast Asia?

- What patterns of variation describe the recruitment, selection, training and evaluation of Southeast Asian school leaders?

- How do different expectations of what comprises leadership success (such as central governments and principals themselves) impact pathways to success?

3

Australian and Pacific Perspectives

Simon Clarke and Helen Wildy

Introduction

For both of us, investigating the efficacy of the preparation and development of school principals has been an enduring area of interest and we have been researching the broad theme of the principalship for the best part of two decades. As Southworth (2010) has rightly pointed out, there seems to be little point in investigating leadership without also understanding how leaders can be produced for both the present and the future. It is this understanding, as Southworth also points out, that will improve how we develop successful leaders on a continuous basis.

In this chapter, we consider the crucial question of how we can develop successful leaders now and into the future, especially in the Australian context. For this purpose, the chapter is divided into four main sections. First, we examine, briefly, the reasons it has become imperative for policy makers, practitioners and researchers to devote their attention to developing high calibre school leaders. Secondly, we describe the research we have undertaken that has helped to reveal some key considerations for successful leadership. Thirdly, we present a conceptual framework that has been generated from our research and can be used as an heuristic tool for engaging with the realities of the school leaders' world and the professional knowledge, skills and dispositions that are required to perform their work effectively. Finally, we comment on the potential of the heuristic as a means by which individual school leaders can be encouraged and supported to take responsibility for their own learning agendas, rather than being overly reliant on the normative requirements of a system.

The importance of developing successful school leaders

The importance of garnering successful school leaders has, of course, been well documented in the literature on school effectiveness for many years and we have no intention of lingering in such familiar territory. By way of setting the scene for the ensuing discussion, however, it is useful to reiterate the more salient reasons that have been suggested for placing the development of school leaders centre stage. Most importantly in this respect is the significance of school leadership in making a difference to children's lives. Indeed, school leadership has been identified as being second only to classroom teaching in its potential to influence student learning (Masters, 2008).

In addition, there is the complexity of exercising school leadership in the contemporary education environment. In this regard, Dempster and his colleagues (2011: 7) have captured well the connection between the increasing complexity of school leadership and the need for powerful professional learning in their comment below:

> The policy environment in which principals are expected to lead their schools is complex and demanding. It involves far-reaching initiatives, most with mandated requirements, all with high political and public expectations, explicit competition and transparent accountability, and some with tangible rewards. All are aimed at driving improved performance by schools, principals, teachers and students. It is in this roiling milieu that the question of how best to help school leaders to develop the knowledge, skills and dispositions necessary for productive careers must be addressed.

Given these circumstances, it is not surprising that for many novices there is considerable adjustment required in becoming a principal, a process that involves relinquishing the comfort and confidence of a familiar teaching role and embracing the discomfort and uncertainty of the new role of principal (Browne-Ferrigno, 2003; Cowie & Crawford, 2009; Crow, 2007). Furthermore, the role of school leaders has acquired a negative perception within several quarters of the education profession. For example, Cranston (2007) refers to potential applicants for the principalship being unenthusiastic about becoming principals because the role is perceived to be too daunting. Darling-Hammond and her colleagues (2007) draw attention to other factors that may discourage teachers in the USA from aspiring to the principalship, including the pressures of new accountability systems, expanding roles and responsibilities, inadequate compensation and poor working conditions. Fink (2011) also argues that the principal's role is especially unpalatable to Generation X'ers who consider these kinds of jobs to be incompatible with their lifestyles and goals, an attitude that is likely to be compounded in the future as Generation Y and the 'millennials' consider taking up leadership responsibilities. These perceptions contribute to the difficulty employers in many jurisdictions are experiencing in attracting leaders to the principalship and this, coupled with the baby-boomer retirement phenomenon, means that the need for education systems to embark on succession planning for sustaining leadership in schools is very much amplified.

A further reason for paying close attention to the development of school leaders relates to the efficacy of arrangements that have already been established to achieve this purpose. In Australia, until very recently, the ways in which interest and capacity in school leadership were enhanced depended entirely on location; there was, in effect, no coherent and comprehensive strategy in place either across the nation as a whole or within a single system (Caldwell et al., 2003). Arrangements for the preparation, development and support of school leaders continue to vary considerably from one state to another, as well as between educational jurisdictions. Some educational jurisdictions provide courses related to preparation for leadership, some have induction processes, some have programmes of support for specific issues. Most school authorities across the country have now produced standards and competencies frameworks used to inform professional development of school leaders and in some cases for their selection and promotion as well (Dempster, 2001). In addition, Australia's first Australian Professional Standard for Principals was endorsed by the Ministerial Council for Education, Early Childhood Development and Youth Affairs (MCEECDYA) in 2011.

It might be argued that this fragmented approach to developing capacity in school leadership is problematic. According to current disjointed arrangements, school leadership development cannot be based on any consensus about what it means to be a school leader. There is also a danger that the learning and development of school leaders will be drawn towards system initiatives, priorities and policies, rather than concentrating on what practising professionals require of themselves and their colleagues (Dempster, 2001). In other words, there is a risk that leadership programmes will lean towards a focus on system priorities rather than a people focus that promotes professional sustenance (Dempster, 2001). This is a key point to which we return later in our commentary.

Our approach to investigating the realities of school leadership

Having reiterated some of the reasons that warrant a close scrutiny of school leadership development from the education community, we now turn our attention to the research we have undertaken aimed at understanding the complexity of school leaders' work. To this end, our investigations have been informed by three connected lenses through which organizations may be viewed, namely social constructivism, micro-politics and complexity theory. These lenses have been described in detail elsewhere (Clarke & Wildy, 2010). In essence, however, they promote the view that schools are places inclined to be disorderly, complex, chaotic and unpredictable, and these are the circumstances school leaders contend with on a day-to-day basis.

Contiguously, we also recognize that reality is a function of personal interaction and perception and is, by definition, a highly subjective phenomenon requiring interpretation. It follows that to develop understandings of individuals' interpretations of their everyday reality, it is necessary to observe and sense what is occurring in the natural setting. In connection with studies of school leadership, this interpretive approach is premised on the belief that the subjective dimension is at the core of what (school) leaders do in terms of decision making, interrelating and communication. Meanings of events and phenomena, therefore, should be investigated from the subjects' perspectives. The notion that theories of organizational life should be generated inductively by examining the perspectives of practitioners themselves is fundamental to representing what is going on in schools and is an especially important consideration in creating appropriate content as well as 'pedagogy' for use in processes of leadership development.

In accordance with these theoretical assumptions we have engaged in research aimed at revealing the complexity of leading small rural and remote schools in order to provide in-depth and rich understanding of the dilemmas, tensions and challenges faced by the principal in such settings (Clarke & Wildy, 2004; Wildy & Clarke, 2005). Relatedly, under the aegis of the International Study of Principal Preparation (ISPP),[1] we have also engaged in research with the intention of finding out what novice school leaders do 'on the job' to ascertain the extent to which principals perceive their preparation aligns with their professional needs in their first year of appointment (Clarke et al., 2007).

Our research endeavours have led us to interview principals in their workplace on numerous occasions. In doing so, participants are encouraged to reflect on their experiences and practice. Using the interview data gathered in this way we have constructed short narrative accounts of problems, issues and challenges principals encountered and how these were handled, as well as reflections on their experiences. From our research activities conducted in Australia over more than a decade we have come to believe that the narrative account offers an effective means of depicting the complexity of principals' work characterized as it is by dealing with dilemmas, interacting with colleagues and the community, and coping with a diversity of professional responsibilities. We have argued previously that narrative writing generates lifelike accounts that can contribute to both theory for understanding and theory for improvement (Clarke et al., 2007; Wildy & Clarke, 2008).

A conceptual framework for engaging with school leaders' work

Over the years, our interpretive approach to investigating school leadership, and especially the principalship, has yielded a rich and realistic portrayal of Australian principals' day-to-day work from the perspectives of practitioners themselves. This comprehensive depiction of the problems, issues and challenges principals encounter and the ways in which these are handled, together with reflections on their experiences, has enabled us to articulate a conceptual framework with four focal points for informing school leaders' leadership development: *place, people, system* and *self*. We now provide a description of these focal points before discussing the potential application of the framework to the process of school leadership development. This description is based on our original articulation of the framework (Clarke & Wildy, 2010), but also includes useful refinements that have since been made by other scholars located in the field (Lovett et al., 2014).

Place

The first focal point of the conceptual framework is *place*. Having the knowledge and understanding of *place* means that school leaders are able to read the complexities of their context, especially the people, the problems and issues, as well as the culture of the school and the community in which it is located. The necessity to be 'contextually literate' (NCSL, 2007) is pertinent to all contexts insofar as it facilitates leaders' capacity to determine the school's priorities and interests, particularly in connection with leadership for learning. At the broader level, this 'literacy' entails familiarity with the socioeconomic, demographic, cultural and historical composition of the community which governs the intake of the school. At the school level, it means acquiring data about students' achievement and progress, turning it into useful information and ultimately into strategies for action. In other words, if student learning is to be the main focus of school leadership, principals require the ability to read the contextual circumstances so they can act in ways which are responsive to the situation. Lovett et al. (2014), however, argue, quite rightly, that school leaders' consideration of place should not be confined to circumstances occurring in the micro-context but should also embrace developments arising in the macro-context. In particular, these authors suggest that school leaders require a comprehensive knowledge of international trends and issues in education as well as their implications for national and local arrangements for enabling them to explain changes in policy, curriculum and practice at a more parochial level.

People

In our initial iteration of the conceptual framework, the focal point of *people* related mainly to school leaders having the knowledge, understanding and skill for handling a range of complex interactions on a day-to-day basis with diverse constituent groups, such as staff, parents, system personnel and community members. These interactions highlight the importance of the interpersonal, political and ethical dimensions of the school leaders' role as well as the need to understand human nature and the motivations of individuals (Begley, 2008). We have also come to realize, however, that the significance of *people* lies in its application to the development of human agency. In similar vein, Lovett et al. (2014: 7) emphasize the desirability of school leaders harnessing and mobilizing the capabilities of individuals in pursuit of common goals. Given the recent focus on the notion of 'distributed leadership' (Bush & Jackson, 2002) for facilitating school improvement, the ability of school leaders to cultivate positive and productive relationships seems to be an especially vital consideration in the formation of principals (Duignan, 2006). Starratt (2011: xi) goes further in his observation that educational leadership needs to be 'grounded in a deep appreciation of the richness, complexity and enormous potential of people'. Such an appreciation of people's potential, it may be argued, will be contingent on the extent to which leadership is perceived to be invited, necessitating that messages are communicated to people promoting their worth. In this connection, Stoll and Fink's (1996: 109) conceptualization of 'invitational' leadership is instructive. According to these authors, invitational leadership is predicated on optimism, or the assumption that people have untapped potential for growth and development; respect, which is manifested in vigorous discussion and reasoned dissent; trust in people to behave as though they are able, worthwhile and responsible; and being intentionally supportive, caring and encouraging. The combination of these tenets in use, it is suggested, helps to create an environment in which the energy and creativity of others are released. It is in these ways that a learning community is more likely to be established, which is characterized by sustained conversations around matters of school improvement. Swaffield and Dempster (2009) have referred to these conversations as 'disciplined dialogues' requiring school leaders to develop a range of effective frameworks for engaging in professional discussions, which ideally start from an evidence base.

System

Having the knowledge, understanding and skill to deal with the education authority, or *system*, means that school leaders are able to navigate their way through complex and often quite baffling bureaucratic regulations, policies and protocols. Lovett et al. (2014: 10) provide an extensive inventory of 'matters' about which school leaders need to be familiar if they are to contend successfully with the legal and regulatory environment of the *system*. These matters include, *inter alia*, risk management, financial accounting, facilities management, child safety, as well as workplace health and safety. They also embrace staff and student rights, workplace relations, employment and work conditions, student enrolment and exclusion procedures, and sexual harassment and discrimination regulations.

This raft of regulatory requirements generated by a *system* engenders knowledge and skill on the part of school leaders that are described as 'compliance' (Lovett et al., 2014). Compliance, however, can be contrasted with the knowledge and skills that entail 'discretion' or, in other words, the ability to consider the unique context of a school in the application of *system* demands. Ideally, school leaders do not descend into simply implementing the policies and values of the *system*, but are also able to question or adapt *system* imperatives.

Dealing with the *system*, therefore, takes not only functional knowledge, understanding and skill for contending with matters of compliance, but also confidence, determination and political sophistication for assisting discretionary decision making. This political sophistication may result in an ability to adapt external *system* imperatives in accordance with the internal purposes of the school. The ability of school leaders to go beyond following *system* prescription is especially pertinent to achieving a balance between, on the one hand, developing the capability to focus on leading learning and, on the other, developing the competency to manage multiple accountability demands. To this end, the use of data and evidence has become an increasingly important dimension of educational decision making (Earl et al., 2002). It is also fair to say that 'data literate' school leaders who can collect, interpret and use data effectively have a capacity to contribute to *system* policy and enhance the intelligence of accountability at that level.

Self

The inclusion of *self* as a focal point of the framework resonates closely with Loader's notion of the 'inner principal' (1997, 2010). According to Loader, a fundamental aspect of this concept is the idea that 'a leader's dominant style arises from their inner person, from their feelings values, beliefs and experiences' (2010: 195). This deep-seated, existential dimension of leadership, therefore, has implications for personal resilience in the job. From this perspective, self-knowledge and the ability to contextualize, understand, accept and deal with the emotional demands of the job is a key focus of our framework for informing the development of school leaders.

The significance of *self*, however, extends beyond considerations of school leaders' well-being and also takes into account their values and intentions. This is what Duignan (2006: 143) has referred to as personal formation and transformation, which engenders a deep understanding of personal values and a conviction that leadership is concerned fundamentally with developing the capacity of colleagues and students. This suggestion resonates with Dempster's observation (2009) that at the heart of leadership for learning is a well-defined sense of moral purpose. As he points out, 'principals are not there to make students' lives worse, they are there to see that schools concentrate on improving students' learning and ultimately their achievement' (n.p.). Indeed, it is the embracing of moral purpose at the very core of school leaders' work that prevents their leadership from being distorted into the uncritical management of agendas that are defined by others and for whom students' interests may be subsidiary (Lovett et al., 2014). In this connection, Higgs' observation (2009) that leader traits tend to be more significant factors in the emergence of 'bad' leadership than inadequate skills is salutary.

Pedagogy

Although our conceptual framework was generated from principals' perspectives of their experiences, we were somewhat baffled that learning, per se, did not emerge as a focal point. We have argued previously (Clarke & Wildy, 2011) that the connection between leadership and learning needs to be emphasized to a much greater extent in the formation of school leaders and for this reason it should be incorporated more explicitly than was the case in the initial iteration of the framework. Dempster and his colleagues agreed (2011) and contended that such is the significance of the leader's educative role, a further 'focal point' needed to be added to the conceptual framework that they have labelled 'pedagogy'. They went on to suggest that this addition strengthens the application of the framework because it reinforces the key purpose of school leadership, namely, the improvement of learning and teaching. The additional focal point has since been further elaborated (Dempster et al., 2012; Lovett et al., 2014). In particular, these authors (Lovett et al., 2014: 7) refer to the importance of school leaders gaining a good understanding of students' and teachers' growth, learning and development from a longitudinal perspective;

effective strategies for teacher professional learning; the planning, coordination, implementation, monitoring and evaluation of teaching and learning; and the use of data for engaging in evidence-based professional discussions.

The use of the conceptual framework for developing successful school leaders

We believe that our framework – *place*, *people*, *system* and *self*, and now, *pedagogy* – has potential to be used as a heuristic tool for dealing with the complexities of school leadership and the professional knowledge, skills and dispositions required to perform school leaders' work successfully. First, it serves as a reminder that if school leaders are to be equipped to take responsibility for others' learning, they need to be powerful learners themselves. Indeed, effective school leadership demands personal formation and growth to the extent that taking responsibility for nurturing the growth and development of others becomes natural (Duignan, 2006). Secondly, the framework emphasizes dealing with people and relationships – a key focus of leadership as opposed to management. Thirdly, and connectedly, the framework is grounded in the realities of the school as a complex workplace. As such, the framework is fundamentally descriptive rather than one which is integral to a normative theory or model.

Taking into consideration the latter comments, we are especially interested in the framework's utilization by individuals themselves as a heuristic tool to guide and plan their participation in professional learning. On this, Huber (2008) has commented that leadership development for school leaders seems to be shifting from focusing on a specific role to a broader concept that concentrates on personal learning and individual needs applying to knowledge, dispositions and performance that are of value in a more complex environment. Along similar lines, McCall (2010) makes reference to the benefits derived from leaders and managers enriching their experience by being aware of what they are doing and what they are learning from it. Robertson (2011) also suggests that the process of leadership development is enhanced when leaders employ meta-cognition to understand and take responsibility and ownership of their own learning. In this respect, we believe that the framework has a number of strengths.

In particular, the proactive application of the conceptual framework on a regular basis might assist school leaders to place an emphasis on their own learning and the learning of students. In doing so, the heuristic has potential for individuals to identify those aspects of leading self and others that have already been established as well as those aspects that have yet to be acquired

(Dempster et al., 2012). From this point of view, there is capacity for individuals to engage in professional learning that is not determined by employers and can enable leadership deliberations to be oriented around the needs of learning rather than the needs of the system (Dempster, 2011). Somewhat paradoxically, perhaps, the need for school leaders to take responsibility for their own learning has been heightened by the plethora of standards and capability frameworks that has evolved over the last few years in both state and national jurisdictions of Australia. As Dempster and colleagues have commented (2012), although standards frameworks have important uses, the choice of subject matter for school leadership development included in these frameworks is decided by employers and systems. Furthermore, standards frameworks tend to be embedded in contemporary understandings of school leadership, which make it difficult for them to offer a basis for planning future leadership considerations. It might be argued, therefore, that the heuristic tool, explicated here, could contribute to creating more balance between individual school leaders' learning needs and the normative requirements of a system.

The extent to which the heuristic is able to prompt personal agency in school leadership development depends, however, on promoting a culture as well as abundant opportunities in the initial preparation, development and support of school leaders that encourage individuals to take responsibility for their own leadership development. In this regard, DeRue and Ashford (2010) have made the pertinent observation that this is an area about which little is currently known and they urge researchers and practitioners to concentrate their attention far more rigorously on enhancing individuals' ability to learn from their own experiences. Lovett and colleagues (2014) also advocate undertaking further research aimed at gauging the degree to which individual school leaders exercise personal agency in their pursuit of leadership knowledge and skills. They have already started on this agenda by conducting trials of the heuristic framework reported here with Australian and New Zealand principals (Dempster et al., 2012). In particular, they have sought to operationalize the heuristic by using it to help school leaders identify ongoing professional learning experiences that are likely to enhance their leadership knowledge, dispositions and skills.

Final thoughts

In sum, we have argued in this chapter that the development of successful school leaders in Australia, as well as further afield, will hinge, at least to some extent, on individual leaders having the inclination to take personal ownership of their professional learning needs and not to rely exclusively on arrangements that are provided by the system in which they are employed. For this purpose, we have articulated a conceptual framework that may be used as an heuristic device to guide personal leadership learning and to encourage investigation and questioning. It would be absurd for us to purport that we are offering a panacea to the vexed issue of enhancing the quality of school leadership either in Australia or, indeed, anywhere else. At the very least, however, the heuristic may serve to highlight the critical importance of personal agency in the process of leadership development. Southworth (2010: 193) expresses this need persuasively in his comment that: 'More than ever before we need school leaders who are learners. And because school leaders are, at heart, educators they should exemplify the power of learning upon their leadership development.' It would seem, therefore, that as understandings of 'successful' school leadership evolve in line with the changing demands and pressures influencing leaders' roles into the future, processes of personal and proactive learning for leadership development will need to be located very much in the ascendant.

4

North American Perspectives

Elizabeth T. Murakami and
Wowek S. Kearney

Introduction

The preparation of school principals (i.e. headteachers, headmasters) is an instrumental piece in the improvement and sustainability of schools around the world. When reviewing the school principals' needs for professional development at an international level, Pashiardis and Brauckmann (2009: 120) in fact recognized the 'importance of school leadership in supporting change and providing for educational quality'. Moreover, the preparation of principals needs to be timely and dynamic in relation to improvement in both intellectual and socioeconomic demands. Hess and Kelly (2007: 2) added how 'school principals are asked to lead in a new world marked by unprecedented responsibilities, challenges, and managerial opportunities'.

Indeed, international and comparative discussions related to the preparation and professional development of principals have been occurring quite intensely. Such discussions include considerations of what are the expectations, training and requirements supporting the preparation of principals (Murakami et al., 2014; Ylimaki & Jacobson, 2011). Variables in preparation programmes for principals in the USA include not only a focus on the knowledge, skills and dispositions principals will need in their job, but also include innovations in the content, form and delivery of preparation which can lead to the sustainability of school and leadership success (Day & Leithwood, 2007; Gurr et al., 2011; Moos et al., 2011).

In this chapter, we recognize that even though leadership preparation in the USA is highly formalized (Ylimaki & Jacobson, 2011), there is variability in the preparation of principals. There are programmes which are concerned with a context-based preparation, depending on the geographical area or state requirements. Considering such variability in the preparation of principal candidates, what do leadership preparation programmes need to do in order to ensure their graduates are prepared to be successful school principals? We begin this chapter by providing a brief overview of the work of principals in the USA, followed by innovative programmes which have been recognized as successful in the country. Our analysis reflects on these modes of delivery in the context of the USA – providing a point of departure for a larger and global discussion of the ways in which the preparation of principals can lead to improving and sustaining successful schools.

A brief overview of principals and guidelines for their preparation in the USA

The national character of the USA can be understood as a federal republic with individual characteristics and freedoms present in its fifty states, federal districts and sixteen territories, including Puerto Rico and the Virgin Islands. The diversity of peoples in states and territories is reflected in the diverse representation of children in schools. Public schooling in the USA is compulsory until high school and free under the jurisdiction of government, state and local districts, who govern schools through elected local boards. There are different types of schooling including public, private, charter (which can use vouchers like schools of choice) and home schooling.

In 2011–12, principals in the USA served approximately 49.5 million students in public elementary and secondary schools. Twenty-one per cent of school-age children in the country are from families living in poverty (NCES, 2014). Approximately 116,000 principals were serving kindergarten–12 grade schools in the USA according to the National Center for Education Statistics (NCES, 2014). From this total, 89,810 principals served in public schools, and 25,730 principals served in private schools. A summary of the most recent characteristics of principals in listed in Table 4.1.

Several guidelines have been created by national organizations for the purpose of articulating the knowledge, skills and dispositions needed in the preparation and evaluation of principals. These include the Interstate School Leaders Licensure Consortium (ISLLC) standards (CCSSO, 2008), the Educational Leadership Constituencies Council (ELCC) standards (NCATE, 2011), the Interstate Teacher Assessment and Support Consortium's (InTASC) 2011 Performance Expectations and Indicators, including leadership roles for teachers and administrators (CCSSO, 2011), and frameworks generated by the National Association of Elementary School Principals (NAESP, 2008) and

TABLE 4.1 US principals' characteristics in 2011–12

Type of school	Gender	Ethnicity	Average age	Degrees held	Average salary	Average years of experience
Public 78%	Female 52%	White 82%	48–52 years	Doctorate 10%	US$85,400	8 years
Private 22%	Male 48%	African American 9.4%		Masters 59%		
		Hispanic 6%		Specialist 23%		
		Other 2.7%				

Source: NCES (2013).

the National Association of Secondary School Principals (NASSP, 2012). All these guidelines have provided individual states with leverage to review their own preparation programmes, performance evaluations and certification policies and processes. There has been strong advocacy towards generating a sustainable principal pipeline (Canole & Young, 2013). Such sustainability efforts at a national level have been led especially by the Council of Chief State School Officers (CCSSO), the Council of the Great City Schools (CGCS), the University Council for Educational Administration (UCEA) and the Wallace Foundation.

ISLCC standards have been a recognized set of guidelines more broadly informing individual state expectations for principals. These guidelines are not necessarily adopted in their entirety by individual states, but many of the ISLCC standards can be identified in guidelines from different state organizations, and state education departments, showing a common core in the expectations and standards for school principals. These highlight important areas such as school vision, school culture, organizational culture, collaboration within a diverse community, ethics and integrity and knowledge of political, social, economic, legal and cultural contexts.

Principal preparation programmes

The preparation of principals can be delivered by a number of agencies within the country. These are often approved by the Department of Education in individual states. Preparation and training sites can include universities, state agencies, school districts or privately-owned agencies. The most traditional programmes are the ones delivered by universities. Different from countries where candidates first seek a position before being trained, in the USA expectations for aspiring principals include a formal preparation (such as a teacher certification, teaching experience, a masters degree) and most often a state certifying examination as a condition to obtaining an administration certification or licensure (Murakami et al., 2014). Around 2005, Adams and Copland (2005) reported that approximately half of the US states required a licensure exam.

Even though university-based principal preparation programmes are the most sought by hiring districts, they are not free of criticism. Sometimes they are perceived as too formal – focusing more on theories and failing to keep pace with the realities principals face when entering the workforce (Levine, 2005; Wallace, 2010). This is a legitimate concern, especially when recognizing that student success in schools depends, to a great extent, on the quality of the school's leadership (Educational Research Service, 1998; Lashway, 2003; Pashiardis & Brauckmann, 2009). Another criticism relates to preparing principals who have no demonstrated leadership experience, as opposed to principals in other countries, who need to obtain a job first, before being certified. Moreover, principal candidates need exposure to current problems in schools, such as school reform issues in the era of accountability, demographic disparities, budget and funding, to name a few. As a result, many principal preparation programmes now embrace the responsibility of ensuring that their candidates receive a good balance of knowledge, skills and dispositions, and enhanced exposure to context-based challenges.

Recognized university programmes

Recognized principal preparation programmes in the country include those demonstrating ways of bridging the gap between theory and practice. One such innovative programme is at the University of Louisville, in which applicants must be nominated by their principal before being accepted into the leadership programme (Darling-Hammond et al., 2010). The logic behind the requirement is that current school principals are well positioned to evaluate the future leadership potential of current teachers. The idea is that once admission practices into the programme become more closely aligned with the perceived needs in schools, principal preparation programmes would be able to ensure they are recruiting candidates who are likely to be successful as school leaders (Browne-Ferrigno & Shoho, 2002).

The Urban School Leaders Collaborative (USLC) in Texas is another university–district partnership focusing on supporting inner-city districts. Housed at the University of Texas at San Antonio, they prepare and retain principals in challenging districts serving a majority of Latinos. Recognized by the University Council for Educational Administration, this programme prepares principals in partnering district facilities, and aligns district needs with university delivery courses (Murakami-Ramalho et al., 2010a). With an emphasis on reflective leadership, candidates are similarly appointed by current principals. The programme focuses on social justice issues to address the school performance of Latino students in socioeconomically underprivileged areas (Hollingsworth, 2009).

A programme demonstrating an extraordinary commitment to schools in high-need areas is the School Leaders Consortium (SLC) at Texas A&M University, San Antonio. The programme changed from a traditional academic one to a partnership with local school districts. In 2011, the leadership faculty began a multi-district partnership with seven districts in the area. This coalition of superintendents generated critical conversations with local school and district administrators, and faculty at Texas A&M University to jointly collaborate in the preparation of school principals who would be instrumental in generating turnaround and change in high-need schools. High-need schools in the area present school demographics showing a high number of families in poverty, a highly diverse ethnic composition of students and restricted educational resources.

Provided with opportunities to exchange ideas of what students and their families need, these leaders drive the development of a leadership preparation programme through a collective vision, featuring five key components:

1 *Courses are co-taught by school leaders working alongside university professors.* This model was designed to blend theory with practice. University professors provide the theory base for students, and district practitioners provide site-based district practices. District officials, such as curriculum directors, finance and law experts co-teach with university faculty to provide principal candidates with most updated trends in research and practice as adapted to the needs of students in the area. Principal candidates in this programme have been more visible among district officials due to the opportunity to meet local district leaders.

2 *Principal candidates are selected by local school principals and district officials.* These candidates are interviewed and assessed for their commitment to contributing to the communities' needs.

3 *Courses are taught within local school districts which facilitates hands-on experiences in real K-12 schools.* District officials work directly with each principal candidate, providing real-life experiences relevant to the district's focus and needs.

4 *Course content is delivered through a combination of face-to-face and online modes to accommodate working schedules.* Principal candidates have taken advantage of the flexibility of this model, where they have the opportunity to carry out lively discussions of concepts covered during online sessions.

5 *Course content is made available free of charge* for any employee of the participating school district who is not pursuing university credit, but is interested in attending for their own professional development.

The expertise these principal candidates are acquiring is instrumental especially in schools in need of improvement, and capitalizes on the knowledge from the collaborating districts. It is important to observe that in the USA there is a strong relationship between poverty and decreased student academic achievement as compared with their more affluent peers (Hopson & Lee, 2011). Thus having an understanding of what can be done to help close the socioeconomic achievement gap is an important consideration when preparing aspiring school leaders (Kearney & Herrington, 2013).

In relation to the preparation of principals in high-need areas, some scholars have proposed the preparation of principals for social justice issues – by focusing on 'critical consciousness, knowledge, and practical skills focused on social justice with their students' (Capper et al., 2006: 212). With this concept, Capper et al. provided a framework for preparing educational leaders for social justice. Their framework has been employed in many ways by the aforementioned programmes.

Another way to provide a more realistic job preview for aspiring leaders is to increase the required number of hours spent in schools during the programme. Students at East Tennessee State University are required to complete 540 internship hours (Klein, 2007), roughly four times the national average of required hours. Wichita State University has a different approach in increasing school-based contact hours. Aspiring leaders receive reduced class contact hours in order to maximize students' experiences by having them work on action research projects with local school districts (Orr, 2006).

Some programmes attempt to ensure that their graduates meet the university's own expectations through the establishment of exit criteria. At California State University in Fresno, students are required to complete exit interviews at the end of each semester with programme faculty and district supervisors to ensure that they are prepared to lead local schools (Jackson & Kelley, 2002). Finally, some states are now requiring support for new administrators beyond programme graduation. For example, the state of Louisiana requires that new school leaders participate in a mentoring programme and complete a professional growth plan as a follow-up support after these candidates obtain their university degree and principal certification (Southern Regional Education Board, 2002). All these innovative programmes demonstrate a common need for a strong partnership with surrounding districts, and a vision for the improvement of schools.

The search for the effective preparation of principals

Based on the new programme initiatives illustrated in this chapter, we can attest that principal preparation programmes in the country have undergone a significant shift over recent years. These recognized programmes seem to be effective in selecting candidates, and in matching the curriculum with the needs of students, schools and local districts. In part, this shift has to do with the changing expectations of what it means to be a successful school leader (Gale & Bishop, 2014). In this section we reflect on the significance of the development of principal preparation programmes within the context of this country.

The programmes introduced in this chapter show that universities can no longer simply prepare individuals in leadership theory. In the current age of accountability, school leaders are now expected to be data analysts, instructional leaders and change agents both inside and outside the school walls (CCSSO, 2012). It is therefore incumbent upon principal preparation programmes to provide their students with the requisite knowledge, skills and dispositions to help them be successful as school leaders. There is pressure in having these principals ready to take on the leadership of schools and generate improvement. Currently, the Council of Chief State School Officers (CCSSO, 2012) perceive that principals in US schools must be prepared and 'ready-on-day-one'. CCSSO defined an effective principal as follows:

> A school-ready principal is ready on day one to blend their energy, knowledge, and professional skills to collaborate and motivate others to transform school learning environments in ways that ensure all students will graduate college and career ready. With other stakeholders, they craft the school's vision, mission, and strategic goals to focus on and support high levels of learning for all students and high expectations for all members of the school community. To help transform schools, they lead others in using performance outcomes and other data to strategically align people, time, funding, and school processes to continually improve student achievement and growth, and to nurture and sustain a positive climate and safe school environment for all stakeholders. They work with others to develop, implement, and refine processes to select, induct, support, evaluate, and retain quality personnel to serve in instructional and support roles. They nurture and support professional growth in others and appropriately share leadership responsibilities. Recognizing that schools are an integral part of the community, they lead and support outreach to students' families and the wider community to respond to community needs and interests and to integrate community resources into the school.
>
> CCSSO, 2012: iv

Beside their preparation, these principals are evaluated on their success according to a number of national indicators which can be found in the Condition of Education report (NCES, 2014). The indicator includes students' demographic characteristics; their participation in education; dropout and graduation rates; and student performance in reading, maths and sciences. To put these indicators into context, the report shows that 3.1 million public school students or 81 per cent of high-schoolers graduated on time with a regular diploma in 2011–12. Schools are also considered effective when preparing students to enroll in college. In 2012, about 66 per cent of high school completers enrolled in college, compared to 60 per cent in 1990. Most concerning in the report is that one in five school-age children lived in poverty in 2012, as opposed to one in seven in 2000. There is a strong relationship between poverty and decreased student academic achievement as compared with their more affluent peers (Hopson & Lee, 2011). There is also a correlation between poverty and college enrolment since higher education can be expensive. Thus having an understanding of what can be done to help close the socioeconomic achievement gap is indeed an important consideration when preparing school leaders.

Identifying effective principal candidates

In our experience preparing principals in university-based preparation programmes, we have been part of many discussions in relation to the admission of candidates, programme design and quality of delivery, including concerns expressed by Levine in 2005. Levine acknowledged that no other professional school is held responsible for intractable social, economic or systemic problems as education schools, different from, for example 'schools of agriculture [which] are not faulted for the decline of the family farm' (p. 6). In the report, Levine also indicated a number of areas in preparation programmes which needed improvement, such as admissions, curriculum, faculty preparation and clinical instruction. Not surprisingly, he received much criticism for this report – by many national leaders who responded that the report failed to acknowledge any of the innovative practices in successful school leadership programmes across the country (Young, 2005). Nevertheless, a number of researchers have since identified similar areas most commonly associated with ineffective school leadership programmes (Creighton & Jones, 2001; Jackson & Kelley, 2002; Murakami-Ramalho et al., 2010b; Normore & Jean-Marie, 2010).

One of the concerns addressed by the aforementioned scholars relates to the low entry criteria required for admission to principal preparation programmes. In a review of 450 principal certification programmes across the USA, Creighton and Jones (2001) found that educational administration candidates had the second lowest GRE scores of any education majors (second only to physical education). We agree with Normore and Jean-Marie (2010) when they argued that the selection of students into graduate leadership preparation is as critical as the quality of the programme or the candidates' experiences. Hence there may be great benefit in partnering with school districts to identify potential principals through a nomination process. Many of the programmes considered innovative seemed to be conducting these selective processes with the purpose of strengthening the pool of future principals.

Preparing principals as change agents

At the heart of effective school leadership is the ability to recognize, understand and respect the needs, values and goals of others through constant communication (Nelson & Low, 2011). Principals are sought to become change agents – requiring that they enhance their communication skills in order to support students and their communities. In the search for effective principals and effective schools, we argue that leadership effectiveness is directly related to the leader's ability to recognize others' needs and respond using the appropriate leadership style suited for the situation (Kobe et al., 2001). This, as Levine indicated, may be even more evident in educational settings, and is highly visible when compared to other organizations (Moore, 2009). With the intent of providing principal candidates with opportunities to understand the importance of communication prior to obtaining a position, leadership programmes may be well served to include internship opportunities and mentoring opportunities with district officials. Cai (2011) found that school administrators who have high levels of social awareness develop strong and productive relationships which have a positive impact on school climate. This is largely due to the fact that the stronger the relationships principals are able to build with their team, the more able they are to involve teachers and community members in collaborative change efforts (Sadri, 2012). One way that principals can maximize teacher involvement is by engaging with them in stimulating conversations about the technical aspects of education (Louis & Wahlstrom, 2011).

Another essential disposition for school leaders is the ability to make mindful decisions collectively, continuously and thoughtfully (Dufour et al., 2004). The ability of a school principal to lead in a thoughtful manner can have a profound effect on school mindfulness and the faculty's ability to take risks (Hoy et al., 2006). Critical opportunities to review concepts of mindfulness reside in sessions where potential principals are allowed to reflect on the broader concept of emotional intelligence. However, accounting for the emotional intelligence of programme participants presents a problem for school leadership programmes. Part of this difficulty is the question of whether the dispositions required of effective leaders can effectively be taught to adult learners, or whether, by the time students enrol in graduate programmes, their behavioural attributes are already firmly established. Some North American institutions currently use personality inventories in order to ensure candidates have the dispositions they are looking for before admitting candidates into their leadership programmes (Ann-Lumsden et al., 2005). Programmes that have adopted the philosophy that dispositions can be taught include the School Leaders Consortium at A&M San Antonio, where they have incorporated emotional intelligence training within their curriculum (Kearney et al., 2014).

Evaluating the quality of principal preparation programmes

Since Levine's report, common characteristics shared by high quality school leadership programmes in the USA have been disseminated by national organizations. Quality in principal preparation programmes included considerations such as whether a programme showed a strong theoretical base in leadership for school improvement, coupled with a curriculum that emphasizes instructional leadership, the integration of theory and practice, quality internships, knowledgeable faculty, social and professional support for students and internal evaluation of programme effectiveness (Orr & Orphanos, 2011). Young et al. (2012) further articulated the importance of clearly defining the purpose of a university programme in order to generate best practice among school administrators. In a report from the University Council for Educational Administration (UCEA) a list of eleven programme quality attributes (see Table 4.2) was included, which proved helpful in our own examination of the innovative programmes reviewed in this chapter.

Towards global discussions of leadership effectiveness and sustainability

By providing this examination of innovative programmes in the context of the USA, with examples of how traditional university programmes are modifying their approach in order to strengthen the experiences of future principals, it is our hope that we ignite a larger and global discussion about the ways in which the preparation of principals can lead to effective leadership in sustainable school environments. In this chapter we have explored the task of preparing successful school leaders by recognizing that there has been an investment to raise the quality of the preparation of principals. We explored what leadership preparation programmes need to do in order to ensure their graduates are prepared to be successful school principals. At an international level, research could include a discussion of the different expectations, training and requirements in different countries. Whereas some countries require

TABLE 4.2 Criteria in the examination of principal preparation programme quality attributes

1. University faculty efforts in promoting relevant knowledge of best practices
2. Courses taught by a critical mass of full-time faculty who exhibit excellence in scholarship, teaching and service in the field
3. Involvement of advisory boards of field stakeholders to plan, teach and support interns
4. Collaboration with other universities, school districts and appropriate agencies
5. Focused on problems of schooling, leadership and administration
6. Engaged in evaluation and enhancement
7. Includes periods of study and supervised clinical practice in diverse student and teacher environments
8. Has a systematic recruitment process to attract applicants with leadership potential
9. Contains efforts for placement and career advancement
10. Faculty that develops, delivers, and evaluates quality programmes in cooperation with professional associations
11. A programme that encourages the professional development of faculty to improve preparation, research and research utilization

*Source: Young et al. (2012: 3).

training after principals are hired in their positions, it would be significant to discuss the content, form and delivery of these programmes as informing the sustainability of schools and leadership success.

Even though we only focused on university-based programmes, non-university training has also been subject to criticism. Flessa (2007), for example, points out that non-university-based school leadership programmes often lack the ability to meaningfully critique substandard local district policies that may be in place. Thus if one school district trains all of its own future leaders from within, they will likely perpetuate whatever norms and expectations exist within the district without being exposed to a broader range of ideas or possibilities. One could logically conclude that neither the status quo nor solely district-based leadership training are independently sufficient to adequately prepare educational leadership candidates for the difficult job of leading schools. What forms of non-university programmes can we find in different countries? How are they structured so that they meet the needs of students and their contexts? These are but a few of the potential research questions that can be developed around this topic.

In summarizing the US experience, we recognize that throughout the centuries, local schools faced a number of historic challenges which still shape the foundation of schools, including democratic goals, end to discrimination and high accountability goals. We learned that academic performance presses principals to be school-ready from day one, as the CCSSO articulated, and requires principals to transition from management to true leadership that motivates students and teachers, as well as generates a supportive instructional environment, especially with concerns towards poverty.

When examining university-based programmes in the USA, we recognized that universities cannot simply prepare individuals in leadership theory, but need to engage in high degrees of collaboration with districts, allowing for plenty of opportunities for the clinical practice of principal candidates, and continued sustainability in professional development efforts. To this end, we provided a number of examples of innovative programmes, including the one offered at our university, with the intent of motivating a continued conversation about the improvement of the profession, programme and modes of delivery, as well as the effectiveness of preparing principals in schools. We hope that this chapter ignites a larger conversation about improving the preparation of principals to potentially serve in the most significant goal in education – that of providing every child with the best education they deserve.

5

South American Perspectives

Candido Alberto Gomes, Alexandre Ventura and Magali de Fátima Evangelista Machado

The recent history of education in South America

The South American authoritarian regimes, established during the Cold War, crumbled in the 1980s, succumbing to the foreign debt crisis and the consequent economic recession. Budget cuts in public education opened the doors to new policies. Founded on the three pillars of decentralization, funding diversification and external evaluation, these new policies were ushered in under the aegis of international financial organizations. At the same time, democratization led to the increasing participation of social actors and school autonomy.

In the 1980s, countries in South America, along with the whole Latin American region, suffered the consequences of the oil crises and high levels of external debt. Ultimately, this led to recession and a moratorium for a number of countries on the international debt markets. This became known as the 'lost decade'. This was the deepest economic crisis since the 1920s (Velloso, 2000), obliging governments to make big spending cuts, especially in the social services, as well as structural adjustments. Education was one of the targets – with significant intervention by international organizations – in a bid to increase efficiency, quality and equity (Trojan, 2010). The unrest that accompanied the economic situation was partly responsible for the fall of the authoritarian regimes that had taken hold during the Cold War that started in the 1950s (Argentina, 1966–75; Brazil, 1964–85; Chile, 1973–90; Colombia, 1954–7), clearing the way for political liberalization.

With economic recovery still elusive, the Jomtien Conference (1990) represented a big step forward in educational policy, with its effects also reaching the continent. The participating countries agreed to raise the quality of basic education with the objective of improving social equity and reducing regional differences, both between countries and inside them. The country representatives met several times, organized by UNESCO, looking to implement an educational development project for the region. This project forged new alliances (especially public–private partnerships), sought the active participation of the school community and drove the decentralization of educational systems and the creation of national evaluation systems. The agenda revolved around the need to reduce public spending. However, ideals of participation and decentralization were also driven by the democratic forces that followed the dictatorships. Increasing efficiency was essential given the shrinking resources, while a results-focused policy also met with the demands for better education. Accordingly, school management emerged as a change factor.

Repositioning education on the list of priorities was a collective effort of public officials and international organizations, such as UNESCO, the Organization for Economic Cooperation and Development (OECD), the World Bank (WB) and the Inter-American Development Bank (IBD). A number of countries made use of the loans by the development banks, which were tied to certain objectives. As such, the reforms being contemplated led the WB to recommend (among other things) that priority should be given to primary education and improving the overall quality of education. This would help ensure excellence for all students (World Bank, 2006).

The reform agenda: decentralization, funding diversification and education evaluation

All the countries studied here were centrally managed, with a high proportion of enrolment depending on central governments. Political authorities appointed principals on the basis of partisanship, fidelity and merit. The most important role of the principals was to keep schools running, ensuring all the numerous bureaucratic requirements were met. Sometimes they were expected to construct good schools, as expressions of governmental achievement. This heritage, a hangover from the authoritarian regimes, survives in large sectors of public education, including the principals' traditional role. Education colleges (and occasionally normal schools) offer preparatory courses for principals, which very often consist only of theoretical instruction. However, the reforms carried out, starting in the 1980s, were based on three pillars: decentralized management, funding diversification (that is, a reduced role for the state) and external evaluation. Decentralized management has meant that more executive powers have been transferred to subnational governments and schools have been awarded more autonomy. With external evaluation, schools received more responsibilities and supplementary funding, generally through per student allocation for current and small capital expenditure. As a region, South America keeps selection, hiring, payment and retirement of personnel centralized at municipal and state levels. For instance, Kracwczyk and Vieira (2008) point out that countries such as Argentina and Brazil (both federative states) and Colombia (a unitary state like Chile) transferred the responsibility for the different levels of schooling to state and municipal governments. In these countries, the previous military rule used centralization to maintain control. However, the economically liberal reforms in Chile devolved responsibility for basic education to the municipalities, with the Ministry of Education acting as a coordinator, although political control remained tight. In Argentina, decentralization started in 1996 with secondary schools. In Brazil, the Federal Constitution of 1988 instituted the process. In later years, a constitutional amendment (1996) established a minimum funding allocation per student and carried out a small tax reform, so as to raise the level of efficiency and equity in public primary education. With this success already behind it, a subsequent amendment (2006) widened the financing to include all basic education. The most notable decentralization in Chile was carried out while still under the military regime, beginning in 1984, and maintained after the regime's fall. As mentioned before, Chilean education is composed of a set of different markets, divided into public institutions, institutions subsidized or maintained by government, and private institutions. Colombia embarked on the process in 1986, with a partnership between the private and public sectors. The country adopted a policy of school municipalization with the Constitution of 1991.

These changes meant that the local managers and school principals gained a strategic importance that they did not have before. In many cases, this meant increased responsibility and involvement in school financial management tasks. However, at the same time, these models minimized the state's responsibilities during the decade, repositioning it more as a regulator than a provider (Kracwczyk & Vieira, 2008).

If one side of the reforms brought decentralized management, the other side added external evaluation to record the results of those responsible for the networks and schools. From another perspective, while the managers had gained more freedom to use their resources, they had become subject to demands for results. These processes meant that leadership became more important for encouraging teamwork. As such, the systems for evaluating the quality of education – using standardized tests applied to students – were introduced starting at the end of the 1980s (Chile, 1987; Brazil, 1989; Colombia, 1991; Argentina, 1993). In 1995, UNESCO's Latin American Laboratory for Assessment of the Quality of Education started its first comparative study involving fourteen countries (Casassus, 2007). The results of the external evaluations led the countries to adopt new education management concepts, including efficiency, efficacy and effectiveness.

The last of the three pillars consisted of diversifying the financing, directly stimulating the rise in the enrolments in private institutions or state subsidized private schools. In this case, private management was seen as superior to state management and also underlined the idea that school leadership can make a significant impact on the quality of education provision. Besides the financed networks that exist in some countries (e.g. Catholic schools), the most enduring experience was the vouchers used in Chile. In this system the state allows parents to choose the school where they enrol their children. The voucher can then be complemented with a top-up payment, thus creating a quasi-market for education.

Successful schools: convergence on school leadership

Under this new perspective, education began adopting the terminology and approaches used in general management, including 'effective school' and 'effectiveness in the school', reflecting international movements. The success of a school is assessed against the objectives achieved and the improvements made in using available resources, particularly with the results becoming ever more public and individually detailed. With this change in direction, emphasis was equally placed on achieving objectives and the internal functioning of the school environment. To this extent, a school may have sub-standard infrastructure, but, if for example it has interested and committed teachers, the students can achieve higher levels of learning. However, it is possible that this perspective also helps disguise the failings of the state in providing resources, shifting the blame to the teachers.

The emphasis placed on leadership in the educational sphere and its level of complexity has led to studies that characterize and systematize the distinctive skills associated with school leadership, seeking to define the ideal profiles for management roles (OECD, 2009). New research by the aforementioned laboratory (LLECE, 2010) gives support to earlier studies, showing that socioeconomic and cultural status are the most important factors influencing student performance. This result is not surprising in a continent with marked social inequalities. However, emphasis continues to be placed on the educational processes inside the school (particularly the environment), leadership by the principal and the satisfaction and performance of the teachers. Successful principals focus on their pedagogical leadership, promotion of learning and support to the teachers in classrooms. Moreover, they construct a positive climate directed towards work and learning. In other words, for the most part, performance is related to a web of complex social factors, where material resources are necessary but not sufficient. From a qualitative perspective, this network was also revealed in a study of successful schools identified in the research carried out by Casassus (2007) looking at socially disadvantaged students (Machado, 2013). Important elements of the school environment included the leadership by the principal and the teachers, respect for teacher opinions, sharing responsibilities and a low level of teaching staff turnover. Particularly in the case of the principals, they supported teachers' work in teams, they shared administrative and pedagogical responsibilities and contributed to building a democratic organizational climate, as well as a pleasant working environment. Furthermore, principals were fundraisers, encouraged parents' participation at schools and did not concentrate leadership, that is, the school was a non-authoritarian organization (Mella, 2002). Thus, their profile has moved away from that of the bureaucrat.

The literature does not show the same picture for school autonomy, which has been patchy, with compromised results (Gomes, 2005). The PISA results show only a limited association between autonomy and performance, depending on the country (OECD, 2011).

Theoretical perspectives on school management

If we have seen such characteristics in practice, how are principals being prepared? Numerous studies in the West and Latin America have shown conflicts between the theoretical models of management and the relation between these models and the structure and running of educational systems. In reality, the concept of management in schools comes down to 'collective involvement and dialogue' (Cury, 2002: 165), built up inside the schools. Libâneo (2007) identifies five theoretical approaches in this area (although they tend to appear less clearly in the teacher training), with one dominant style:

1 A technical-scientific approach (bureaucratic), based on a hierarchical order for the organizational structure and favouring a more conservative,

centrally located role for the manager. The bureaucratic manager ensures that the rules and regulations governing the running of the educational institution are enforced. The management models of effective schools (and others), associated with specific results targets, tend to incorporate some elements of this approach.

2 A self-managing approach, envisaging the participation of all the members of the school community in developing the objectives and in the search for effective means of achieving them, respecting the principles and standards laid down in the current legislation.

3 A collegial management approach, relying on the collaborative culture of the school as an institution. In other words, objectives are shared and a 'co-responsibility' exists between the social stakeholders of the school as an institution, through a process of dialogue and group decision making. The school community participates in collegial management via a collegial body, usually composed of representatives from all stakeholder segments.

4 An interpretative approach, seeking to consolidate social interactions by using the way the school works as a tool for social construction, with the subjective experiences of the individuals as supporting basis. This approach is designed to be a link between the interaction and the action, between the theory and practice, between education and society and between the individual and the social surroundings (Sander, 1995).

5 A democratic-participative approach, based on the institutional relationship between the management and the participation of the team members. This ensures participative management and at the same time management of the participation. This approach is designed to help achieve objectivity when studying organization and management, using the collection of real data and without influencing the study of the subjective and cultural meanings.

While somewhat of a generalization, it can be stated that the re-democratization process on the continent meant that the first approach lost ground – under varying circumstances and political settings – to the last four approaches. It should also be noted that these theoretical approaches became interwoven into management training courses and, in practice, depending on public policy, have become far removed from pure or idealized types. In any case, as will be seen, administration has not been successful in providing future leaders with training.

School leadership in South America

Re-democratization and decentralization

Re-democratization and decentralization have led to increased similarity among the criteria for training principals – commonly as part of undergraduate or postgraduate higher education courses – as well as selection and career progression processes. The often brusque changes that have occurred in public policy have meant that a wide range of different systems have been observed over time and space: the same region may have principals elected by parents, students and teachers; principals who are nominated using party-political criteria; and principals selected by examination in a public competition, among other possibilities. There may be teachers (who may or may not have specific training in school management) who rise to the position of school principal and then return to being teachers; and there may be principals that are part of a special career track. In some places, the debate on the need for school management courses is still ongoing. However, consensus of opinion holds that principals should have classroom experience. These changes make it difficult to gauge the effects of the different alternatives. At the same time, the laws of the different countries have provided some common baselines, as shown below. To this end, four of the largest and most populous countries were selected, recognizing the diversity in the continent and the uneven development of the literature in the area.

Argentina

The educational reforms in Argentina were laid out in the 1993 Federal Education Law no. 24.195. This established an educational system based on principles of equity and equality. Educational services were outsourced to the provinces in the expectation that decentralization would help increase quality and efficiency; in such a big country, this would help bring the services closer to the public.

Decisions on working regulations and contracting procedures for teachers and principals were left to each province. The Teacher Statutes (Law no. 14.075/1986) stated that the teaching career provided the access path for a teacher to become a principal in most provinces. However, in two provinces different statutes coexisted: one covered teachers at pre-/primary school (that cannot become principals), and the other covered secondary/higher education teachers (who can become principals).

Becoming a principal is dependent on a two-stage process: the first stage involves an assessment of the candidate's history (years of service, training, skills and professional career path) while the second stage is based on theoretical and practical tests. The candidate must present a proposal for the institution which is subject to an oral exam and interview. Such competitions are standard in all the provinces, with one exception, which has its own regime for selecting managers. Public schools in Argentina adopted a self-management approach in selecting their school principals (Kracwczyk & Vieira, 2008).

However, higher education institutions have not shown themselves capable of building leadership capacities in the students that will become future principals. They are faced with problems of endogamy, a lack of rules covering critical areas, teachers contracted on a per-hour/class basis and minimal autonomy. As a result, those being trained lack sufficient professionalization (Aguerrondo & Vezub, 2011).

Turning to democratization, it is important to note that experiments with school councils were still being carried out in the country in the 1980s. These had varying results but suffered obstacles such as a lack of support from regional authorities, resistance from principals and efforts concentrated on obtaining material resources (Garostiaga, 2011).

Brazil

The Constitution (1988) implemented democratic management of public education throughout Brazil. Immediately following the lead given by the federal constitution, the states and municipalities introduced the principle of democratic management in schools as part of the state constitutions and municipal organic laws. In 1996, the Education Act (Law no. 9.394/96) introduced and formalized community participation as part of school management, allowing the education systems to adapt their particularities to the ideals of democratic management in public schools providing basic education.

In this respect, democratic management is one of the dimensions of decentralization, bringing with it demands and responsibilities that are shared across different administrative levels and segments of schooling, requiring the participation of the educational community and the family in decision making processes. Following the publication of the legislation regulating the Constitution, the federal, state and municipal governments produced increasingly frequent programmes which transferred financial resources directly to schools, usually based on the number of enrolments. This reduced political pressures, as the distribution of resources became subject to universal criteria, covering small investments and operating expenses.

At school level, a development plan is normally a prerequisite for transferring funds. This plan is approved by a board covering the diverse segments of the school community. It is this same board that analyses and approves the accounts of the teaching institution, which are then sent to the bodies responsible for control and verification in the respective governmental authority. Distributing control of funds strengthened these boards, which, despite some operational difficulties (such as a having little prior tradition of participative roles and resistance from the principals), have contributed to increased access and a reduction in students repeating years. However, they frequently became a front for the formal administrative model required by law (Garostiaga, 2011).

Brazil is both the most populous and the largest country in South America. This fact (together with its three levels of government) means that it also exhibits the largest differences in the way autonomy and the selection procedures for principals are implemented. Basically, the selection process for school principals in the public network is frequently based on five methods. In the first method, no restriction is placed on the choice of principal, which is the responsibility of the political powers. The second method involves an internal selection procedure, with the candidate having to show proof of their knowledge and achievements, which is restricted to those who are part of the public education career path. The third method involves a public competition for the position of principal. The fourth model merges two methods: a list is drawn up with three or six names (or a mixture of processes) followed by an election. Lastly, a fifth method exists where the post of principal is awarded to the winner of a direct election. Estimates show that in 1996–8 some 53 per cent of the municipal and state networks had elected principals. This helped significantly reduce political influence, but problems emerged with personal agendas, populism and lobbying within schools (Gomes, 2005). In turn, in-depth study showed that school performance was associated with principals having the following particular characteristics: a firm, objective and participative leadership style; good relations with the community; motivation to win over the teachers; and a desire to help students in difficulty, in a joint effort with parents and teachers. It has also been shown that good performance is highly associated with principals who are selected by examination, in contrast to those selected by a board (Soares et al., 2011).

Starting in 1996, the decentralization process (in a country that today has 5,561 municipalities) created new leaders – municipal education managers and education councillors. Since then, their level of schooling has been constantly rising and their role has become more technical and pedagogical. Meanwhile, most of them still have only limited control over their funds (Brazil Ministério da Educação, 2011). The boards – which were born mainly out of legal requirements rather than local necessities – faced structural problems, such as their submission to executive power, their role as government as opposed to state bodies and a series of obstacles to citizens taking control of education (Souza, 2013).

Chile

The education sector in Chile is a set of markets, split into public institutions, private institutions subsidized by government and private unsubsidized institutions. This reform dates back to 1981 and the period of the military regime (1973–90), reflecting part of a larger market transformation in the economy, including decentralization, school external evaluation and a universal voucher mechanism based on a per student allocation by the government. Despite later changes after democratization, strictly speaking private institutions are the most expensive and maintain the highest level of socioeconomic selectivity. They are followed by private subsidized schools, which require money from parents or students to supplement the governmental allocation. The public institutions work with the public allocation only. Studies of the system (e.g. Mizala & Torche, 2010) reach the conclusion that educational achievement became socioeconomically stratified, thus reinforcing differences. This is one of the main reasons for the political protests by students in the last decade.

This reform introduced differences for school principals, with one example being the selection process. Nowadays they have job stability in both the public and the subsidized institutions, which is reflected in their low level of mobility. Law no. 19.070 (published in 1991) states that potential principals must have a teaching career. The 1991 teacher statutes require only that teachers have additional training (in school management/supervision and evaluation/educational guidance) for them to be promoted to management positions. The 1995 law (no. 19.410) set out the regulations governing the public competitions for teachers wishing to take on management roles.

Law no. 20.206 (2005) meant that the municipal education institutions became obliged to hold public competitions for principals and abolished the position of 'lifetime principal'. One of the stages in the competition consists of the candidate defining a work proposal for the institution where they wish to become principal. The other stage of the competition is a written test.

Private institutions contract principals following the laws of supply and demand in the market. Each education institution decides its own rules for carrying out management functions. These differences between the three types of school mean that the education system lacks cohesion (Donoso et al., 2012).

Research confirms that principals have a verifiable impact on students in Chile. However, the impact of different leadership styles lacks research (Horn & Marfán, 2010). In any case, training of principals lacks adequate attention to leadership and management (Galdames-Poblete & Rodríguez-Espinosa, 2010). As in other cases in South America, theoretical concerns may prevail over practical capabilities.

Colombia

After various attempts at producing education legislation, Colombia passed Decree no. 2.277 in 1979, defining the rules for pre-school, primary and secondary education. This Decree stated that only those having qualified as an education professional or who were enrolled in the National Teaching Register could practise as teachers. The management roles in public education are carried out by teachers, that is, by qualified education professionals. These roles are: school principal or group principal; coordinator or registrar for the institution; rector of the campus for basic, secondary or middle education; principal of the teaching centre or group of institutions; and education supervisor or inspector.

The approval of Law no. 715 brought educational matters under sovereign control. The Decree no. 3391 which followed in 2003 set out the regulations, defining and establishing the general rules and mechanisms for evaluating and training teaching and management personnel.

The management of private schools in Colombia is characterized by the fact that it is one of sixteen Latin American countries where the Fe y Alegría Catholic schools operate. Combining public funding with private management, they give preference to poorer students, whose income is the same or less than that of similar students in other schools (Parra Osorio & Wodon, 2011). They are institutions that have their own culture and leadership, usually with great success.

Overall, the liberal policies adopted in recent decades (including decentralization and government subsidies) negatively affected the quality of education, creating a trade-off between access and quality (Miranda M., 2011).

Converging and diverging themes

The education reforms in South America all follow a similar pattern, responding to identical challenges. As a result, they also share some difficulties, including:

1 Little tradition of participation, resulting from the engrained social history of the continent, with its colonial past and succession of oligarchies and dictatorships. Frequently, increased participation by parents and students encounters the resistance of teachers and principals. This reflects a stance by leaders in the field who see themselves as experts in education. For them, the opinions of citizens and students, the subjects of the educational process (or as they supposedly should be), are not welcome. This attitude frequently contradicts what is said publicly, showing how theory and practice diverge.

2   The reforms and new pedagogical ideas call for principals who are open to participation. However, in reality they dedicate their time to bureaucratic tasks, either due to the pressures from the hierarchy within the educational organization, or due to their adopting a traditional interpretation of their role. Torrecilla and Carrasco (2013) showed that primary school principals in Latin America dedicate an average of 80 per cent of their time to bureaucratic tasks and only 20 per cent to pedagogical tasks. In Brazil, bureaucracy takes up no less than 93 per cent of their time. The impact of the principal's actions on student performance is directly linked to their pedagogical leadership, gaining the support of the system actors, stimulating them, encouraging them and creating high expectations.

3   Besides the contradiction between bureaucratic tasks and pedagogical leadership, a review of the literature shows that it is the 'community model' rather than the bureaucratic model that is effective at producing results. Schools that have a flexible organization, that are participative, relatively autonomous and with high levels of consensus are more successful and have a notable impact on the performance of the students from lower income groups (Fernández Aguerre, 2004). As such, after around three decades of re-democratization the different states still retain a certain level of rigidity and are still working towards participative models.

4   This panorama reveals a need for the state and education to make structural changes, such as curricular changes and reform of educators' education, both to improve the return on the taxpayers' money and to increase the quality of education and help democratize it (Donoso, 2011). Protests by Chilean secondary students (Zibas, 2008), followed by higher education students, show the discontent created by the oldest and most far reaching liberal reforms in South America.

5   A sizeable part of the difficulties that principals experience in acting as leaders is due to the poor training they receive from higher education institutions. Even though there are well founded theoretical positions, higher education has found it difficult both to develop leadership and to clearly understand how it can influence the results of educational processes.

6   Research supports the importance of the leadership role of principals; however, one area needing further study is leadership by teachers, since they are strategically decision makers in classrooms. Further

issues are: (a) the explicit and implicit theoretical perspectives practised by school administrators; (b) the criteria and processes of principals' selection and the impact on their quality; (c) challenges and responses of higher education institutions in preparing principals; (d) patterns and trends in teacher education, as well its attention to leadership.

6

Caribbean Perspectives

Paul Miller

Introduction

Research on successful and effective school leadership has been around for some time with different positions being taken up in relation to what is meant by 'successful' and 'effective'. Indeed, several studies and reports from researchers, school inspectors and others have claimed that leadership is arguably the most important factor in organizational effectiveness and the key to success and improvement (Earley, 2013). It is now widely acknowledged that high quality leadership is one of the key requirements of successful schools and that leaders can have a significant positive impact on student outcomes. Leithwood and Seashore-Louis (2012: 3) summarize the consistency of these findings when they state 'to date, we have not found a single documented case of a school improving its student achievement record in the absence of talented leadership'. In Earley's (2013: 7) view, 'the Caribbean is no different and leadership, leaders and their development are crucial to the future success of all educational systems'.

The role of the principal is repeatedly emphasized in the literature on school leadership. Yet, according to Kruger and Scheerens (2012: 1), 'despite the many researchers and the many definitions of leadership appearing in the literature, there remains very little consensus concerning what leadership is and what it comprises'. In the context of the Caribbean, Miller (2013a: 195) argues that: 'It may not be possible to construct a unitary definition of Caribbean school leadership particularly as school leadership is exercised in multiple ways across territories.' Similarly, Earley (2013: 7) proposes there is no 'identikit' leadership style, pointing instead to the need for principals to interact sensitively with local contexts, peoples and communities.

The international literature on effective schools cites leadership that is firm and purposeful, involves others in decision making, uses data to help make decisions, exhibits instructional leadership, monitors performance and standards and promotes a culture of high expectations (Kirk & Jones, 2004; Lezotte, 2001; Mendels, 2012). As Earley (2013: 8) notes, 'Effective school organisations also demonstrate a positive culture where a shared vision is shown, and an orderly environment and positive reinforcement emphasised.' Miller (2013a: 183) cautions against 'Westernised school leadership influences being deployed en-masse without contextual modifications in the Caribbean'; a point also supported by Pashiardis et al. (2011) but which contrasts with that made by an influential report from the McKinsey Corporation which concluded 'good leadership is the same irrespective of context, and "what works" is surprisingly consistent' (Barber et al., 2010: 3). The McKinsey Report highlights a set of practices which effective leaders share, and a common set of beliefs, attitudes and personal attributes which they possess. Similarly, Miller and Hutton (2014), in a small-scale comparative study of principals' values and beliefs in Jamaica and England, found that both countries are driven by, broadly speaking, the same beliefs, attitudes and personal attributes.

Principals influence school success regardless of culture or context. Studies have specifically considered the relationship between leadership and school success (e.g. Day et al., 2011). Hallinger and Heck (2010) argue that the effect of leaders is largely indirect; what leaders do and say, how they demonstrate leadership, does affect the learning outcomes of students, but it is largely through the actions of others, teachers for example, that the effects of school leadership are mediated. Day et al. (2009, 2011) found that a small number of personal traits explained the variation in the effectiveness and success of leadership. Principals' values, strategic intelligence and leadership strategies were key 'in shaping the school and classroom processes and practices which result in improved pupil outcomes' (Day et al., 2009: 2). Leaders were found to 'improve teaching and learning and thus pupil outcomes indirectly and most powerfully through their influence on staff motivation, commitment, teaching practices and through developing teachers' capacities for leadership' (Day et al., 2009: 2).

School leadership research in the Caribbean

Sustained research into the theory and practice of school leadership and management in the English-speaking Caribbean is an emerging field. For example, over the three years between 2012 and 2014 there have been three publications aimed at providing understanding and assessment of educational leadership and management issues through a regional lens (Miller, 2012,

2013a, 2014). These have been supplemented by national studies covering such topics as high-performing principals (Hutton, 2013); curriculum planning and implementation (Roofe, 2014); universal secondary education (Knight, 2014); 'inclusive education' (Brown & Lavia, 2013); teacher and principal development (Bissessar, 2013); transformational leadership practices in emergency situations (Shotte, 2013); and educational policy and secondary schooling (Beepat, 2013).

Although school leadership practice in the Caribbean is by no means uniform, several issues have been observed between countries. For example, career progression to the principalship has been found to be problematic in Guyana and Trinidad (Miller, 2013a) and in Jamaica (Miller, 2013b). Similarly, the preparation and development of principals throughout the region is not standardized (Bissessar, 2013; McCallum, 2013), although Jamaica, through the National College for School Leadership, is trying to lead regional improvements in this area. This chapter examines what principals know and do as successful and effective leadership in the Caribbean. In answering the question, 'What does successful and effective school leadership look like in the Caribbean?' it considers both individual and national contexts.

Conceptual framework

Successful and effective school leadership is dependent on several discrete yet overlapping components, the most obvious of which may be training. Inputs that are not as obvious, for example experience, can play an equally important part throughout an individual's professional life, since, over time, they will encounter, interact with and engage with several individuals, some of whom they may even come to mimic, admire or resent. Kolb's (1984) experiential learning theory provides that experience is *the* source of learning and development and that experiential learning is not rationalist but is instead an evolving process not defined by fixed notions and ideas. Knowledge and interventions such as formal training however ought not to be seen as oppositional to experience since, according to James (1980), knowledge is derived from and is continually tested out in the experiences of the learner.

Similarly, tacit knowledge is contrasted with explicit or propositional knowledge (Polanyi, 1958) as important constructs in how knowledge is created and how knowledge and experience interact. Explicit knowledge is captured in words, writing and drawings; knowledge that has possibilities of being universal, supporting the capacity to act across contexts. Tacit knowledge, on the other hand, is unarticulated, 'as yet unspoken', tied to the senses in movement skills and accumulated physical experiences. It 'indwells' (Polanyi, 1966) and is rooted in local action, procedures, routines, commitment, ideals, values and emotions. Not everyone sees the notion of tacit knowledge as a distinct or, indeed, useful form of knowledge (Fodor, 1968). For example, Hildreth and Kimble (2002) also make the point that tacit and explicit knowledge are seldom entirely distinct and inherently inseparable, but interact dynamically along a continuum. Resolving these tensions is beyond this chapter. However, suffice to say that effective and successful leadership is a factor of tacit and explicit knowledge, and when used together this can positively impact an organization's direction. As suggested by Ambrosini and Bowman (2001), to speak a sentence that captures explicit knowledge one needs tacit knowledge to utter it, to pause, shape sounds, find and use rhythm.

Literature review

Notions of successful and effective leadership vary and overlap depending on who is doing the defining and on the context. In general however, successful and effective leaders are believed to shape the future of their institution, lead learning and teaching, develop self and others, manage and improve their institution, secure accountability and strengthen internal and external links between institution and community (Department for Education and Skills, 2004). The following may illustrate the contested nature of the field.

Successful leadership

Drawing on several research studies on successful leadership, it is possible to gain insights into what successful school leadership is. For example, Leithwood et al. (2006) proposed *seven strong claims about successful school leadership*. Furthermore, from their meta-analysis of leadership, Robinson et al. (2009) identified five dimensions which influence success in schools. Drawing on previous studies, in their IMPACT research study, Day et al. (2009) proposed eight key dimensions of successful leadership, in the form of: vision, values and direction; improving conditions for teaching and learning; restructuring the environment (roles and responsibilities); enhancing teaching and learning; redesigning and enriching the curriculum; enhancing teacher quality and succession planning; building relationships inside school; building relationships outside school and common values.

Taken together, the studies recognize that successful leaders have different starting points and that successful leadership requires a combination of cognitive and emotional understandings connected to clear sets of standards and values, the contextual application of strategies, and enduring commitment to people and education (Day & Leithwood, 2007). Nevertheless, from the available literature, it appears that there are five characteristics which successful principals are expected to demonstrate: show passion, commitment and personal accountability (Robinson et al., 2009); articulate moral purpose and manage tensions and dilemmas (PricewaterhouseCoopers, 2007); focus on learning and development of others in the school (Leithwood et al., 2006); make emotional and rational investment (Leithwood et al., 2006) and emphasize the personal and the functional (Robinson et al., 2009).

Effective leadership

The relationship between school leadership and student learning has been considered in the following terms:

> Effective headteachers provide a clear vision and sense of direction for the school. They prioritise. They focus the attention of staff on what is important and do not let them get diverted and side-tracked with initiatives that will have little impact on the work of students. They have a clear view of the strengths and weaknesses of their staff. They know how to build on the strengths and reduce the weaknesses. They can focus their programme of staff development on the real needs of their staff and school. They can gain view through a systematic programme of monitoring and evaluation. Their clarity of thought, sense of purpose and knowledge of what is going on mean that effective headteachers can best out of their staff, which is the key to influencing work in the classroom and to raising the standards achieved by students.
>
> NCSL, 2001: 1

From their meta-analysis of leadership, Robinson et al. (2009) identified three dimensions of effective pedagogical leadership. In addition, the Wallace Foundation (2012) provides eight characteristics of effective leadership which give important pointers about the work of effective leaders and bespeak the importance of principals showing emotional intelligence (Harris, 2006). From their review of school leadership practices in international contexts, Barber et al. (2010: 47) found that 'high-performing principals did not necessarily work longer hours than other principals; however, more time was spent with other people in their school: they walk the halls more, spend more time coaching teachers, interact more with parents and external stakeholders, and spend more time with students'. Similarly, Hutton (2013), found that 'high performing principals' in Jamaica spent time getting to know staff and were passionate, committed and possessed a clear vision. Furthermore, Hallinger and Lee

(2013) reported that how principals used their time was influenced by sociocultural and institutional factors.

Methodology

This study was conducted to gain an initial understanding of what principals in the Caribbean (a) know about what successful and effective leaders do; and (b) from their own practice, what they 'do' as successful and effective leaders. A quantitative approach was used in order to provide useful baseline data for a more extensive study to be conducted on a regional or national basis. The data presented in this chapter was elicited from a short questionnaire comprised of two main sections with two subscales each. The two main themes were: (a) knowing and doing successful leadership and (b) knowing and doing effective leadership. Under each section there were two subscales each with seven items. Each item required respondents to rank them on a scale of 1 to 5, 1 being the highest and 5 being the lowest. Snowballing sampling was used to select the participants for the survey questionnaire which was emailed by the researcher to university contacts in Guyana, Trinidad and Tobago, Cayman Islands, Jamaica, Barbados and Grenada. There were twelve respondents: one secondary principal and eleven primary principals. Three principals were from Guyana and nine from Jamaica. There were two male primary principals, both from Jamaica and one secondary principal, also from Jamaica.

The survey was developed by the researcher drawing on several studies on successful (e.g. Day & Leithwood, 2007; Leithwood et al., 2006) and effective leadership (Kirk & Jones, 2004; Lezotte, 2001). Section A required principals to identify what they know about successful and effective leadership, and Section B required them to note what they do in relation to successful and effective leadership. The same questionnaire was used for 'knowing' and 'doing', thereby allowing the researcher to gauge the extent to which what is known is practised. The main question was, 'What does successful and effective school leadership look like in the Caribbean?' Data were analysed with the use of Microsoft Excel Mega Stats Add Ins.

Findings

Knowing and doing successful leadership

This section has two parts: knowing about successful leadership and doing successful leadership. Figure 6.1 shows a summary of the responses for the

FIGURE 6.1 *Knowing and doing successful leadership.*

subscales of knowing and doing successful leadership. Since the lower the scores the higher the ranking, it is noted that Jamaican participant 4 scored lowest in both knowing and doing. Participants 10, 11 and 12 are Guyanese principals and obtained high scores. Participant 12 scored highest in both doing and knowing successful leadership which is a low ranking. Of twelve participants, five scored below 8 points in their responses to knowing about successful leadership.

Knowing and doing effective leadership

This section also has two parts: knowing about effective leadership and doing effective leadership. Figure 6.2 shows a summary of the responses for the

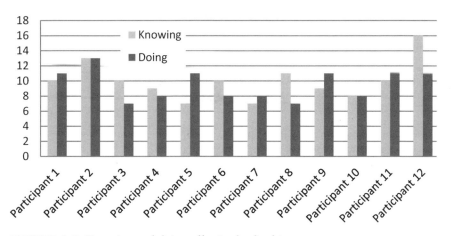

FIGURE 6.2 *Knowing and doing effective leadership.*

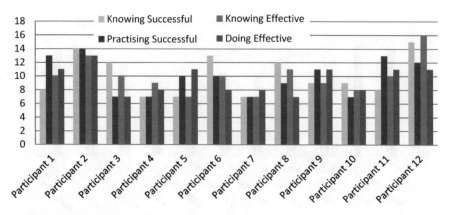

FIGURE 6.3 *Summary of leadership.*

subscales of knowing and doing effective leadership. Since the lower the scores the higher the ranking, it is noted that Guyanese participant 10 scored lowest in both knowing and doing effective leadership. Jamaican participant 2 scored the highest in knowing and doing effective leadership.

Figure 6.3 shows a summary of the responses for the subscales of knowing and doing successful leadership, and knowing and doing effective leadership. For several participants their knowing of both successful and effective leadership lagged behind their doing. Since the lower the scores the higher the ranking, it is noted that Jamaican participants 4 and 7 scored lowest in both knowing and doing. Participant 10, from Guyana also had a low score. However, principals 2 and 12 scored highest in both doing and knowing successful leadership which is a low ranking. Of twelve participants, five scored below 8 points in their responses to knowing about successful leadership whereas three participants scored below 8 points in their responses to knowing effective leadership. Three participants scored below 8 points in terms of doing successful leadership whereas three participants also scored below 8 points in terms of doing effective leadership.

Discussion

Successful leadership and effective leadership practices are crucial to a school's success, and where principals provide these kinds of leadership an entire school community is better placed to achieving short-, medium- and longer-term goals. In this small-scale study, the doing of successful leadership outstripped the knowing. Their doing of effective leadership was ahead of the knowing, although the knowing and doing of effective leadership was behind the knowing and doing of successful leadership. Nevertheless, the evidence also suggests that principals 'know' and 'do' successful and effective leadership in a relatively consistent manner. These findings point to three clear issues: doing ahead of knowing, individual and contextual issues and the need for continuing professional development of principals. These are discussed in turn below.

Doing ahead of knowing

There was clear evidence among participants that their knowing and doing of successful and effective leadership was irrespective of school phase level (e.g. primary or secondary), gender and country location. For example, their knowing and doing of Leithwood et al.'s (2006) claim that 'successful leaders draw on the same repertoire of leadership practices' was mirrored in their responses, receiving a score of 16 in both cases. This was also the case for successful leaders applying 'leadership practices contextually' (receiving a mirrored score of 17) and successful leaders 'directly and indirectly improve[ing] teaching and learning' (receiving a mirrored score of 15). This uniformity of knowing and doing was also the case for their knowing and doing of 'effective leadership', as regards the claim that effective leaders 'promote and value positive home-school relations' (Kirk & Jones, 2004), which received a mirrored score of 15.

An important finding of this study is that in all but one case the actual doing of successful and effective leadership was ahead of knowing. This finding is as cathartic as it is problematic. It is cathartic for two main reasons. First, it shows that principals do not readily have command of the leadership language 'toolkit' (Earley, 2013). Second, it shows principals are doing 'what works', pointing to a form of 'on-the-ground' approach to leadership, which highlights the role of experiential learning, supporting James' (1980) assertion that knowledge is derived from and is continually tested out in our experiences.

These findings are also problematic because, as the evidence suggests, these principals are already doing well and could possibly exceed their current doing of both successful and effective leadership, through more knowing. In other words, tacit knowledge on its own will not be enough to sustain and improve practice. As suggested by Ambrosini and Bowman (2001), to speak a sentence that captures explicit knowledge one needs tacit knowledge to utter it, to pause, shape sounds, find and use rhythm.

Individual and contextual issues

Individual and contextual differences among principals could be influenced by several factors, for example leadership preparation, leadership experience, size of school, a school's geographic location (Pashiardis et al., 2011) and a school's culture and the principal's personal characteristics (Hutton, 2013). Whereas principals know that effective leaders 'ensure a culture of positive beliefs and high expectations among staff and students' (15), their doing did not always reflect this (20). This is undoubtedly problematic and requires further investigation. Similarly, cultivating leadership in others (13) was a point well known among principals, although doing it (16) lagged behind. Participants were however relatively consistent in their overall knowing and doing to ensure a safe and orderly environment (scoring 11 and 13 respectively).

Kolb's (1984) experiential learning theory could provide some possible explanations and answers for some of these variations. How did principals in Jamaica and Guyana come to do more than they know? Kolb argues that experience is *the* source of learning. That is, learning is an evolving process and activity that happens from any interaction. In other words, learning can take place through informal means as much as it can take place through explicit rational structures. This study did not ask principals how they came to know and do what they know and do. Instead, it asked them *what* they know and do. Nevertheless, principals may have come to shape their doing based on observations, the influence of mentors and/or other principals and from 'learning on the job'. These explanations highlight the interlocking between tacit and explicit knowledge (Fodor, 1968; Hildreth & Kimble, 2002) but once more foreground the position that knowledge is derived from and is continually tested out in the experiences of the learner (James, 1980).

Continuing professional development of principals

The overall scores arrived at for all principals in terms of their knowing and doing of successful and effective leadership were fairly consistent. This suggests that through targeted intervention and support for groups of principals, as well as for individual principals, doing plus knowing can lead to a more effective form of doing and knowing. But this requires the interlocking of tacit and explicit knowledge (Hildreth & Kimble, 2002) or experience and rational knowledge (Kolb, 1984), defined in terms of 'book knowledge' and joint critical reflection and 'sense-making' among principals. Transforming lives is the foundational role of a school organization and the power to sustain and develop a school rests with successful school leadership. No two schools are the same and successful school leadership is highly dependent on principals knowing their organization's culture and temperature. Similarly, effective leadership is highly dependent on principals being responsive to the needs of everyone in their organization, and not only students. In other words, principals need to be attuned to the social, political, economic, physical, human and cultural aspects (Kowalski, 1995) of their schools.

There are many external factors that could impact the provision of fit for purpose training to school leaders in the Caribbean. Miller (2013a) highlights socioeconomic differences, political diversity, geographic dispersion, location of resource personnel, situated cultural problems and insufficient educational research. Despite these factors however, principals in this study have acted according to the sociopolitical contexts they inhabit, as well as in response to the particular needs of staff and students. Although in operation for less than five years, it is clear that Jamaica's National College for Educational Leadership will have a lot of work to do in providing appropriate continuing professional development opportunities for principals on the island. Indeed, its programmes and their impact could be a test case for the entire region.

Conclusions

Principals in this exploratory study have shown that it is possible to do successful and effective leadership, even if their knowledge of the theory that informs what they do is missing or not up to date. When doing is met with more knowing, this creates the potential for much more effective practice, driven by critical reflection and reflexive actions. The most important thing that can be seen from these findings however is that principals need appropriate continuing professional development if they are to improve upon what they already do. Additionally, successful and effective leadership in schools is not something to be seen 'out there'. Instead, successful and effective leadership must be theorized and understood in the contexts in which people are located and in line with the values present in a society (Miller, 2013a; Pashiardis et al., 2011). Successful and effective school leadership for the Caribbean must therefore focus on school leaders and their development, simultaneously grounding itself in an awareness of what visions schools have, where schools are and what experience and skills principals have, in order to take them to the next stage.

7

European Perspectives

Helene Ärlestig

There is no doubt that schools can make a difference. Almost everyone has individual memories that can be valued as good or bad signs of how effective and successful schools are. Besides the importance for the individual student, schools and how they function are connected to society and a nation's status and well-being. Large international surveys like PISA and TIMMS[1] have become a concern for politicians, media and school personnel all over the world. Learning and knowledge are often seen as a way to develop the future for individuals, communities and societies. Therefore, it is both understandable and necessary to discuss and research how organizations like schools are governed and led.

Research can have a powerful impact on how schools and their leadership develop, which involves an understanding of what is going on in the local, national and international arenas. This complexity requires many sources and perspectives to capture the various components and aspects that impact schools and their development.

This chapter begins with a section that elaborates on current challenges for successful and effective schools on a national level as well as on a European level. The aim is thereafter to give examples of collaborative European research projects, discuss the research challenges in understanding success, and provide support to schools to create a better society around Europe. In this chapter I only focus on an inter-European perspective, even if there are similarities (as well as variations) in other parts of the world.

Successful and effective schools: various interpretations based on history, politics and local context

Europe consists of forty-four countries. Size, economy, history and culture differ considerably among them. The countries in the east have a history of controlling the economy with one-party systems. Some of the countries in the middle have gone through severe internal conflicts, and new countries have thus emerged. In some countries, teachers and schools have a high status, and here there is little variation between schools and their outcomes. Finland is often used as an example of this. In Estonia, on the other hand, teachers were, during the Soviet regime, seen as ideological tools, which still results in low trust from the public (Kukemelk & Ginter, 2015). In many countries, economic recessions have affected both individuals and institutions like schools. In the north, on the other hand, the countries are welfare states with a high degree of democracy.

Schools as organizations are governed by a mix between national, federal and local interests. Most principals need to navigate and meet expectations from a number of levels within the governance system. Some countries have a higher degree of centralization and external inspections, while in others the local school has a high degree of autonomy. Centralized national ambitions as well as federal and local actors and routines guide the process. Many countries have local committees, including elected representation of parents, teachers and so-called co-opted members (invited influential representatives of politics and the economy). These can be viewed as signs of democracy – for example, in Latvia and Estonia (Ärlestig et al., 2015). In England, the school committee has the authority to recruit principals, and principals need to confirm and discuss their decisions and strategies with the board of governors (Day & Armstrong, 2015).

The degree of administration and bureaucracy differs as well. In Germany, for example, it is typical that the principal also has teaching duties (Huber, 2015), while in France the principal mainly works with administration and discipline (Norman, 2015). The mandate and responsibility connected to the individual school and principal differ considerably among countries. In Sweden, principals can set teachers' salaries, have their own school budget and can decide how teachers spend their time during the working day, while in Germany principals cannot even recruit their own teachers. In Finland, the principal leaves what happens in the classroom to a great extent to the teachers. In Austria, principals need to be present at schools during teaching hours; otherwise, they need a substitute. Some schools in Switzerland and in the lower grades in France do not even have a principal (Ärlestig et al., 2015).

These examples show that the prerequisites for schools differ in relation to national history, culture and structure. What is considered as successful and effective is clearly something that requires both interpretation and contextualization. Despite this variation in national context, the definition of success is often taken for granted and connected to an individual student, principal or school that has good academic results and, through good behaviour, can meet others' expectations.

Looking at successes from a societal perspective, there are challenges and issues that are the same for all European countries. Cooperation between European countries took a huge step forward in the mid-1950s when some countries started to cooperate economically and politically to avoid future wars and conflicts. Today, twenty-eight countries are members of the European Union (EU), and more countries are candidates to become members. The EU, as well as the OECD have, during the last decade, influenced European school politics and policies to a great extent, even if the different countries' school systems were historically and culturally in various stages of development.

Europe is also to a great extent influenced by transnational trends, even if they are filtered through a national political culture (Seashore Louis & van Velzen, 2012). Concepts as well as ideas travel, and since school leadership in many ways is socially constructed and depends on language and interpretation, a highly diverse context contributes to more challenging communication (Möller, 2011).

Three of the most challenging issues from a European policy perspective are closing achievement gaps, working for inclusion and meeting the needs of increased multiculturalism. In the EU, 6 million students have only secondary school training or less when they leave school and 20 per cent of our young people do not have basic skills in reading, mathematics and science, which in turn affects employment and health.[2]

The EU has encouraged mobility; besides the European demographic changes internally, an increased number of refugees are entering Europe. This raises issues both at a national level and at the local school level about multiculturalism, inclusion and lifelong learning. The global trends of accountability and a focus on subject content, as well as a higher degree of market-driven policy (including free choice and private actors running public schools), external control and higher centralization are obvious in Europe (Nordin & Sundberg, 2014).

Taken together this means that principals, despite their national context, have some common missions. The EU advisory board clarified in 2009 that school leaders are important factors in relation to the general teaching and learning environment in terms of raising expectations and supporting students, parents and teachers. This requires that principals have the capacity and qualities to cope with an increasing number of tasks, paying less attention to administrative tasks and concentrating on the quality of teaching, education plans, pedagogical issues and their personnel's achievements, motivation and development (EU Official Journal 2009: C 302/04).

Changed expectations and norms of successful school leaders

There is much effort in the EU as well as in individual countries to develop European schools to become more effective and successful. This includes both ambitions related to academic knowledge as well as social and civic objectives. The schools' role in contributing to an inclusive and democratic society is a prime issue in many countries. Using tax money also raises issues about effectiveness and how to create the most value within an existing system. Today we can see different logics competing in terms of how to develop. For principals, this means that they are expected to work more as managers, which includes, for example, more documentation and control. Principals are expected to be clearer and firmer in relation to what their task and mission are. At the same time principals are expected to work with a leadership that increases students' learning through a distributed and more collaborative approach with teachers. Professional communities and distributed leadership are examples of this approach (Harris, 2008; Leithwood & Seashore Louis, 2012).

A research overview (Ärlestig et al., 2015) focusing on recent domestic research about principals in thirteen participating European countries showed that there are many countries with a limited research base on school leadership. England, together with North America and Canada, has been influential on European research, policy and practice for decades. In the German-speaking countries, many studies are only published in German and have therefore not reached a wider audience – a phenomenon that also applies to other countries belonging to a minor language group. Many of the current European studies on principals are small case studies, and in many countries it is hard to get research grants to study school leadership. As a result, we see more and more mixed method approaches, and the tradition of mainly having qualitative or quantitative methods has shifted in many countries. Even if some of the topics and aims are general, it is hard to form overall conclusions that can be informative at a European or global level.

As values and norms in a society change, the expectations of principals and what they ought to do to become successful also change. Two figures that describe changes in German-speaking countries as well as in Nordic countries point in the same direction.

Schratz (2015) refers to Lohmann, who described a change during the last forty-five years in German-speaking Europe. Schools have gone from self-contained to self-dependent. Principals have changed from being *primus inter pares* to more systemic leadership. One aspect here that is important to mention is that leadership is not always connected to something good or positive. In German-speaking countries, the concept of *führung* is used instead of leadership. *Führung* relates to *führer* and the leadership during the Second World War, and has a negative connotation (Schratz, 2015). The hierarchy is flat, and principals do not always have the authority to make and implement decisions concerning a school's work. At the same time, new public management as well as the debate on standardization and accountability influences the prerequisites and indicators of success for principals.

A study of Nordic countries on how principals' professionalism has developed points in the same direction. To illustrate this development, Figure 7.1 was used.

The principal in the nation-state was often an experienced teacher from the same school – a person with high status among colleagues. Since school to an extent was rule-based, the principals' main task was to understand and learn the rules and how these could apply to the local school. Twenty-five years ago, there was a wave of decentralization. It was built on a belief that problems should be solved close to where a problem is. Teachers and principals were given a high degree of autonomy and the task to interpret complex objectives with high ambitions. Today curricula are more detailed and connected to national tests. External evaluation and inspections have increased, and principals are required to act as managers to a greater extent (Uljens et al., 2012).

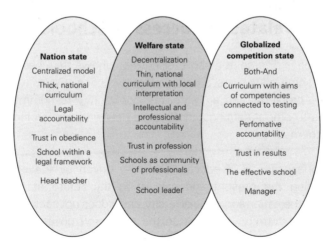

FIGURE 7.1 *School leadership development in Nordic countries.*

Source: Uljens et al. (2012)

Both these examples show development affected by global trends and how expectations on principals change over time. To be able to get a deeper understanding of success from a broader perspective, it is necessary to trace how expectations and norms change depending on time and context. Visible academic results thus become a concern for everyone.

Another trend that has attracted attention is high mobility. Due to increased mobility norms, mutual collaboration and understanding have become even more necessary. To protect and increase democracy and keep a high respect for the individual student, inclusive education is a huge concern in Europe. As we become more and more multicultural, it becomes more and more obvious how important it is to have a critical view of norms and normality. Schools' ability to enhance every individual's learning and close achievement gaps is often seen as the most important task to create successful schools and societies. This area is often demanding because it is connected to ethics and social justice. One way to describe what inclusion and social justice mean in relation to practice is as follows:

1 A redistribution of goods, including social as well as physical goods.

2 A recognition and cultural approach, through which marginalized groups are more strongly acknowledged and supported.

3 Relational or participatory justice, where people are empowered to fully take part in relationships and in society (Lumby, 2013).

International cooperation and studies related to successful schools

Even if Europe is diverse, the above discussion shows that, besides national challenges, some issues are a concern for everyone. Curiosity about how others solve problems and an increased opportunity to communicate and have access to official data has encouraged networks and projects focusing on various themes.

The European space of education is now driven by the political work of producing the present and calculating the future. It is aiming to strengthen the nation and value diversity, and it does not seek harmonization or a global uniformity. It is built on the same soft governing approach—it cajoles, persuades, and enables—but it is powered by data and standards.

Lawn & Grek, 2012: 153

This indicates that we need research projects with contributions from various countries to understand each other, ourselves, and today's global society, as well as being able to work together towards a multicultural region with low achievement gaps. Below I give four examples of recent European projects related to quality and school leadership.

The International Successful School Principal Project (ISSPP) involved twenty-four countries; almost half of them (eleven) were European. Based on case studies, a framework for an initial knowledge base was founded. Four broad categories were identified related to leadership practice in successful schools (Day & Leithwood, 2007):

1 Building vision and setting direction.

2 Understanding and developing people.

3 Designing the organization.

4 Managing the teaching and learning programme.

Successful principals benefit from a well-defined mission together with a cognitive and emotional understanding of what and how to do and act. To build and sustain success, principals need to combine principles and practices.

● Sustaining passionate commitment and personal accountability.

● Managing tensions and dilemmas and maintaining moral purpose.

● Being other-centred and learning-focused.

● Making emotional rational investments.

● Emphasizing the personal and the functional (Day & Leithwood, 2007).

The conclusions were general in relation to leadership and leading a school. The selection of participating schools was related to the national context and therefore differs among countries. Mainly, it was related to students' academic achievements.

The project is now starting a second phase where the researchers will study underperforming schools. This approach is partly inspired by a Swedish project called Structure, Culture, and Leadership – Prerequisites for Successful Schools. The project studied twenty-four schools during a five-year period (Höög & Johansson, 2011, 2014). It was mixed-method research in which students, teachers, principals and superintendents contributed their views. The project showed that the twenty-four schools could be divided into four different categories. Five were successful in academic, social and civic objectives; only seven were successful in relation to academic results; eight were successful in relation to social and civic objectives; and four did not succeed at all. Considering academic, social and civic success was an attempt to come closer to the complexity that affects how we understand schools and their results.

Other projects that have studied principals are the LISA and Pro-LEAD projects. The aim of the LISA project was to study how principals perceived their role, leadership style and effectiveness in enhancing the overall quality of education. In the Pro-LEAD project, the aim was to study the relationship between principals' leadership styles, their epistemological worldviews and their beliefs about the structures in which they operate (Pashiardis, 2014). The theoretical model was validated for eight countries: Cyprus, England, Norway, Germany, Slovenia, Hungary, Italy and the Netherlands. The findings indicated that the instructional style forms the baseline for effective school leadership and that the dominant trends are the entrepreneurial and structuring styles. This can be interpreted as an increased level of awareness with regard to the expanded responsibility of the school or an internal organizational stability effort to cooperate with leaders outside the school on an equal footing, thus guaranteeing the willingness and capacity of the school to collaborate both internally and externally (Pashiardis, 2014: 85).

One of the conclusions is that research on leadership styles has important implications for policy, practice and research. Despite this conclusion, it is evident that there is not a best 'cocktail mix' of leadership styles for all school leaders in their various contexts (Brauckmann & Schwarz, 2014; Pashiardis, 2014). This is another example where the results and conclusions become more general and overarching instead of more narrowly focused on achievement gaps and inclusion.

A third project has focused on leadership competence. Huber and Hiltmann (2010) invented a web-based instrument for self-assessment called the Competence Profile School Management inventory, or CPSM (German *KompetenzProfil SchulManagement*, KPSM). The inventory offers participants the opportunity to reflect on their individual competencies related to peers from the same context. The inventory has been developed and evaluated, and since 2013 it has been organized in two main areas. General education leadership competences incorporate nineteen disposition dimensions, including motives and attitudes relevant to all leadership activities. The other area covers task-specific education leadership competences, which incorporate nine leadership activity dimensions based on concrete job-related activities by educational leaders in central fields of school management. An EU project involving twelve countries – Switzerland (coordinating partner), Germany, Austria, Czech Republic, Cyprus, Denmark, England, Norway, Spain, the United States, Sweden and Australia (Queensland) – has contributed to the inventory being translated into eight languages and it is currently being piloted in all involved countries (Huber, 2010; 2015).

These three projects are examples of collaborations where common interests both try to consider national culture and structure as well as find more general aspects that constitute school leadership. What they have in common is that the studied dimensions and the results often become general and sometimes normative or ideal. Each country's context and issues, such as achievement gaps and inclusion, are not given any specific attention.

A still-ongoing project during 2015 is the European Policy Network on School Leadership (EPNoSL). The project is an EU-founded network of researchers, practitioners and policy makers seeking to suggest a common framework for school leadership in Europe. A basis for their discussion has been a changed society with increased mobility, which creates challenges in areas such as inclusion, democracy and social justice. The aim has been to use what we already know from research to look forward and position school leadership in a reform agenda. The network is in itself a sign of what we will probably see more of – namely, researchers, policy makers and practitioners working together. This means that researchers need to be faster in doing their analyses and reporting on processes as they occur rather than viewing them retrospectively. The network has constructed a school leadership policy toolkit. The toolkit is related to distributed leadership, policy response, accountability, autonomy, capacity building and stakeholder collaboration, with the aim of generating knowledge and reflection to enhance work within a changed society and promote learning, democracy and inclusion (see http://www. schoolleadership.eu/portal).

Taking a closer look at accountability, which can be related to effectiveness and success, EPNoSL defines it as the management of diverse abilities. To clarify these abilities they are divided them into three categories: (1) managerial expectations (to work with national and local policy evaluation and standards) include demands in relation to finance and the marketplace; (2) expectations of the public (the local community and parents) require that the school seeks legitimacy; and (3) professional expectations require teachers to be autonomous professionals who work with processes rather than results: 'The different types of expectations relate to different logics, which emphasize societal concerns, political pressures, bureaucratic concerns, top-down management, and responses to market dynamics, professional responsibility, and ethical principles. These logics can exist in combination or parallel to each other and they can easily conflict' (Koren, 2013).

These expectations are reflected in both more policy-friendly research about successful schools and in more critical research related to new public management (e.g., Ball, 2003; Hall, 2013). What we can see is probably the first steps towards a more nuanced view of results and the positive and negative effects. This is an important step, especially if inclusion and democracy are seen as aspects of successful and effective schools. What is considered normal and how all children are included in learning become important internal issues because the 'normal' and ideal student affects teachers' behaviours (Mac Ruaric, 2013).

The future for school leadership research in Europe

These four examples of European collaboration show that there is an important base of research about successful and effective schools in Europe. At the same time societal changes are creating tension and challenges. To meet these it is important to have a wide definition of success that includes issues that do not care about national borders. School leadership is closely related to policy issues and the local context, therefore it is important that research about success and effectiveness mirrors and relates to policy and societal changes. To take a step forward and avoid repeating the dilemmas we know exist, the research community has to struggle with several challenges.

One challenge in distributing and spreading new knowledge is the language barrier. Europe has many languages besides English, German and French, which are seen as the major languages. Many educational leadership researchers mainly write and publish articles and books in their own language. In several countries, only a few books are translated from English to the national language, which contributes to making a lot of the globally published research unknown to practitioners and policy makers. Researchers within these countries have a great responsibility to select and connect their own research and understanding to a wider perspective. Another effect is that research from countries with languages that are spoken by smaller populations is not known to a wider international audience.

Another challenge is to increase the influence of theory and conceptual work. This is because European research is, to a great extent, built on case studies. Even if research articles on educational leadership often use a third of the number of pages to refer to earlier research, actual theories or more cumulative research are missing. When the authors refer to theory they often use classical communication, organization, learning and leadership theories connected to Habermas, Foucault, Weick, Yukl, Dewey and Weber, among others. There is also a growing number of theories building on poststructuralism, neoinstitutionalism, and economic and governance theories, as well as educational leadership researchers including Leithwood, Spillaine, Harris and Seashore Louis. These theories are not specifically European, but that is not the point. Theory and concept building are necessary to move the field forward and not simply repeat earlier studies.

Funding for school leadership research is a challenge in many countries. Often, funding is connected to national traditions and challenges. At the same time it is necessary, especially for countries with little research on school leadership, to work and learn together with others. Participating in international research projects can create opportunities to both strengthen and challenge individual countries' norms and governing structures.

There is a danger that international projects might not pay enough attention to societal challenges such as closing achievement gaps and increased inclusion. There are tendencies for schools with high results situated in middle-class areas to receive more resources and thus better qualified and experienced teachers and principals (Gu & Johansson, 2013, TALIS[3]). If international research projects decline to handle such issues, the indirect effect could be that the research project instead contributes to strengthening nations, schools and school leaders that *already* are successful.

This is especially true in a time when many countries are market led with increased juridification and bureaucracy. Researchers have various aims and target groups for their research. Some are more interested in writing research reports for other researchers, without taking account of ongoing national or global societal changes. Interest in the effects of research and how it is received in the larger community is limited. Some write mainly for practitioners. Their research is primarily descriptive, trying to capture the ideal and normative dimensions of how to handle the opportunities and challenges principals are facing. A third group has policy makers as their prime target. They are often interested in more structural and critical perspectives. Sometimes it is unclear who the assumed reader is. This variation includes authors who are descriptive, authors who want to give a more general view, authors who mainly focus on the context or specific actors and authors who are critiquing aspects of current development. These different approaches can contribute to a fragmented and complex picture of successful and effective school leadership, which creates confusion about aims and quality in educational leadership research.

As we can see in the projects mentioned earlier, we know a lot about more general leadership issues. The results are often published as concrete advice and general recommendations. Sometimes these conclusions hide the dilemmas that occur as a result of governing chains, reforms and changed norms. We have an increased number of more critical perspectives on leadership and policy that, together with more descriptive and general knowledge, can add new dimensions. 'Measures aiming at improving quality, effectiveness, and efficiency become mechanistic and bureaucratized when they are not tempered with an understanding of complex organizational processes and then they do not reflect the need for a learning culture that focuses on the human side of the organization' (Halasz, 2012: 220).

To summarize, in Europe we have active research networks that have made important contributions to general knowledge about successful and effective school leadership, knowledge that needs to be interpreted and transformed, depending on each country's (and school's) unique prerequisites. To capture the local culture and structure and at the same time bring research results to scale is a challenging task but one that can at the same time create new perspectives that might lead us to further discussions rather than presenting unique cases and being in favour of or against today's trends, including test- and market-driven policy making. Success is to a high extent a qualitative concept formed by today's norms. To develop research on schools and how they work in order to contribute to both today's and tomorrow's societies requires courage, good scientific methods, ethical considerations and increased cooperation. The research projects discussed in this chapter show that international research collaborations can be important for school leaders' development and education, which besides important general knowledge can be one way to reduce achievement gaps and increase inclusion.

PART TWO

Practising Successful and Effective School Leadership

8

African Perspectives

Raj Mestry

Introduction and background to the problem

There is a growing global concern that public schools are not functioning optimally. Many nations have undertaken wide-ranging reforms of curriculum, instruction and student assessment with the intention of better preparing children for the twenty-first century higher education demands and the world of work (Blasé et al., 2010). The rapid rate at which education changes have taken place and are still taking place, together with the increased volume of administrative work, has placed school leaders under enormous pressure, resulting in ineffective leadership. Today, the position of principal is far more sophisticated and the job far more complex than in previous decades. This complexity can best be seen in the various functions that principals are expected to perform daily and often simultaneously. The maintenance of quality and standards in education depend largely on the extent to which principals effectively carry out their leadership responsibilities (Ibukun et al., 2011).

Goslin (2009) argues that ineffective leadership is inherent in principals and headteachers who overlook their curriculum or instructional leadership responsibilities because they are not fully cognizant of their primary tasks and are inclined to concentrate more on their administrative responsibilities, resolving organization conflict and maintaining student discipline. This is prevalent in many African countries. For example, research conducted by Sifuna and Sawamura in 2010 revealed that the inadequate capacity of principals was one of the contributory factors to the low quality in teaching and learning and high dropout rates in Kenya (Ayiro, 2014). Children leave the public school system without having obtained a sustainable level of basic reading, writing and numeracy skills. In Nigeria, it was found that some schools experience poor learner performance and more conflicts than others, and this was mainly attributed to the principals' level of leadership effectiveness (Ibukun et al., 2011). Similarly in South Africa, researchers such as Bloch (2009), Fleisch (2008), and Mestry and Singh (2007) contend that there are many managers who lack the requisite knowledge and skills to lead their schools effectively in the twenty-first century. Ineffective leadership is reflected in the poor academic achievement of students in many public schools. For example, in the Annual National Assessment (ANA) for 2011 in South Africa, grade 3 students achieved an average of 35 per cent in literacy and 26 per cent in numeracy, while grade 6 students achieved an average of 28 per cent in language and 30 per cent in mathematics (Joseph, 2011). Grade 12 students also fared poorly in the recent National Senior Certificate (NSC) examinations. Although the overall pass rate for the country's NSC examinations appears to be relatively high (in 2012, 73.9 per cent and in 2013, 78.2 per cent), the minimum requirement to pass a subject at this level is 30 per cent. Thus, the low student performance in subjects such as maths and science has qualified less than 30 per cent of the grade 12 students to study at higher education institutions. These disconcerting statistics exemplify the generally poor academic standards (Bloch, 2009; Fleisch, 2008) and could be symptomatic of a lack of effective leadership.

A school's management team (SMT) (principal, deputy principal and heads of departments) plays a leading role in students' academic achievement by engaging in the school's instructional programmes (Glanz, 2006; Sergiovanni, 1984). It is expected that education leaders steer their schools effectively through the challenges posed by increasingly complex environments. Curriculum standards, such as those prescribed in the new Curriculum Assessment Policy Statements (CAPS), achievement benchmarks and policy directives generate complicated and unpredictable requirements for schools. Leaders are expected to respond to increasing student diversity, including cultural background, immigration status, income disparities, physical and mental disabilities and variations in learning capacity. They are required to collaborate with external stakeholders. Rapid developments in teaching and communication technology require adjustments in schools' internal workings. These are some of the conditions that make schooling more challenging and effective leadership more essential.

Based on the above, the research problem investigated was: *What leadership traits should members of SMTs master in order to practise effective school leadership?*

The research problem is encapsulated in the following questions:

- What do we mean by effective leadership and successful leadership?
- What traits are essential for effective leadership in education organizations?

- What are the SMT members' perceptions of practising effective and successful leadership?

This chapter describes an empirical investigation to determine essential effective leadership traits and the SMT members' perceptions of practising effective and successful leadership in the Gauteng East school district of the Gauteng Province of South Africa. Leadership traits exhibited by SMT members offer a new and important theoretical lens through which effective leadership practices in schools can be reconfigured and conceptualized.

Understanding the concepts 'successful leadership' and 'effective leadership'

The Concise Oxford Dictionary (Soanes & Stevenson, 2004) defines 'effective' as an adverb that describes an action or accomplishing tasks. Management guru Peter Drucker (2001) explains that 'effectiveness' is a habit constituted of a complex of practices. These practices are always exceedingly hard to do well but once acquired they become an unthinkable, conditioned reflex, and a firmly ingrained habit. Webster, on the other hand, defines 'effective' as 'producing a decided, decisive, or desired effect (result or outcome), producing an intended effort' (McKechnie, 1983: 577). 'Successful', very closely connected to 'effective', is defined as the attainment of outcomes or accomplishing what was aimed for (e.g. academic success).

Twenty-seven years ago, Fred Luthans (1988) used promotion rates – those who had been rapidly promoted over a five-year period – to identify successful and effective leaders in a business context. He found that effective leaders were those who achieved results that consistently beat the competition, while successful leaders spent considerably more time networking and staying on top of office politics, and relatively little time managing people, teams and business results. Effective leaders focused on people and teams rather than office politics. From an educational perspective, leader effectiveness is defined as the amount of influence a leader has on individual or group performance, followers' satisfaction and overall effectiveness (Derue et al., 2011). From an African perspective, Nahavandi (2000: 4) asserts that leaders are effective when their group performs well and when followers are satisfied. Effective leadership is determined by the upliftment of the villagers/community and the way that they progress (Masango, 2002). Leadership is a function to be shared by all (distributive leadership) rather than leadership invested in one person. Central to this perspective is that the philosophical traditions of Africa offer an important contribution to the theory and practice of effective leadership in the world today. African humanism or *Ubuntu* evokes both reason and empathy as the basis for ethical leadership. *Ubuntu* means that a person is a person because of other people (Khoza, 2012). It is further contended that the reciprocal relationship between the individual and the social collective stimulates caring and progressive thought and action. Nowhere is this more apt than in the relationship between leader and followers.

Successful leaders differ from other people and possess certain core attributes or leadership traits that contribute significantly to their success. Understanding the importance of these core traits that predict leader effectiveness can help organizations with their leader selection, training and development practices (Derue et al., 2011). Leadership traits are described as integrated patterns of personal characteristics that reflect a range of individual differences and foster consistent leader effectiveness across a variety of group and organizational situations (Zaccaro et al., 2004).

Research (see Gunter, 2001: 33) shows that there is a fundamental set of leadership traits that form the nucleus for effective and successful leadership in almost all educational contexts. Effective leaders are 'firm and purposeful' in leading school improvement, participative by sharing leadership and delegating, and 'the leading professional' through their pedagogic and curriculum knowledge. Effective leaders have the ability to facilitate team problem solving; resolve conflicts in a win-win way; 'sell' an idea, programme, plan or solution; understand and control their own emotions; motivate themselves when feeling negative; give credit to others; self-diagnose their own leadership style; and place the good of the group ahead of their own.

McEwan (2003) identifies ten traits of highly effective leaders (principals): the *communicator*, who has the capacity to listen to, empathize with and connect with students, teachers and parents; the *educator*, a self-directed instructional leader with a strong intellect and deep knowledge; the *envisioner*, who has a vision of what schools can be and is guided by a mission that has the best interests of all students at heart; the *facilitator*, who has outstanding human relations skills; the *change master*, who has the ability to motivate and manage change in a positive and enduring fashion; the *culture builder*, who models a strong and viable vision based on achievement, expectations and accountability; the *activator*, who has the gumption (drive, enthusiasm and energy) to lead the institution; the *producer*, a results-oriented person who translates high expectations into academic achievement; the *character builder*, who is a role model with high moral values such as integrity, respect and trust; and the *contributor*, whose priority is to contribute to the success of others.

Thus, from an educational perspective, effective leadership refers to all the appropriate actions that school leaders take to manage their schools. Successful leadership implies that academic excellence is achieved through the actions of SMTs effective leadership. Effective leadership is viewed as fundamental to the success of any organization.

Leithwood et al. (2006) and Leithwood and Riehl (2003) posit that leadership is all about organization improvement; more specifically, it is all about establishing a widely agreed upon and worthwhile direction for the organization and doing whatever it takes to urge and support people to move in that direction. At the core of most definitions of leadership are three broad categories of practice that have been recognized as important for effective leadership and success in most education organizations: setting direction, developing people and developing the organization.

Setting direction

Evidence suggests that leadership practices associated with setting direction account for the largest proportion of a leader's impact (Leithwood et al., 2004). This dimension of leadership includes inspiring staff and other stakeholders with a vision of the future and action aimed at achieving goals for effective schooling. Although a vision can be inspiring, action requires that goals have to be accomplished in order to realize the vision. Important organization goals need to be identified in such a way that individuals take ownership of them. Unless this happens, an organization's goals have no motivational value. Leadership traits required for setting direction include relationship behaviours 'aimed at promoting cooperation among [teachers] and getting them to work together toward a common goal' (Podsakoff et al., 1990: 112).

Setting direction also entails setting high performance expectations of staff and students. While high performance expectations do not define the substance of organization goals, they demonstrate the leader's values and 'the leader's expectations of excellence, quality, and/or high performance' in the achievement of those goals. Demonstrating such expectations is a central behaviour in successful leadership (Podsakoff et al., 1990: 112). To set the direction for an institution, effective leaders should be able to convey their expectations for quality and high performance and help others see the challenging nature of the goals (Leithwood & Riehl, 2003). It is imperative for effective leaders to sharpen awareness of the gap between what a school aspires to and what is presently being accomplished, and promote cooperation in the pursuit of common goals. In the past, teachers often worked under conditions of relative autonomy, but new models of schools as professional learning communities emphasize the importance of a shared vision. Effective school leaders ask critical and constructive questions, emphasize the use of systematic evidence and encourage careful monitoring of both teacher and student progress.

Developing people

Effective leaders provide opportunities for staff development. Their primary aim is capacity building, building not only the knowledge and skills staff need to accomplish organization goals but also their commitment and resilience (Day & Schmidt, 2007) and the disposition to persist in applying that knowledge and those skills (Harris & Chapman, 2002). Effective leaders are characterized by three key practices (Leithwood & Riehl, 2003; Podsakoff et al., 1990): the first is individualized support to staff. Leaders know their followers' needs and promote their development. In this way, leaders demonstrate respect for their colleagues and provide emotional understanding and support. Second, effective leaders encourage intellectual stimulation. This includes encouraging staff to take intellectual risks, re-examine their assumptions, look at their work from different perspectives, rethink how their work can be performed and challenge the status quo concerning leader effects on student achievement. Finally, effective leaders lead by example. They demonstrate transparent decision making, confidence, optimism, hope, resilience and consistency between words and deeds.

Developing the organization

Very little is achieved by increasing people's motivation and capacity if working conditions do not allow their effective demonstration. The three practices described below are about establishing the conditions of work which will allow staff to make the most of their motivation and capacity.

- Building collaborative cultures such as the development of professional learning communities and the improvement of student learning. Success depends on prior conditions, such as a history of working together successfully, which may in turn build trust, making further collaboration easier. Trust is increasingly recognized as a key leadership trait in encouraging collaboration. Individuals are more likely to trust those with whom they have established good relationships (Bryk & Schneider, 2002).

- Restructuring: this includes leaders creating common planning times for teachers, and establishing teams and group structures. Restructuring includes distributing leadership for selected tasks and increasing teacher involvement in decision making.

- Building productive relationships with families and communities: successful leaders embrace a meaningful role for parents.

Establishing a close relationship with the broader community has been identified as a factor contributing to effective school leadership.

School culture sets a tone and context within which work is undertaken and goals are pursued; adjusting and monitoring a school's structure, including how tasks are assigned and performed, the use of time and space, the acquisition and allocation of equipment, supplies and other resources, and all of a school's routine operating procedures; enhancing the performance of a school by providing opportunities for staff to participate in decision making about issues that affect them and for which their knowledge is crucial. In this way, leaders help others to shape the school in ways that can accomplish shared goals and address individual concerns, and working with various role-players in the school's environment – including parents, community members, business and government – and influencing them to participate in school activities (Leithwood & Riehl, 2003). It should be emphasized that the leadership traits of SMT members will contribute to the effective implementation of the practices discussed above.

Research methodology

In order to gain an understanding of how SMTs perceive what traits contribute to them being effective and successful leaders, a generic qualitative study was used. Generic qualitative studies 'simply seek to discover and understand a phenomenon, a process, or the perspective and worldviews of the people involved' (Merriam, 1998). As such, this study was located within the interpretivist paradigm which emphasizes the importance of understanding (Connole, 1998).

An open-ended questionnaire was used to collect data. Where more information or clarity was required from participants, it was followed up with telephone interviews. Some questions included in the questionnaire were: What personal qualities contribute to you being effective or successful? Explain how you set about developing the school as a learning organization. How do you promote continuing professional development among teachers in your department? How do you create and maintain a positive school culture?

Seven principals, four deputy principals and three heads of departments (HoDs) with over five years' experience were purposefully selected from five primary schools and nine secondary schools out of a population of fifty-six primary and 134 secondary schools in the Gauteng East school district in South Africa. Schools that were characterized by regular attendance of teachers and students, effective student discipline and excellent examination results, having attained over 80 per cent for the ANA in grades 3 and 6 in the primary schools and over 80 per cent for the NSC examinations (grade 12) in the secondary schools were selected. Male and female participants were also selected. However, as more males occupy leadership positions, eight males and six females formed part of the sample.

The questionnaires were distributed to all the selected schools and collected from them personally. Participants were requested to complete the questionnaires independently during their free time.

Tesch's approach (Creswell, 2009: 186) was used to analyse the data and to search for themes and patterns in the participants' perceptions that address the aim of the study. To ensure the trustworthiness of the study, Lincoln and Guba's measures were applied throughout the research process (Shenton, 2004: 64). Transferability was addressed through purposive sampling and the provision of rich, thick, detailed descriptions (McMillan & Schumacher, 2006: 319). Dependability and confirmability were obtained through a detailed report of the processes followed in the study, so that future researchers can repeat the work as well as determine how defensible are the constructs that emerged from the study (McMillan & Schumacher, 2006: 324).

Consent for the study was obtained from the Gauteng Department of Education and the SMTs of the selected schools. Participants were made aware that they could withdraw from the research at any time and were assured of the confidentiality of data sources and that no personal information would be revealed without their consent. All information was secured for the duration of the study and was accessible to participants upon request. The findings of the empirical research are discussed in the following section.

Findings

The following are themes that emerged from the data analysis and consolidated with relevant literature.

Key attributes that contribute to successful leadership

The SMTs were unanimous that having a shared vision for the school was the core of their leadership and it was crucial for this vision to be communicated to teachers, students and parents. An HoD (school 9) emphasized that a shared vision contributes to the SMT achieving the school's goals. According to a principal (school 4): 'The vision and mission of our school is a starting point because it is what all schools should aim for – namely: the delivery of quality education and creating of opportunities for students to excel. These expectations form the basis of a positive school culture.' Another principal (school 5) emphasized that 'shared decision making was essential when developing a vision. Regular positive feedback helps in motivating and inspiring staff. Acknowledging and celebrating individual and collective successes as teachers and SMT was another important characteristic for successful leadership.'

The principal of school 1 emphasized that he was a 'visionary, hands-on, and prepared to face challenges head on. I encourage teamwork, share a common vision with the school community and put agreed and working systems in place. I am committed and hardworking.'

Most of the participants felt that good working relations with the students, staff, parents and the district office contributed to their success. It was also apparent that their style of leadership underscored the value of collaboration, collegiality and effective teamwork. A principal (school 5) explained that a good working relationship with other school principals in the area was essential and that collaboration with staff was indispensable to achieving the school's goals. It also emerged that effective school leaders have expert knowledge of the curriculum and keep abreast of new knowledge and developments in education. Although none of the participants used the term 'instructional leadership', what they described as their leadership style was effective instructional leadership. One HoD (school 8) agreed that instructional leadership is a core responsibility of SMTs: 'I think my best quality in terms of leadership is that I've shown that I was in the first place a successful teacher and knowledgeable in my subject field. Therefore I believe that my staff has respect for me on curriculum matters.'

The principal of school 5 described the attributes that made him successful. He felt that 'a successful leader should have a strong sense of commitment and a persistent determination to improving his knowledge and skills; to take command in his position as principal – improving his qualifications; having a flexible style of leadership – being autocratic when needed to be and consultative during negotiations'. He asserts that 'shared decision making is crucial to having a very supportive staff. They required drawing motivation and inspiration from the leader. Decisiveness, effective communication, giving direction to staff and students, and developing a theory of action and a shared vision were also crucial traits.'

Leaders should be an inspiration to their followers (Leithwood & Riehl, 2003). This view is supported by Spillane (2001), Davies (2005), Crow et al. (1996) and Bush and Glover (2003). For them, leadership is about direction-setting, inspiration and supporting others in the achievement of a vision which is based on clear personal and professional values. Leadership does not occur in isolation but in the context of an organization and the wider society. The involvement of society is crucial for a school to achieve its goals.

Creating a positive school culture

Most of the participants were of the opinion that SMTs are instrumental in creating a positive school culture. A principal (school 1) said that: 'We are definitely responsible for creating a positive culture for our school. This can be achieved by promoting teamwork, working closely with other community structures like non-governmental organizations (NGOs) and community-based organizations (CBOs). School leaders should ensure continuous communication with parents, students, staff and the school governing body (SGB), inducting newly appointed personnel, setting targets and time frame for upward movement of academic results, recognizing expertise in the school community and then creating space for performance of tasks assigned.'

A principal (school 2) explained that to create and sustain a positive school climate, school leaders, especially principals, should be good role-models and 'when someone is found doing the right thing then praise, praise, praise'. He added that he 'sets high expectations for his staff and if these expectations are set, people tend to live towards meeting these expectations. A leader always strive for effective communication with all role-players.'

The participants were in agreement that successful school leaders ensure that SMTs, teachers and parents take joint responsibility for effective school discipline and that teamwork is maintained. A principal (school 9) asserted that: 'The most important aspect of creating a positive school culture is that of promoting quality teaching and learning and this is achieved by instilling discipline among students/teachers. There should be no late coming amongst teachers and students, ensuring an effective discipline policy through classroom management, instilling values whenever there is an opportunity.'

Crow et al. (1996) assert that school culture is the 'glue' that holds a school together. It blends the efforts of teachers, students, parents and administrators in creating a school with a particular character. A school's culture determines how role-players view a school and shapes their attitudes towards and their relationships with others in the school. The maintenance of a school's culture is a source of stability and predictability. Leadership is critical in the creation of a school culture. In addition, effective leaders initiate the development of teachers, students and non-teaching staff by instilling values in them and shaping their attitudes (see Leithwood & Riehl, 2003).

Developing the school as an organization

Successful leaders develop schools as organizations. Two principals (schools 1 and 2) provided similar responses. One of them (school 1) explained how he sets about developing the school as an organization: 'We draft policies that are in line with the legislation and departmental policies and make sure that the policies are implemented. We also ensure that everyone is fully conversant with the policies so that they can effectively implement these policies. We also consider treating everyone equally and fairly. We collaborate with other institutions about policy matters.'

The principal of school 4 stated that: 'Team leadership is essential. You have to ensure that the right people are in the right posts and then allow them to do their work without you trying to micro-manage. Trust people and allow them to do their work. Developing policies and assigning work as a team, the principal takes on a leadership position and provides direction when people start floundering.'

Successful leaders create conditions which support and sustain staff and students' performance. According to Davies (2005) and Leithwood and Riehl (2003), effective leadership practices acknowledge the importance of building professional communities, strengthening school cultures and creating collaborative processes to ensure broad participation in decision making. Further, and in view of the importance of continuing professional development as an important ingredient of successful schools, this is discussed in more detail.

Promoting continuing professional development

One of the most important functions of successful leadership is to ensure that SMTs and teachers are provided with continuing professional development programmes. The Department of Education through the IQMS (Integrated Quality Management System) strongly recommends that all schools engage in professional development programmes. Most of the participants follow similar continuing professional development processes in their schools. The deputy principal (school 7) explained how the IQMS and Professional Management Development System (PMDS) tools and processes are used to identify individual staff strengths and weaknesses. SMTs then plan intervention strategies to help develop those staff members who need support. Furthermore, knowledgeable and competent staff members develop new and existing staff. When the need arises, experts are called in to assist. He explained further that: 'We have Identified post level 1 teachers to assist with management tasks thereby making management more efficient whilst at the same time developing potential leaders. Many such members who have assisted with management tasks have now been promoted and are doing well in promoting teaching and learning in other institutions.'

A principal (school 2) observed that as a leader he 'reads extensively and brings latest trends in education to the attention of the SMT who then cascade this new body of knowledge to teachers. Furthermore, the school sends out questionnaires to teachers and parents so that the SMT can be assessed by the teaching staff and staff in general can be assessed by parents. As a successful leader, I arrange for specialists or experts in various fields to provide training to the SMT and teachers. We also welcome visits from the Department to provide professional development.'

An HoD (school 11) expressed concern that very little attention is paid by school leaders to 'succession planning and that leaders usually feel threatened when the time comes to replace all those in leadership positions. However, professional development is still considered a priority and leaders should ensure that staff development opportunities are provided for the staff.' A HoD (school 13) listed a few aspects pertaining to school development. These included: mentoring and coaching of staff; team teaching; in-house training of staff; sending staff to circuit or district training sessions, if available; and working with other cluster school teams to share ideas on improving teaching practice. Providing school leaders and managers with continuing professional development is of paramount importance if leaders wish to turn around underperforming schools, or even turn good schools into great schools (Roe & Drake, 1980).

Personal qualities required for successful and effective leadership

Most participants believed that their personal qualities make a very significant contribution to their success as leaders. Some of these personal attributes include trustworthiness, honesty, integrity, sense of humour, being friendly yet firm, being exemplary, commitment, being hardworking, transparency, being a good communicator, self-confidence, being self-disciplined, having strong moral and ethical values, having a sense of responsibility, being accountable for one's actions and being results driven. Other attributes include decisiveness, being a fast-student, 'thinking on your feet', patience, always striving for continuous improvement, and being fair and consistent.

The principal of school 4 added the following traits required of successful leaders: 'Understanding and interacting with people; caring and consideration for others; planning and organizing skills; delegation of duties according to strengths; dedication and loyalty to my work; and being a lifelong learner – the aspiration of keeping abreast with changes.' The principal of school 5 asserted that: 'I am not totally task-driven and neither too lenient. A balance should be kept between getting things done and motivating and managing the staff. I see myself as open minded team leader – listening when required to and assertive when demanded.'

A head of department of school 8 also touched on the caring aspect of leaders. She articulated the following that contributes to her success as school leader: 'Being human is what your team needs. They don't want a super-hero, but someone who is honest and real, sometimes sad, mostly optimistic. A real person with real feelings, someone they can relate to. If you are always in control you are likely to demotivate them. Your team need to know they can trust you to being fair to them, to back them when necessary, to listen to them and to support them, to try and help in any way you can the same for them and for anyone else in the team.'

These remarks are closely interrelated to the African philosophy of *Ubuntu*. It is described as the capacity, in African culture, to express compassion, reciprocity, dignity, humanity and mutuality in the interest of building and maintaining communities of justice and mutual caring (Bekker, 2007). Leaders with *Ubuntu* are welcoming, hospitable, warm and generous, willing to share. They are open and available to others, willing to be vulnerable, affirming of others, do not feel threatened that others are able and good, for they have a proper self-assurance that comes from knowing that they belong in a greater whole (Tutu, 2004).

Conclusion

The role of SMTs has become complex and multifaceted and can create serious leadership implications. This research has confirmed that there are three very important practices as advocated by Leithwood and Riehl (2003): setting direction; developing people; and developing the organization that contributes to effective and successful leadership. The amount of influence a leader has on individual or group performance and overall effectiveness is also dependent on the leadership traits being displayed by SMTs. In African countries such as Kenya, Nigeria and South Africa, effective schools emphasize the need for continued professional development where SMTs set the example as 'lead learners'. Further research on the continued professional development for principals leading schools in Africa therefore becomes imperative. Effective leaders know the art of balancing their leadership and managerial responsibilities in ways that move their schools forward. Based on the African philosophy of *Ubuntu*, if leadership functions are distributed across the many formal and informal roles in a school, leaders are likely to be successful. Effective leaders differ from other people and possess certain core traits that significantly contribute to their success. Understanding the importance of these core leadership traits that predict effectiveness can help organizations with their leader selection, training and development practices.

9

South Asian Perspectives

Elson Szeto, Yan Ni Annie Cheng and Allan David Walker

A series of recent studies exploring educational leadership across Asia (e.g. Hallinger & Chen, 2015), and East and Southeast Asia in particular (Hallinger & Bryant, 2013a, 2013b, 2013c), have made a significant contribution to the international knowledge base on Asian school leadership. However, subsequent analysis shows much of this regional output to remain dependent on western theoretical perspectives, although several comprehensive country-specific literature reviews have been produced (e.g. Walker et al., 2012). These reviews suggest that school leaders in Asia display indigenous patterns of leadership and integrate western and indigenous approaches through contextually adaptive cultural schemas. Despite some progress towards an understanding of school leadership across the countries that make up East Asia, there remains a serious lack of supportive empirical work. Hallinger and Bryant's (2013a) broad-brush review of the East Asian literature on the topic highlights a very low level of output from the region relative to other regions, despite a discernible but insignificant increase in publications, as well as low publication impact rates and a remarkably uneven distribution of output by Asian scholars.

For example, two recent reviews (Hallinger & Bryant, 2013a, 2013b) of research publications on educational leadership and management in eight core international journals revealed Hong Kong to be the source of more than 50 per cent of publications from East Asia and more than 25 per cent of those from Asia as a whole between 2000 and 2011. A further study (Hallinger et al., 2013) of the corpus of published research articles on these topics concluded that Hong Kong is an outlier in achieving unusual success in knowledge production in this context. Hong Kong scholars are responsible for more educational leadership research output than any other country in East Asia.

Like other East Asian countries, Hong Kong schools serve a diverse mix of students and many face the challenges of complex social, cultural and economic changes such as low birth rate and a hybrid of western and Confucian cultures (Bloom et al., 2010; Marginson, 2011; Szeto, 2014). We therefore chose Hong Kong as our site of inquiry to offer an Asian perspective on effective school leadership and management.

In fact, there is no simple formula for what makes an effective, or successful, school leader. How leadership plays out, and how much of a difference it makes, is influenced by many and diverse contextual factors that vary by person, by school, by locality, and by culture and country. It is therefore unsurprising that there is a lack of clarity and consensus when it comes to defining successful and effective school leadership across societies (e.g. Drysdale & Gurr, 2011; Ngcobo & Tikly, 2010; Pashiardis, 2012; Pont et al., 2008). Even within the same system, practices recognized as constituting effective leadership in one school may not be entirely transferrable to another. Thus, any understanding of what produces successful school leaders is necessarily context specific.

This chapter reports a small-scale empirical investigation of successful school leaders in two schools serving underprivileged populations in Hong Kong. Its aim is to contribute to the school leadership knowledge base in three ways: first, by identifying what constitutes effective leadership in two Hong Kong primary schools, thereby contributing to the indigenous knowledge base; second, and more specifically, by exploring leadership enactment within schools serving underprivileged students, an area that has received very little attention in Hong Kong or more widely in Asia; and, third, by viewing what makes for effective leadership practices through the eyes of two principals of underprivileged schools in an East Asian educational context, thereby contributing to an international understanding of such practices. The chapter addresses the three following research questions.

1   What challenges have the principals faced in leading underprivileged schools?

2   How have the principals successfully addressed these challenges?

3   What lessons can be learned about successful, effective leadership from these two cases?

Exploration of principal leadership practices in underprivileged schools

The reasons for choosing the two principals for our case study were that, first, there has been widespread recognition of their practices as successful leadership from the Hong Kong media and the local community in terms of emphasizing holistic student development. Their recognition is not based on their schools' academic performance, but rather on individual student development in a context of diversity. Some studies (e.g. Muijs et al., 2010; Ross & Berger, 2009) call for alternative perspectives on school leadership practice as it relates to student development in schools that are culturally, socially and individually diverse, and others (e.g. Goldring et al., 2008; Hallinger, 2011) argue that individual organizational factors such as location, structural differences and school culture shape leadership practices in different ways. In our view, the challenges of student diversity, if not perceived as a barrier, can actually broaden leadership perspectives by examining evidence of successful school leadership practices in various local contexts.

Second, we further argue that the practices in local school contexts can contribute to the construction of alternative perspectives. The key is to adopt a framework suitable for exploring the characteristics of successful leadership practices in individual local contexts. In their discussion of the basic characteristics of successful leadership proposed by Yukl (1989), Leithwood and colleagues (2006) argue that a successful school leader needs to be a visionary. A principal with the capability to lead change by turning challenges into opportunities can set a new developmental direction for the school as a whole. The basic characteristics outlined by Yukl (1989) are as follows.

- The ability to build a shared vision that serves as a positive driving force.

- The ability to motivate teachers and students alike to perform differently.

- The ability to cultivate a whole-school culture conducive to taking advantage of new opportunities.

- The ability to build a school–parent–community partnership that extends learning beyond the school walls.

Third, we adopted Yukl's (1989) basic leadership characteristics as our framework in this small-scale case study designed to examine the richness and depth of phenomena in a real-life context (Yin, 2014). We chose this framework to identify whether or not the basic characteristics of successful leadership practices from a western perspective can contrast with those in an Asian context. We began with the contextual characteristics of the two schools, and then moved to the leadership practices perceived by the two principals. Data were collected through in-depth interviews with the principals, examination of accessible school documents such as school external reports and development plans, as well as walk-throughs of the school environments (Creswell, 2012). Interviews are regarded as a useful reflective self-report method for examining participants' values and responses to a changing context (Cohen et al., 2007), thereby affording an understanding of the thoughts and meaning construction characterizing their leadership practices. The interview method allowed us to examine the context of each case, as well as the embedded units of analysis (Yin, 2014), thereby enhancing the overall richness of the study.

The limitation of this study is that the results were based on the principals' self-reporting. The school plans and external review reports of the schools were also used for data analysis to minimize the possible bias associated with self-report data. We believe this reflects the principals' values and why they practise leadership as they do. We acknowledge that deeper data will be required from the next phase of the study into order to cross-check our finding here; this might include, for example, student and teacher views.

In this chapter, we present the two cases in two parts. Part I covers the contextual characteristics of the two schools, including their respective backgrounds and responses to challenges and changes in their student profiles, and the principal leadership practices therein, including the principals' renewal of the school vision, preparation of the teaching team, curriculum innovation and parent–community partnership. To elucidate the similarities and differences between the two cases, Part II summarizes the contextual characteristics and leadership practices of the two schools under study, with the results presented in Tables 9.1 and 9.2, respectively. These tables support further discussion of the characteristics of successful school leadership from an Asian perspective, given the previously mentioned distinct knowledge development furthered by Hong Kong.

Part I

School A: Contextual characteristics

Background

School A is a government-aided primary school[1] sponsored by a Buddhist organization. It was founded in 1931, and is situated in one of the wealthiest districts of Hong Kong Island, and is thus surrounded by many high-performing schools. School A is constructed in a Buddhist style, and boasts many traditional Chinese architectural features, thereby projecting its cultural foundations in Buddhist and Chinese traditions.

Principal's responses to the threat of closure

When she took up principalship of the school in 2005, Cherry (a pseudonym) viewed it as a traditional aided school admitting primarily students of Chinese ethnicity living in surrounding districts. The principal declared that she had a clear vision, which was to serve the needs of local students. Not long after becoming principal, however, Cherry recognized an imminent threat, that is, the waves of primary school closures due to the steady decline in the birth rate in Hong Kong at that time. She recalled her response to the news: 'The government might have its own considerations, but I believe that education is not a commercial business. We should consider other factors instead of [emphasize] the number of enrolments only' (Cherry's interview: excerpt 1). She continued: 'increasing revenue and cutting expenditure is inevitable in today's commercial world. However, when it comes to education, it makes us feel sad' (excerpt 2).

The threat of closure was accompanied by opportunities to recruit a more diverse mix of students from the surrounding community. With the aid of social workers, Cherry was introduced to a group of non-Chinese-speaking ethnic minority children from various districts who were seeking primary school places. Most of these children were from Southeast and South Asian countries, including Thailand, the Philippines, India and Pakistan. Cherry decided to admit this group of children in the 2005/6 academic year as a novel way of preventing the school from being closed down. At the same time, it also constituted a meaningful initiative to provide a quality education to ethnic minority children. To expand enrolment to these children, Cherry first had to convince the school's sponsoring organization, then its incorporated management committee, and finally the parents of existing students. Equally important, the teaching team needed to revise the curriculum and medium of instruction (MOI). Cherry was not only successful in gaining the sponsoring organization's approval, but also teacher and parental support for the school's new direction.

Change in student profile

In contrast to the school's previous profile, today over 90 per cent of its students are the children of non-Chinese-speaking immigrants from South and Southeast Asian cultures with a variety of religious beliefs, and the school also accommodates a small number of special educational needs (SEN) students. Also, in contrast to the wealthy district in which they attend school, most of the students come from low-income[2] families living in other areas. According to Cherry, most parents have refused to apply for the government's Comprehensive Social Security Assistance (CSSA[3]) scheme. In sum, the school is not only culturally distinct, but also socially distinct from the district in which it is located.

School A: Principal leadership practice

Building a shared vision as a positive driving force

Cherry envisaged cultivating a caring and stimulating environment in support of all-round student development in a multicultural educational context. She shared this vision with staff members whenever staff meetings were held and during individual interactions with the teachers. As a result, the majority of the teachers were motivated to teach the diverse students regardless of their ethnicity, culture or religion. She also sought their assistance in helping the students to realize their full potential as responsible citizens. In particular, the school now views the Buddhist motto of 'benevolence and fraternity' as the foundation stones of character. Realizing this vision in practice, Cherry set out to offer quality education to her diverse population through drawing on Buddhist ideology. Her school offers multicultural education in support of communal harmony.

Motivating teachers and students to perform differently

Cherry's new vision of multicultural education was a pioneering notion in Hong Kong. Undoubtedly, sharing this vision with the teaching team who would play the most significant role in creating a multicultural environment constituted a major challenge. Cherry was fully cognizant of the fact that without the teachers' support for the necessary changes, her renewed vision was unlikely to bear fruit. She launched the change with a core team of teachers who had shown willingness to take up the challenge. She first conveyed her vision to the teaching team at a school planning meeting. All teachers were encouraged to express their concerns over and willingness to take on board the possible changes involved in moving towards multicultural education. Less than 10 per cent of the teachers initially expressed willingness to teach non-Chinese students, with 90 per cent being reluctant because of their lack of experience teaching such students, the language barrier or individual cultural and learning differences. Some teachers remained reluctant and decided to leave the school. Cherry was not surprised by the teachers' resistance, because the concept of learning diversity in a multicultural context was novel at the time. She saw the high turnover as an opportunity to rebuild the teaching team, and ultimately ended up with a mix of newly recruited and seasoned teachers who shared her passion for multicultural learning. Reducing inequality is seen as a high education priority in Confucian heritage cultures (Lee, 1996). Therefore, cultivating teachers' willingness to teach underprivileged students is regarded as successful leadership practice that is conducive to effective student learning and academic excellence in East Asian societies.

Language is a critical issue for non-Chinese-speaking ethnic minority students living in Hong Kong. Under the 'bi-literacy and tri-lingual' language and primary education language policies, the MOI for most subjects in mainstream primary schools is Chinese/Cantonese.[4] However, most non-Chinese students possess very low Chinese and Cantonese proficiency levels. To enhance both the Chinese and English proficiency of her school's non-Chinese students, Cherry initiated the innovative school policy of a flexible MOI in developing a school-based curriculum to cater for students' diverse learning needs. Accordingly, the MOI of mathematics and general studies, which are commonly taught in Cantonese, is now English, to maximize students' understanding, whereas music, visual arts and physical education remain taught in Cantonese, as in other primary schools, to enrich the Chinese-language learning environment.

The teaching of religion in school is another critical issue in multicultural schools. To cater for the religious diversity of the new student population, the previous lessons on Buddhism were revised as multicultural religion lessons. In addition to introducing students to Buddhism, the lessons also encouraged them to share the tenets of their own religions in class. This curricular innovation was well received, with students' learning mode changing from passive to active participation. Although such curricular innovations may be common in the West, School A was a pioneer in Hong Kong, if not in all of Asia, in implementing them.

Cultivating a whole-school culture for new opportunities

The next step was to help the whole school, including the teaching team and support staff, to gain a better understanding of ethnic minority children and their learning needs. To do so, Cherry collaborated with social workers from non-governmental organizations (NGOs) with experience of working with these children. Cherry considered a whole-school culture supportive of diverse students' learning needs to be essential and organized a series of seminars and training workshops to raise awareness of multiculturalism and learning diversity. For the first few years, she continued to work on building and consolidating the school culture in this direction and put considerable effort into induction and training programmes aimed at conveying multicultural practices to new teachers.

Utilizing the school–parent–community partnership for learning beyond the school walls

Cherry places a high value on parents' voices as a salient channel for building a mutual understanding of the school's development. She regularly carries out parental surveys to collect parents' opinions of their children's development. Cherry learned through these surveys that ethnic minority students' major struggles are: (1) learning written Chinese (a long overlooked educational issue in Hong Kong); (2) gaining acceptance from the community; and (3) searching for their own identity. In response, Cherry encouraged the parents to build partnerships with NGOs and other organizations in the community in which the school is located and the communities in which they live, and to participate in communal cultural activities such as street dance performances. She was thus successful in facilitating greater recognition of non-Chinese families in communal events.

Cherry's most recent innovative project uses mobile apps as an interactive platform to enhance ethnic minority students' Chinese-language learning. She first found sponsors to donate iPads to the school, and then collaborated with NGOs to develop apps for the school Chinese curriculum. These apps have been successful in stimulating students' interest in learning Chinese, and the school received a Best Inclusive Digital Silver Award in the 2014 Hong Kong Information Communication Technology (HKICT) Awards[5] organized by the Hong Kong Council of Social Service. More importantly, the school has won social recognition for its care of underprivileged students through the use of information technologies. In the eyes of both the media and the community, Cherry's school leadership has been recognized as constituting good multicultural practice grounded in harmonious student development.

School B: Contextual characteristics

Background

School B was a government-aided primary school sponsored and operated by a local charitable organization with a history of over sixty-five years. It has been located in a poor area of a wealthy district on Kowloon Peninsula since 1945, and has witnessed the changing face of the community over the years. School B was initially a charitable school offering free education to its students. Its mission was to serve the community through free education aligned with the core values of the sponsoring charitable organization. In accordance with these values, the school building features boxy, inconspicuous architecture that makes effective use of its open floor area. Although the school is still operated by the same charitable organization, it is now an aided school.

Principal's response to the threat of closure

As the vice-principal of a high-performing school, Paul (a pseudonym) was initially reluctant to accept the position of principal at School B, which was threatened with closure at the time. He recalled that his initial mission as principal was simply to save the school: 'the school would be "killed" [forced to close down] if the external review report conducted by the [then] Education and Manpower Bureau was unsatisfactory' (Paul's interview: excerpt 1). This crisis is regarded as an immediate indicator of an effective principal who can prevent the school from being closed down.

Changing student profile

The district's declining birth rate has been offset by a growing number of ethnic minorities and new immigrants in the past ten years. The latter have gradually become the majority student population in the years since Paul saved the school. Around 150 students of mixed backgrounds are currently enrolled in the school, of which 70 per cent are newly arrived migrants from the mainland, most with a low socioeconomic status (SES). A further 15 per cent or so are the Hong Kong-born children of ethnic minority parents from South and Southeast Asian countries, including Thailand, the Philippines, India and Pakistan. The families of 60 per cent of students are supported by the CSSA scheme. The school also admits a number of SEN students. Since Paul joined the school, its student profile has become more culturally, religiously and individually diverse.

School B: Principal leadership practice

Building a shared vision as a positive driving force

Paul accepted the offer of principalship of School B in 2002. Despite having extremely limited resources, he was determined to save the school, first by satisfying the EDB's requirements with a new three-year school plan and then by rebuilding it in accordance with his long-standing vision of 'nurturing the students for all-round development in the domains of ethics, intellect, physique, social skills and aesthetics, [thereby laying a] foundation [for a] successful future' (Paul's interview: excerpt 2). Such a vision, Paul believed, would maximize students' advantages and potential.

After less than nine months under Paul's leadership, School B received a satisfactory performance rating in the EDB's Quality Assurance Inspection report, and was thus allowed to recruit new students for the following year. The school subsequently introduced the new concept of 'invitational education'. For Paul, invitational education is an approach to creating, sustaining and enhancing an authentic and truly welcoming learning environment based on trust, respect, optimism and care that facilitates better learning outcomes and enables students to realize their full potential (see the International Alliance for Invitational Education[6]). Accordingly, School B was rebuilt with a clear focus on student growth through joy, care, creativity, trust, respect and confidence.

Motivating teachers and students to perform differently

To achieve the two goals of preventing School B from being closed down and practising invitational education, Paul needed to raise morale and build a strong teaching team. This was easier said than done because he intended to bring about changes in teaching to demonstrate to the EDB that the school was serious about providing quality education. To motivate the team to move in the desired direction he introduced the invitational education concept to all teachers because he believed it was important to kick off the necessary changes with a shared understanding. He closely watched the teachers' implementation of this concept through classroom observations and frequently evaluated their progress through both individual and collective meetings. The two-month temporary school suspension necessitated by the outbreak of severe acute respiratory syndrome (SARS) in 2003 gave Paul an opportunity to offer teachers a two-month intensive training course on quality teaching.

Paul further extended the team approach to a set of school-based curricula designed to meet diverse student needs and accord with the tenets of invitational education. It was decided that both English and Cantonese would be used as the MOI. The school-based curriculum team redesigned and adjusted the assessments for every subject to cater for students from a diversity of cultural and social backgrounds. This reform was considered effective as Paul improved both teachers' practices and the overall quality of the school. He recalled that many teachers mentioned that he behaved like a dedicated teacher educator.

Cultivating a whole-school culture for new opportunities

Paul's determination and deep commitment to cultivating a new school culture, and the role model he presented in doing so, impressed his staff. Despite being very demanding, Paul turned the school around and put it on the right track. His educational vision also inspired new opportunities to change students' lives through an invitational and joyful learning environment. Consequently, the school as a whole realized its potential to address individual student needs and differences with confidence. Paul's leadership and efforts to cultivate a strong school culture were recognized and endorsed by the EDB in an external review report issued in 2009.

Utilizing the school–parent–community partnership for learning beyond the school walls

Paul had a deep commitment to serving students and their families both within and outside the school. As most of the students lived nearby, their development, he believed, should involve parent–community cooperation. As noted, School B was surrounded by many high-performing schools, and many local residents were of a high SES and did not see School B as a popular choice for their own children. Despite the disadvantaged status of the school, Paul upheld the core values of both the sponsoring charitable organization and his own educational vision. Drawing on the concept of invitational education, Paul saw the school as an invitational school for the local community.

Accordingly, he opened up the school and organized a variety of educational and cultural activities for the students, parents and the community. For example, instead of holding a Christmas party, Paul invited representatives of a community church to give a talk on the meaning of Christmas. His aim was to instil respect for and an appreciation of different cultures and diversity through a school–parent–community partnership. The end result was a revitalized invitational school open to everyone in the community. The school's new status also adhered to the guiding values of the charitable organization, whose mission was to provide a wide range of services to the community, with education being chief among them.

Drawing on the concept of invitational education allowed Paul to put the school motto, 'Benevolence, love, diligence and integrity', into practice. He embedded the motto to develop the teaching team and provide a school-based curriculum focused on diversity. Paul's further promotion of a school–parent–community partnership allowed him to successfully provide quality, balanced student development in the local community.

Part II

The two schools under study developed with different contextual characteristics and are situated in quite different communities. The principals of both realized that the schools were on the brink of closure if they did not implement change. By coincidence, they both sought to save their schools by admitting students with backgrounds different from those they had traditionally served. These students also had different individual learning needs, were from a diverse mix of cultural, religious and social backgrounds and were largely from low SES households. Such a diverse student mix provided the schools with both challenges and opportunities. Table 9.1 summarizes the contextual characteristics of Schools A and B.

Despite their common aims and means of saving their respective schools, the two principals' leadership practices were informed by differing holistic approaches to student development in the context of diversity, although they both chose an educational path that differed from the common focus on students' academic performance in public examinations. Table 9.2 summarizes the principals' leadership practices in the two schools

Characteristics of principal leadership practices in the two schools

It is important to note that we do not wish to generalize the case study findings more broadly. However, by examining the challenges that these two underprivileged schools addressed, we were able to identify the characteristics of successful principal leadership practices as put forward by Yukl (1989).

Visionaries for a new educational direction

The two cases reflect the fate of schools on the brink of closure owing to Hong Kong's declining birth rate. As both of the underprivileged schools considered faced this common threat, their experiences serve to characterize successful school leadership practices in times of difficulty. Both principals first built a shared vision to cultivate a socially and culturally adaptable school conducive to divergent student demographics. Cherry pursued a vision of multicultural education, and Paul a vision of invitational education. They both inspired their schools with these visions (see Tables 9.1 and 9.2) in pursuit of social, cultural and learning diversity (Dimmock & Walker, 2000) for the whole school. In so doing, their practices characterize a form of school leadership that differs from that adopted by high-performing schools. The difference lies in the holistic development of student potential in a context of diversity.

Capability to lead change

Both cases demonstrate the principals' capability to lead school transformation in a situation of diversity (Walker & Dimmock, 2002) and to cope with the

TABLE 9.1 Contextual characteristics of Schools A and B

	School A: Principal Cherry	School B: Principal Paul
Background of the school	• Over 80-year history • Sponsored by a Buddhist organization • Aided primary school • Situated in one of the wealthiest districts of Hong Kong Island, where many high-performing schools are located	• Over 65-year history • Sponsored by a local charitable body first offering free education to the children of local families and then operated as an aided school • Situated in the poor area of a wealthy district and surrounded by many high-performing schools
Principals' responses to threat of closure	• Faced the threat of being closed down due to the decreasing birth rate • Believed a successful school should take into consideration factors other than exam performance • Saved the school by admitting non-Chinese-speaking ethnic minority children • Provided quality education for children • Pursued multicultural education • Obtained the full support of the sponsoring organization and acceptance by the then parents	• Faced threat of closure owing to declining birth rate • Could not compete with high-performing schools in the same district • Believed a successful school could take a different path from that of high-performing schools • Saved the school by satisfying the EDB with a three-year school plan and admitted non-Chinese-speaking ethnic minority, new immigrant and SEN children • Pursued his long-standing educational passion for 'nurturing . . . students for all-round development'
Change in student profile	• Over 90 per cent of the students in the school are now non-Chinese-speaking immigrants from Southeast Asia • Around 10 per cent are local children • A small number of SEN students attend the school • Students are mainly from low-income families • Diverse cultural, religious and language backgrounds	• Over 70 per cent of students are newly arrived migrants from the mainland • Over 15 per cent are ethnic minority children born in Hong Kong to parents of mixed Chinese and Southeast Asian backgrounds • A small number of SEN students attend the school • Students are mainly from low-income families • Diverse cultural, religious and language backgrounds

TABLE 9.2 Principal leadership practice in the two schools

	School A: Principal Cherry	School B: Principal Paul
Building a shared vision as a positive driving force	• Cultivated a caring and stimulating environment in support of all-round student development and multicultural education	• Introduced a new school vision based on the concept of 'invitational education' to facilitate better learning outcomes and help students to realize their full potential through joy, trust and respect
Motivating teachers and students to perform differently	• Practised distributed leadership to start the change with a core team of teachers • Supported the other teachers with professional development to understand non-Chinese students' learning needs. • Implemented innovative school policy by adopting flexible MOI in developing the school-based curriculum conducive to diversity • Revised the previous Buddhism lessons as multicultural religion sharing lessons	• Practised instructional leadership • Shared a common understanding of the invitational education concept with teachers • Built a strong teaching team by raising morale through intensive training in quality teaching in a context of diversity • Adopted a team approach to developing a set of school-based curricula for diverse student needs • Teachers used English and/or Cantonese as the medium of instruction
Cultivating a whole-school culture to capitalize on new opportunities	• Planted multicultural seeds in the school and raised awareness of the cultural, social and pedagogical changes needed for diversity • Collaborated with social workers from an NGO helping the children to build a new school culture • Considerable effort devoted to induction and training programmes designed to convey multicultural practices to new teachers	• Acted as a role model in cultivating a school culture • Infused his educational vision into practice to change students' lives through an invitational and joyful learning environment • Developed a school culture conducive to new opportunities • Efforts to cultivate a school culture for enhanced learning recognized by the EDB in an external review report

| Utilizing school–parent–community partnership for learning beyond the school walls | • Parents' opinions collected in surveys to support mutual understanding of the school's development
• Building partnerships with parents, NGOs and other organizations in the community for active communal participation
• A sense of belonging to the school and the community developed through active participation in various communal activities
• Collaborative mobile app projects sponsored through partnership recognized as an important form of support for students' Chinese-language learning needs | • Integrated the core values of the charitable organization with the vision of invitational education to facilitate school–parent–community cooperation
• Encouraged parent participation in student development in the local community
• Organized a variety of educational and cultural activities for students, parents and the local community
• Opened up the school as an invitational school to parents and the local community |

changing face of the communities in which the schools are located and the students live. Both Cherry and Paul were successful in leading their teaching teams to effect change in the face of a common threat. Although their capability to lead change is contextually specific, their practices provide a broader understanding of successful school leadership conducive to capitalizing on new opportunities.

Turning challenges into opportunities for a new developmental direction

The selected cases demonstrate how to handle the threat of closure and turn it into an opportunity to rebuild the entire school by (1) renewing the school vision; (2) building a strong teaching team with a focus on school-based curriculum development for diversity; (3) constructing a whole-school culture in the context of diversity; and (4) utilizing the school–parent–community partnership to extend learning beyond the walls of the school. Cherry and Paul adopted a similar holistic student development approach to the schools' diverse student mixes, although their strategies for turning challenges into opportunities differed. In fact, adopting a holistic approach to education in East Asia is not uncommon – the holistic concept is embedded in education as the means to educate up all-round human beings, while the aim of education in other contexts is to develop the full potential of an individual (Cheng, 1998). For example, discipline and ethics are seen as two core values of education conducive to effective learning and academic excellence in East Asian societies (Cheng, 1998).

The main difference is that Cherry led in collaboration with NGOs and then gained local parents' acceptance of non-Chinese ethnic minority students. In contrast, Paul worked closely with different components of the school and educated teachers to change their attitudes, thereby gaining their commitment to the new direction, followed by that of the parents. Although a school–parent–community partnership can raise various tensions and issues (Bryk, 2010; Hornby & Lafaele, 2011; Larocque et al., 2011; Tam, 2007), both Cherry and Paul managed to use that partnership as a strategy to address the challenges their schools faced and to create educational opportunities for a diverse mix of students.

Conclusion

Again, it must be reiterated that this chapter cannot provide a set of universal characteristics of successful school leadership practice in the Asian school context. Our aim in presenting these two cases is to further understand how local contextual characteristics shape principals' leadership practices. In response to a common threat, the two principals considered herein adopted both similar and different strategies to achieve desirable educational outcomes in underprivileged schools with a diverse student population. Their strategies differed from those of traditional high-performing schools, which aim for superior academic performance. On the one hand, the threat of closure inspired the two principals' leadership practices in their particular contexts. On the other hand, their leadership practices changed their schools' development trajectory and hence the contexts in which they were situated. This reciprocal relationship between local contextual characteristics and school leadership practices, with reference to western models of successful leadership practices (Bush & Glover, 2012; Day & Sammons, 2013; Leithwood et al., 2006; Yukl, 1989), offers a broader perspective to the school leadership field. Such models have also provided an interesting contrast to the Asian context of educational leadership.

Bringing up all-round human beings and adopting a holistic approach as the criteria of achieving successful leadership seem to be the distinctive characteristics in this East Asian society. How do these characteristics vary across different types of schools in Hong Kong or in other Asian countries? Further qualitative and quantitative research on a larger scale is needed to reflect a broader view of successful and effective school leadership practices.

10

Australian and Pacific Perspectives

David Gurr and Lawrie Drysdale

Introduction

Research about effective and successful school leadership has a relatively short history in Australasia. For example, in our reviews of successful school leadership in Australia (Gurr, 2008, 2009, 2012; Gurr et al., 2010) we describe how substantial research in the area has a fifty-year history, and a predominate focus on principals. The 1960s saw research and teaching on educational administration emerge, particularly fuelled by the work of Walker and colleagues at the University of New England, and Bassett and colleagues at the University of Queensland. This work relied on overseas research and a somewhat unsophisticated view of school leadership, with the overwhelming view that this resided in the male head of a school, in an individualistic and positional pursuit to influence others to improve: effectiveness and success tentatively meant '[a] good school has good staff . . . Given a reasonable basis on which to work, the headmaster can *create* a good staff' (Bassett et al., 1967: 3); '[e]ven if he [the headmaster] (*sic*) already has a good school, he can look forward to leading an infinitely better one' (Bassett et al., 1967: 32).

In the following decade, research and writing remained largely focused on principal leadership, but there continued to be a lack of major Australian research. This changed with the project titled 'The Australian School Principal: A National Study' (see Duignan et al., 1985), a study that heralded a thirty-year interest in exploring successful Australian school leadership. Using interviews with principals, parents, teachers and students from government and non-government schools in all Australian states and territories, a survey administered to 1,600 principals and fourteen case studies of highly effective schools from across Australia, it was the first major study in Australia to explore principal leadership and effectiveness, and presented a model relating principal personal and professional qualities (including leadership) and the nature of their work to improving teaching practice, and indirectly, student learning outcomes. In the ensuing years there have been many more contributions such as the following.

- Several books on how principals lead school improvement and success (e.g. Beare et al., 1989; Caldwell & Spinks, 1992; Simpkins et al., 1987).

- A large survey-based study exploring leadership, organizational learning and student outcomes – *Leadership for Organisational Learning and Student Outcomes* (LOLSO) (Mulford & Silins, 2003; Mulford et al., 2004).

- Many small-scale case studies of successful principal leadership such as exploring innovation and success (Dimmock & O'Donoghue, 1997), market-centred leadership (Drysdale, 2001, 2002) and leadership of a successful Christian school (Twelves, 2005).

- An extensive and ongoing school improvement project that has developed a framework for establishing professional learning communities to improve school outcomes – IDEAS (e.g. Crowtherr et al., 2009; Lewis & Andrews, 2007).

- Research focused on describing successful Australian practice within a world focus (e.g. Caldwell & Harris, 2008), or principals writing about what they do (Anderson & Cawsey, 2008; Fleming & Kleinhenz, 2007; James, 2012).

- Formation of the Australian and New Zealand arms of the International Successful School Principalship Project (ISSPP) and the International School Leadership Development Network (ISLDN).

- Exploration of middle-level leadership through case studies of fifty Australian secondary school subject departments and cross-school programmes – An Exceptional Schooling Outcomes Project (AESOP) (Dinham, 2005, 2007).

- Publication and distribution to all Australian schools of a book of seventeen stories about the exhilaration of being a principal (Duignan & Gurr, 2007a).

For this chapter we focus on the last three contributions to describe a collection of research that provides a description of the practice of good leadership in Australia and New Zealand. We begin by describing in some detail findings from the cases from the Australian group associated with the ISSPP (the ISLDN is still at an early stage although some exploratory research is described in Gurr et al., 2014), before exploring a summary of findings of the cases from the New Zealand ISSPP group. The focus on principals concludes with an exploration of the work of successful principals described in *Leading Australia's Schools* (Duignan & Gurr, 2007a). The chapter ends by broadening the focus of leadership with a discussion of research on successful middle-level leaders in Australian schools. It is not meant to be an exhaustive review of research in Australasia, and while the selections are somewhat eclectic and predominantly Australian, they serve to provide illustrations of effective and successful leadership to complement the chapter on leadership development in Australia by Clarke and Wildy contained in this book (Chapter 3).

Evidence from the ISSPP: Australia

Some history of the ISSPP is needed to locate the importance of this project within the broader educational leadership research landscape. The ISSPP (http://www.uv.uio.no/ils/english/research/projects/isspp) began in 2001, and was established to address the need to better understand how principals contribute to school success. The aim was to examine the characteristics and practices used by successful school principals across countries. With more than twenty countries now involved, it has been a productive research project accumulating more than 100 case studies of the leadership of successful schools and producing many publications including four project books, seven special journal issues and more than 100 chapters or journal articles. It is most likely the largest international educational leadership project ever undertaken. Apart from being involved in the leadership of this project from its early stages, our research involvement has been through the production of cases studies from Victoria, Indonesia and Singapore in association with several graduate research students, and collaborating with Bill Mulford as he produced case studies and conducted a principal and teacher survey in Tasmania (see summaries of this work in Mulford & Edmunds, 2009; Mulford et al., 2009).

The ISSPP established early the protocols to conduct the multiple perspective case studies. Primary data are collected through semi-structured interviews using a standard protocol conducted with the principal (multiple interviews), teachers (individual and group interviews), parents (group interviews), students (group interviews) and members of the school board or council. Secondary data are collected through school documents, minutes of meetings, press reports, school websites, researcher ethnographic notes and so forth. For later case studies, observation of the work of the principal, and of the life of the school, are also included.

Schools were selected using one or more of the following: student learning performance above expectations on standardized tests; reputation of the principal (typically gathered through discussion with system leaders); and other indicators of site-specific success such as school inspection reports.

Having selected the schools, the researchers set about determining the extent that participants in the study could identify and confirm the principal's contribution to the school's success, and identify what participants thought were the characteristics and qualities of the principals that helped them to contribute to that success. Fourteen case studies were conducted in the states of Victoria and Tasmania between 2003 and 2005. The five case studies in Tasmania were conducted under the leadership of Bill Mulford, and the nine cases from Victoria were conducted under the supervision of David Gurr and Lawrie Drysdale. Three of the schools in Victoria have been subsequently revisited, with these studies including observation of practice (Drysdale et al., 2011).

Success defined by the schools

Initially the researchers focused on 'success' rather than 'effectiveness' because success was seen to be a more inclusive and broader concept. It was felt that success would provide another dimension that was not included in previous definitions of effectiveness, which had focused on student achievement within a narrowly defined curriculum. Sergiovanni (1991) had previously noted that 'successful' should be used because it communicated a broader definition of effectiveness. In order to better understand success we wanted to investigate perceptions of success at the school level and explore the contribution of the principal to that success.

A key finding was the difference in the definition of success of the participants in schools compared with the more narrow definition adopted by the researchers; almost universally, participants outlined a broader definition of success than the researchers. Typically school success was defined as school achievements and milestones, improved student outcomes in a range of areas, whole school improvement, and the provision of services, resources and amenities. While these success factors were common, schools also defined success in their own terms and within their specific context. Examples of success included: achieving individual potential; student engagement; self-confidence and self-direction; sense of identity; sense of community and belonging; positive school staff morale; a positive school culture; a focus on the whole child; prizes and rewards; and reputation in the community.

Findings from Victoria and Tasmania

Principals made a difference and contributed to success by being a positive influence on the quality of the education in their school (Gurr et al., 2005, 2006). The contribution was manifest in aspects such as improving the image of the school, setting new direction through a common vision, establishing high expectations, building school capacity (especially in regard to staff development), reorganizing the school, and focusing on improving teaching and learning. In most cases the school community identified the principal as the 'engine room' of school improvement and change, and were able to identify milestones and achievements directly attributable to the principal.

From these cases we explore five common features of the leadership of these successful school principals: values and beliefs; qualities; skills; interventions/practices; and capacity building. The first three features (values, qualities and skills) are to do with principal identity. These were personal characteristics attributed by participants to the principal that shaped their perception of positive leadership, which enabled the principals to influence and have impact. The other aspects were more to do with what principals did – the practices and interventions that led to success and how they built the capacity of staff to enable success.

Values and beliefs

Sergiovanni (1991) noted that style itself is less important than what the principal stands for, believes in and communicates to others. This was clearly one of the key findings from the Australian case studies. Initially we categorized this as the principal's personal philosophy (Gurr & Drysdale, 2007). Subsequently we have defined this as values and beliefs (Drysdale & Gurr, 2011). The principals were able to clearly articulate their values and were observed to act in accordance with their values; they embodied or modelled what they believed. The values were perceived on multiple levels. For example, they expressed core values, such as respect for others, fairness, trustworthiness and responsibility. But they also had universal values, such as social justice, dignity and freedom, empathy for the less well off, compassion and tolerance. Other levels included professional values and beliefs (service to staff, acceptance of diversity, accepting constructive feedback from others, maintaining confidentiality) and social and political values (respect for life and the environment, respect for minority rights, respect for the law).

Qualities

It was obvious from the interviews with participants that successful leaders were attributed qualities and traits that helped to define their leadership. Gurr et al. (2006) found that particular personal qualities and characteristics seemed important for the success of the leadership of principals, and Belchetz & Leithwood (2007) noted these features were important, not so much for what leaders do, but for how they do it. Traits found in the Australian research included passion, optimism, enthusiasm, persistence, determination and assertiveness, and principals were described by interviewees as visionary, inspirational, authentic, collaborative, courageous, having integrity, resilient and intuitive (Gurr et al., 2006).

Skills

Successful principals demonstrated a set of skills that enabled them to align people in collective purpose, empower people to act, push through change and initiate new approaches, remove blockages, provide a clear vision for the future, establish good relationships with a range of stakeholders, and develop strong support networks and alliances. They showed highly developed skills in planning, team building, organizational management, communication, coaching, problem solving, decision making, sensitivity to others, and developing self and others.

Interventions/practices

Values, qualities and skills are only part of the equation. Who they are is important but significantly what they do and how they do it also determines their success. We have found that successful principals used particular kinds of influence and intervention strategies to improve outcomes such as 'enhancing the school and professional capacity of teachers, improving the quality of instruction, redesigning the curriculum, building social capital, and providing a safe and secure environment' (Drysdale, 2011: 454).

Leithwood and Riehl (2005) labelled these interventions as practices. They identified three practices: setting direction, developing people and redesigning the organization, and in later publications (e.g. Leithwood et al., 2006) this list was expanded to include managing teaching and learning. Our ISSPP research confirmed these four key practices and added three additional ones – self-leadership, influencing and understanding the broader context. Principals demonstrated self-leadership by being able to understand themselves to maintain and improve their own effectiveness and overall performance. They showed evidence of personal motivation, self-direction and emotional maturity in order to reflect on, monitor and improve their cognition and behaviour. In respect to the broader context, successful leaders were able to make sense of the changes in the internal and external environment. They were aware of international and national trends and were able to navigate the uncertain terrain by being adaptive and learning from their practice and experience to ensure school success. Finally, they were effective influencers. They were able to build coalitions and establish alliances. They built productive relationships and networks using a range of influence techniques and strategies. The principals acted purposefully and strategically. They engaged in a series of interventions that reflected the contexts and the needs of their schools (Gurr & Drysdale, 2007: 45).

Capacity building

In producing an initial model of successful leadership, Gurr et al. (2006) identified 'capacity building' to be a common intervention to improve student learning across the cases, and this has featured in our subsequent revisions of our model of successful school leadership as we have gone back to several schools to explore the sustainability of success (e.g. Drysdale & Gurr, 2011). The latter model also lends itself to interpretation of leadership influence broadly and helps locate the work of principals and other leaders in schools. In this model we conceptualize leadership as influencing student outcomes through interventions in teaching and learning (Level 1), school capacity building (Level 2) and external influences (Level 3). Level 1 interventions are focused on improving curriculum, pedagogy, assessment and reporting, and have the most impact on student outcomes. This is the area in which many middle-level leaders operate. Level 2 interventions are focused on school capacity building (individual, professional, organizational and community capacity building). Level 2 interventions have a more indirect impact on student outcomes, and principals and other senior leaders typically operate at this level. Level 3 involves the external influences on schools. In this, principals, and occasionally other school leaders, are responsive to the many external influences on schools, and sometimes are able to shape these influences by, for example, contributing to district and system level policy development, and being involved in networks and professional associations.

Evidence from the ISSPP: New Zealand

Led by Ross Notman, the ISSPP group in New Zealand has contributed thirteen cases to the ISSPP including one specialist school, one early childhood centre, one intermediate school, six primary schools and four secondary schools. The early childhood example is the only one in all of the ISSPP cases. Findings from an initial six cases were published in Notman and Henry (2009, 2011) and Notman (2012), a further seven cases were published in a ten-case edited book (Notman, 2011a) and one final additional case (Notman, 2014) contributed to the fourth book of the ISSPP (Day & Gurr, 2014). The selection process and case study methodology adhered to that previously described for the ISSPP, with leadership success denoted in the main through positive school inspection reports (particularly in regard to the leadership and management of the principal), and the acknowledgement by professional peers of their leadership success.

From the initial six cases, the following findings emerged in regard to the 'influential components of a principal's successful leadership and their capacity to maintain that success' (Notman & Henry, 2011: 377):

- **Personal characteristics** – these included having previous life experiences that enhanced their leadership, a passion for education, demonstrating pride and self-belief in school and community, a high work ethic, a high level of resilience and being able to portray the human face of leadership.

- **Leadership skills** – included management skills developed before becoming a principal, use of communication skills to build positive connections and consultation with the school community, knowing when to lead and when to let others lead, expert use of a variety of decision making processes, critical self-reflection and interpersonal connectedness.

- **Leadership strategies** – these included establishing shared vision and purpose, focusing on student achievement for all students, continuous school improvement, consulting with teachers and the community, employment of quality and supportive staff, developing a strong senior leadership team, personnel support systems, integration of different cultures and fostering cultural diversity and inclusiveness, growing other leaders through delegation and shared decision making and having one's 'fingers on the pulse' of events in the life of a school.

- **Sustaining leadership success** – this was supported by developing collaborative leadership, adopting a contingent leadership approach that addresses external influences on the school and good intrapersonal leadership that focuses on a principal's self-awareness and self-management.

In Notman's (2011b) synthesis of the ten cases in the book *Successful Educational Leadership in New Zealand: Case studies of schools and an early childhood centre* (Notman, 2011a) he used the term 'pedagogical leadership' to describe the core focus of the principals' work. This included a vision for teaching and learning that aims to increase student achievement, an orientation to the possibilities and opportunities rather than the limitations of government curriculum mandates, fostering staff collaboration through stimulating learning conversations among staff, encouraging explicit sharing of pedagogical strategies and the use of assessment data to guide student learning programmes, and, in the early childhood and primary settings, building school–parent partnerships to support children's learning. Notman went on to describe how these leaders exhibit a range of common leadership strategies that included:

- Articulating an overarching vision that is communicated clearly to the school/centre community.

- Employing strategies that focus on cultural change, such as being culturally responsive to demographic changes in the school community, and using an ethic of care to promote a positive culture.

- Promoting teacher quality through recruiting, inducting, developing and motivating teaching staff.

- Building individual capacity among staff through professional development and use of distributed leadership practices.

- An acute contextual awareness (both internal and external), resulting in a strong sense of advocacy for students and the school community.

The leaders were people-centred, and were good at developing relationships, modelling appropriate behaviour and establishing relational trust. They could articulate their core beliefs and values and demonstrate these through their actions. Critical self-reflection, personal resilience and demonstrating a range of interpersonal skills that involved and acknowledged others were important elements of their successful practice (Notman, 2012).

Leading Australia's Schools

Leading Australia's Schools (Duignan & Gurr, 2007a) is a book of seventeen empirical stories about the exhilaration of being a principal, with all the principals being highly regarded and successful school leaders nominated by their peers in the Australian Council of Educational Leaders (ACEL). Unlike the ISSPP, this is a book about principals reflecting on their work. Case study writers (esteemed educators nominated within ACEL) were engaged to interview the principals and prepare a chapter that described their work, particularly focusing on the sustaining aspects of being a principal. Partly sponsored by the Australian federal government, the book was distributed to all Australian schools.

Drawing on descriptions from the first chapter (Gurr & Duignan, 2007), some of the aspects of the work of these successful principals can be described. Principals make a difference to the lives of students, as they can help lift a school to extraordinary heights where students are able to perform at a level higher than would normally be expected. Tony Considine at Thursday Island High School in the Torres Strait, and John Fleming at Bellfield Primary School in Melbourne, showed that it does not matter what level of disadvantage exists in a community, students can be provided with a school environment that allows them to be the equal of any. Under the guidance of expert principals, schools can be inviting, exciting, purposeful and humane places that students want to go to. As Lynne Hinton from Buranda commented: 'Our kids enjoy coming to school. But more than that, there is a real sense of purpose about what the kids are doing. A sense that they are here for a reason, and that is to learn.' Principals provide support, advice and a warm smile for parents and they often influence the wider community. The story of Rhonda Brain described how she extended her influence outside of her school and improved literacy in the surrounding rural community. These principals' work is complex and Jodee Wilson used the term 'chaos' to describe her work. She saw herself as a human resource facilitator, an educational expert and a symbolic chief, while at the same time making sure her school operated smoothly. Sister Geraldine, the principal at a small Western Australian Catholic school for young teenage girls experiencing serious behavioural and emotional issues, described her multiple roles as spiritual head, social worker and educational leader. Yet despite the demands of these multiple roles and sustaining a small special-setting school, Sister Geraldine saw her work as a privilege:

> It's a privilege to be trusted by them [the students] and work with them to get the best outcomes. It's a privilege to see them grow day by day at school, to see them improve their behaviour outside school, to see their life in the family improve, to see conflict replaced by harmony. It's a privilege to help them live their lives more fully the way God wants them to live – to reach a greater fullness of life. That is the biggest reward.

It is a job with many tensions and dilemmas that need to be balanced. For example, Mark Doecke at Yirara College in Alice Springs explained the tensions involved in connecting with the school community, and how the clearly-expressed school values and beliefs helped resolve these:

> One of my hopes for the college is that Aboriginal people will feel free to visit, chat, perhaps offer their services for some paid or unpaid work, and that we can accommodate that, as inconvenient as it may be. Yes, there will

be tensions. For example, the needs of family versus the needs for education for the right behaviour. But let us not flee from those tensions, but deal with them in a spirit of openness and love, without compromising our values and beliefs. For it is our strong values and beliefs that are our strength.

Fundamentally though, being a principal is an exhilarating job, one full of possibilities and hope, one that few of us can do, but which, when done well, is one of the most satisfying of all. As John Fleming said: 'I love my job, I love it. It is not all hard work and drudgery, and "how am I going to get through it?" It is actually exhilarating.'

The last chapter in the book (Duignan & Gurr, 2007b) provides a synthesis of the seventeen stories. To construct this, an initial thematic analysis was conducted by Gurr, looking for the big ideas that were being described. Two educational leadership graduate classes were invited to do the same and the analyses compared, with a final thematic review by Duignan, resulting in the production of the chapter. Duignan and Gurr (2007b: 158–64) found that these successful principals had:

- A clearly articulated philosophy and deep moral purpose.

- An unwavering focus on all students and their learning needs.

- A passionate belief in the significance of what they do.

- A commitment to making a difference.

- A focus on, and valuing of, people.

- Strong support for learning, growth and development of themselves and others.

- An expectation of high professional standards.

- Development of a collaborative, collegial and inclusive school culture.

- A view of leadership as service.

- Acceptance of the hard work associated with leading a school.

- A 'can do' attitude to all that they did.

- Enjoyment and satisfaction from what they do.

These individuals demonstrated an orientation to life and work that helped them to be successful as a principal (e.g. use of self-reflection, clear values, love of people), a love of and for learning, a strong sense of moral purpose for what they do, and an unwavering hope for a better future.

Leaders other than the principal

In Australia, there have been several examples of research on middle-level leadership (see Gurr & Drysdale, 2013), and of the leadership of those in more senior roles such as assistant principals or heads of campus (Cranston, 2009 provides a summary of much of this research). Here we explore one research project focused on exceptional middle-level leaders who were heads of curriculum and support areas at the secondary school level, and then relate this to research that highlights the issues for those middle-level leaders that may not be as successful.

In what was termed An Exceptional Schooling Outcomes Project (AESOP), Dinham (2005, 2007, 2008) made a substantial contribution through exploring the impact on student learning of the leadership of fifty subject departments and cross-school programmes (e.g. student welfare) across thirty-eight secondary (years 7 to 12) and central schools (K to 10). All schools were able to demonstrate exceptional student outcomes in years 7 to 10 over at least a four-year period. Outcomes included academic, personal and social, with schools and leaders selected on the basis of public examination results, value-adding measures and nominations from parent groups, principals and system officers. Multiple-perspective interviews were used involving the principal, headteacher/leader of the outstanding department/programme, staff group forum, student forum, parent forum, classroom observation and document analysis. Principal leadership (Dinham, 2005), and leadership of the heads of department/programmes (Dinham, 2007) were both important for student success. The middle-level leaders were found to promote success through:

- A focus on students and their learning.
- High level interpersonal skills, and generally being well-liked and trusted.
- High level professional capacity and strategic resource allocation.
- Promotion and advocacy of their departments and maintaining good external relations with the school.
- Influencing department planning and organization.
- Developing common purpose, collaboration and sense of team within their department.
- Fostering teacher learning, and developing a culture of shared responsibility and trust.
- Clear vision, high expectations of themselves and others, and developing a culture of success.

The support and encouragement of principals was important for the success of these middle-level leaders and Dinham (2005) describes how principals were able to foster exceptional achievement through adopting an outward focus and creating important external networks, having a bias towards innovation and action, having high expectations, maintaining a pleasant school environment, developing a culture of continuous improvement, promoting professional learning and the development of leadership skills, developing a common purpose to unite staff, encouraging staff collaboration, focusing on student welfare to support student's learning, and, above all, focusing their work on students, learning and teaching.

Gurr and Drysdale (2013) reviewed the research of three of their doctoral students – Cotter (2011), Keane (2010) and White (2000). These studies, similar to Dinham's research but without the criteria for leadership success, used multiple-perspective interviews of the work of school leaders with curriculum leadership roles, and showed that their work is heavily dependent on how their roles are constructed and the capacities, abilities and attitudes of the leaders. Some are expected to be leaders that influence teaching and learning, and they may be developed and supported to do so. Too often, however, teachers in these key roles have few expectations or opportunities to exercise leadership. While many have the capacity to be leaders of teaching and learning, others are not sure about their ability to influence teaching and learning. Keane (2010: 153) captured some of the issues well when he stated:

> . . . [middle level] leadership is complex and multi-dimensional and is seen to be central to improvement in student learning outcomes. Their complex role includes the kinds of leadership that is exercised by principals and the senior management team, and yet the learning area leaders often receive inadequate preparation and little time to carry out their role. Moreover they are often removed from discussions about whole school policy and development.

Taken together, these two examples of research on middle-level leaders show that while middle-level leaders have the potential to make a significant impact on school and student improvement, far too often this potential is unrealized. Lack of understanding and organizational support by senior leaders, lack of professional preparation and leadership development by individual middle-level leaders, and underdeveloped professional knowledge and capability contribute to a missed opportunity to make a difference in schools. Middle-level leadership can be enhanced by focusing on opportunities for quality professional learning and leadership development in building professional knowledge and practice in teaching, curriculum, assessment and student learning, and also in helping with developing strategies for building school capacity.

Reflection

The study of successful school leadership is a relatively recent phenomenon in Australasia (Gurr, 2009) and has been focused in the main on principals (e.g. Duignan & Gurr, 2007a; Gurr et al., 2006; Notman, 2011a), albeit with emerging research interest in senior leaders (e.g. Cranston, 2009), middle-level leaders (e.g. Dinham, 2007; Gurr & Drysdale, 2013) and teacher leaders (e.g. Crowther et al., 2009). Beginning in the 1960s the study of school leadership tended to reflect the historical context of the times. In the 1960s and 1970s the focus was on supervision, and in the 1980s and 1990s it was school effectiveness and instructional leadership. From the 2000s the focus has been on success, student outcomes and the complexity of school leadership in a rapidly changing environment. This historical perspective provides a valuable insight into successful and effective leadership. In the 1960s and 1970s a good school had good staff. Good leadership was about creating a good staff (e.g. Bassett et al., 1967). In the 1980s and 1990s leadership of successful or effective schools focused on improving teaching and learning and, indirectly, student outcomes (e.g. Beare et al., 1989). Since then the features of successful school leaders have broadened, as illustrated in the ISSPP studies in Australia and New Zealand. The distinction between successful and effective is not something that has been given much consideration, although in the ISSPP research, indicators of success were used as a way of broadening the more narrow effectiveness focus of previous research, and when participants in this research were questioned about school success, their definition was broader again. The stories of successful school principals by Duignan and Gurr (2007a) attest to a broader definition of successful leadership and successful schools than previously reported. There is also evidence that successful middle-level leadership can foster a range of positive outcomes that include, but go beyond, improving teaching and learning (e.g. Dinham, 2007; Gurr & Drysdale, 2013).

The many cases touched upon in this chapter illustrate the importance of the work of principals. The participants in the studies of successful principals in the ISSPP clearly described their principals as being important for their schools. From this multiple perspective research, and the principal perspective research in Leading Australia's Schools (Duignan & Gurr, 2007a), the contribution to school success by principals is through: holding beliefs and attitudes that encourage success for all, such as having high expectations of themselves and others, valuing all, having a 'can do' attitude and so forth; establishing, communicating and developing a shared vision; developing the capacities of the teachers, with this perhaps best thought of as the establishment of a performance and development culture; inclusive leadership that engages others in the work of school leadership; culturally responsive leadership that fosters community engagement; an ability to understand, respond to, and influence context; knowledge of, and experience in, implementing a range of interventions/practices that improve teaching and learning; and acquiring, developing and using a range of personal and interpersonal qualities that promote success for all. The research on middle-level leadership supports these characteristics, but has a greater focus on improving teacher practice directly and advocating for particular sections within a school, and less focus on whole-school change. The characteristics of principal and middle-level leadership support summaries of leadership practice such as the setting of direction, developing people, developing the school and improving the teaching and learning dimensions of Leithwood (e.g. Leithwood, et al., 2006), but they go beyond these summaries to provide a more complex and nuanced understanding of leadership. It is difficult to describe successful leadership without taking this more complex approach, and so the importance of continuing to do in-depth case study research remains.

One thing that is clear is that principal leadership, and leadership in general, contributes to success and effectiveness however these are defined. What leaders do is important for building success. They engage in key practices or interventions that help to build success whether or not this has a direct or indirect impact on student learning. However, the studies also show that what helps to underpin success are the values, qualities, personal traits, characteristics and skills of the leaders themselves. It is the interplay of what the leader brings to the situation and the context itself. Contributions to success will be played out through this interaction.

11

North American Perspectives

Stephen L. Jacobson

Introduction and overview

The growing consensus in educational research from North America is that when it comes to a school's success, especially in terms of improving student achievement, leadership matters (Leithwood & Louis, 2012). Surprisingly, this was not always the case and as recently as fifty years ago there was a compelling argument to be made that when it came to predicting a child's potential academic success, leadership and/or any other 'in-school' variable, such as per student spending, paled in importance to the effects of 'out-of-school' factors such as family socioeconomic status (SES). Although exogenous variables such as SES still contribute considerably to student achievement, we now know far more about how and in what ways school leaders – particularly principals –influence (both directly and indirectly) the effectiveness and success of their schools (Hallinger & Heck, 1996; Jacobson, 2011; Leithwood & Louis, 2012).

The purpose of this chapter is to review the research literature on successful and effective school leadership, particularly in regards to how leadership is seen to enable improved classroom instruction and student performance in North America. Although the terms 'successful leadership' and 'effective leadership' are often used interchangeably, there are nuanced differences that need to be considered. Specifically, the term successful leadership should be viewed as the more inclusive of the two, with effective leadership as a subset focused almost exclusively on performance results. In the research to follow, an effective school or leader is one that raised student performance beyond what might have been expected based upon the student body's socioeconomic demographics, whereas a leader or a school can be considered successful if it begins to hit targets set in an improvement plan. 'Effective' is a more technical term that derives from the effective schools literature, based upon outliers performing beyond predictions. 'Successful' is far more subjective, often based upon criteria established by different constituent groups. For example, a school can be seen as successful by teachers and parents if students are safe, well cared for and getting a reasonably good education. Yet a researcher might look at the same school and argue it is not effective because it is underperforming based upon its potential. In other words, a school could appear successful without having effectively minimized the impact of its students' backgrounds. Therefore the term 'successful' should be viewed in terms of school processes (often in the short term), while 'effective' is more about student outcomes (especially when considered in the long term). This distinction should become apparent in the research to follow.

The review begins with the Equality of Educational Opportunity report commissioned by the US Department of Education (Coleman et al., 1966). More commonly known as the Coleman Report, this study used achievement data from more than 650,000 students across the USA and produced findings that challenged much of what the educational community previously thought it knew about how schools affected the equality of educational opportunities for children in America. The Coleman findings led to the effective schools research, which focused on commonalities in schools that performed well above predicted levels based upon the composition of their student bodies, and subsequently the process research of the school improvement literature that focused on what was actually happening in schools that were achieving success in trying to improve. These two bodies of research set the table for more recent studies that focus on organizational, instructional and culturally responsive leadership (Ylimaki & Jacobson, 2013), and more directly on how leadership is linked to student learning (Leithwood & Louis, 2012).

The chapter concludes with a review of two cases drawn from the International Successful School Principalship Project (ISSPP) that examined successful and sustained leadership in high-need North American schools (Jacobson et al., 2009; Jacobson & Schoenfeld, 2014). Based on the core leadership practices defined by Leithwood and Riehl (2005), these cases examine the characteristics, behaviours and actions of two successful school leaders. Particular attention is paid to how these principals sustained improvement under very challenging circumstances by setting a direction for their school; developed their teachers, staff, and parents; refined and aligned their schools to build collaborative structures and removed potential obstacles to success; and improved the instructional programme. Also discussed are stability of school leadership and its impact on trust building and capacity, interconnected factors that educational systems in North America need to consider in light of rapidly changing policy mandates and shifting demographic environments.

Research on school effectiveness and improvement

The 1966 Coleman Report provides a significant starting point for this review of successful and effective school leadership in North America, in part because it was the largest educational study conducted to that point in time, but more importantly because its findings landed like a bombshell, exploding long-held beliefs about what schools contribute to the equality of student outcomes. Specifically, the study found that 'out-of-school' factors accounted for more variation in student performance than 'in-school' resources, which countered common wisdom. Put bluntly, the Coleman Report suggested that having the right parents was a more reliable predictor of student achievement than school resources, including the principal. But the data also revealed that students in some high poverty inner city elementary schools were performing at levels in reading and mathematics well above what predictions based upon socioeconomic demographics might otherwise suggest. These statistical outliers indicated that, at least in some situations, effective principals and teachers could make enough of a difference in academic performance to overcome the negative consequences of poverty.

Researchers began to examine 'effective' schools that performed beyond expectations, focusing less on the skill sets that school leaders had previously acquired through preparation and practice, and more on how principals tied leadership skills to measurable student outcomes. Brookover and Lezotte (1979), for example, found that principals in effective schools focused primarily on instruction, giving rise to the idea that 'instructional leadership' was a central if not *the* central practice linking principals' work to student achievement (Hallinger, 2003). Other seminal studies during this period include Edmonds (1982) in the US and Rutter et al. (1979) in the UK. This refocusing of the research emphasis to measurable outcomes of effective leadership practice, as opposed to pre-existing skills, led to a subsequent line of research that sought to understand the processes used successfully by principals to change and improve schools.

These so-called 'school improvement' studies emphasized successful organizational change, school self-evaluation and the extent to which individual schools and teachers owned the change process. While early school improvement studies did not try to connect process initiatives to student outcomes, a 'second phase' of the research drew insights from the school effectiveness work (e.g. Hopkins et al., 1994). This merged perspective included a simultaneous focus on successful processes and effective outcomes, seeking school improvements powerful enough to affect student outcomes, using 'mixed' methods, in which quantitative 'outcome' data plus qualitative 'process' data were combined to measure educational quality and variation in that quality. There was also a growing interest in 'capacity building' through professional training, coaching and staff development, as well as an appreciation of cultural change as an underpinning of sustained school improvement (Jacobson, 2011; Jacobson & Bezzina, 2008).

Leadership as a collective construct

One of the key findings from this merged perspective was that with the right mix of autonomy and support, schools have a better prospect for improvement, especially when school leaders leveraged external mandates that provided additional support. Harris (2002) found that leaders in successful schools believed in the ability of their students and teachers, and focused on classroom improvement through the use of explicit models of instruction, evaluative evidence, professional development and the provision of external support. The school had to become the epicentre of change, with the teacher as the catalyst for classroom development. For these successful school leaders, teaching and learning became central through a commitment to formal and informal job-embedded professional development and diffused leadership (Harris, 2002; Jacobson & Battaglia, 2001).

Note that these findings support a reconceptualization of leadership from being a narrow, individual construct based upon the skills a principal possesses to a broader, collective construct that is critically dependent upon the relationships leaders cultivate (Fullan, 2001). As such, leadership is associated with empowerment, transformation and community, and no longer refers just to a school's titular head (Gronn & Hamilton, 2004; Silins & Mulford, 2002; Spillane et al., 2007). Teacher leadership begins to play a prominent role in understanding school success as distributed leadership expands the principal's role from manager to facilitator (Crowther et al., 2002). But this broader conception of leadership seems not to diminish the influence of the principal on decision making as perceived by the school community (Leithwood & Louis, 2012). And, though the quality of its teacher workforce remains a school's strongest determinant of student motivation and achievement, it is the ability of principals to motivate and enhance the quality of their teachers' work setting that has the second greatest impact on student performance (Leithwood & Louis, 2012; Marzano et al., 2005). Moreover, quality leadership seems to be especially important in North American schools serving low SES youngsters, with leadership effects accounting for approximately 5 per cent of the overall variation in test scores in aggregate – or almost 2 per cent of the in-school variables over which educational policy makers have control (Hallinger & Heck, 1996). In light of the findings from the Coleman Report cited at the beginning of this chapter, it is especially meaningful to recognize that effective school leadership seems to have the greatest impact on student achievement precisely where it is needed the most (Potter et al., 2002).

Core leadership practices for school success and the ISSPP

Through a comprehensive synthesis of research about what was then known about leadership practices linked to successful school improvement, Leithwood and Riehl (2005) developed a set of core practices they described as necessary, but insufficient, for school success, regardless of context. Specifically, these core practices are: (1) setting directions; (2) developing people; (3) refining and aligning the school organization; and (4) improving the instructional programme. For more specific details about these core practices see Leithwood (2012).

Although not rigidly sequential, these core practices suggest a logical progression in how successful leaders translate values and ideas into actions. Specifically, if they are to increase the likelihood of student success, leaders need to create a sense of coordinated purpose within a school, i.e. develop a shared direction focused on improving the instructional programme, supported by the provision of resources and appropriate motivation to enable staff to acquire and utilize the skills necessary for the collective undertaking. Furthermore, leaders must carefully examine existing organizational structures to remove obstacles and enhance opportunities for the creation of a more collaborative school culture. Ideally this is a culture that is not threatened by accountability, but rather institutionalizes high performance as a matter of professional responsibility. Note that this last set of skills fits under the more general heading of organizational leadership (Day et al., 2011) that serves as a critical complement to instructional leadership (Ylimaki et al., 2011) if principals hope to create school structures that build upon short-term gains for long term success. Moreover, schools in America and other developed nations around the world are experiencing increased diversity in the racial, ethnic, linguistic and cultural composition of their student bodies fuelled by waves of immigration, both legal and illegal, as a result of displacement by war, social and economic upheaval and natural disasters occurring in less developed nations. As a result, culturally responsive leadership becomes a necessary addition to organizational and instructional leadership in such school settings, if they are to serve their mission of both educating and socializing a new generation of citizens (Johnson et al., 2011). These three facets of leadership – organizational, instructional and culturally responsive – are all enabled by the core practices and the consistency of the research findings that produced these practices helped to establish them as an analytic framework for the ISSPP.

In its first phase in 2001, ISSPP schools were selected using a combination of indicators of site-specific success during a principal's tenure. Among several overarching questions, ISSPP sought answers to the question: What variables link principals' leadership to student achievement? In essence, the project connected the student outcome concerns of school effectiveness research with the concerns of school improvement researchers about successful processes. (Details about ISSPP can be found at: www.uv.uio.no/ils/english/research/projects/isspp/ and specific details about the research protocols used in the first phase of the project can be found in Jacobson & Day, 2007.)

The sole North American research team in ISSPP at that time, from the University at Buffalo (UB), added an additional requirement for a school to be selected for study, i.e. it had to be a 'high need' school, a categorization based upon the percentage of students eligible for free or reduced lunches. Consistent with the findings reported earlier, the UB team felt that if leadership really mattered these were the schools where it would matter the most. Seven such 'challenging' contexts were identified and three were studied in depth during the first phase of the project (see Jacobson et al., 2007). It is important to note that while the team from UB focused exclusively on high need schools, teams in Australia, England (Ylimaki et al., 2007), China and Norway (Johnson et al., 2008) also reported on similar schools within their cases.

In aggregate, this first round of ISSPP produced over sixty case studies from eight different countries, the scope and breadth of which has helped to overcome limitations typical of small sample case study research (Leithwood, 2005). One finding from the initial case studies that distinguished challenges faced by principals in high need schools in the USA from principals elsewhere was the relatively short time frame they had to achieve student performance goals. Since the early 2000s, schools in the USA have operated under accountability pressures created by required and publicly reported annual testing as per the No Child Left Behind (NCLB) and Race to the Top (RttT) mandates (Leithwood et al., 2011). As a consequence of this standards-based approach, schools that persistently fail to make 'Adequate Yearly Progress' (AYP) face severe sanctions including administrator loss of employment. As in sports, when a team does poorly, it is easier to fire the manager since you cannot fire the whole team. This is precisely the pressure confronting principals in these high need schools; either turn the school's performance around quickly or start looking for a new school or vocation. Meeting AYP expectations is relentless and creates short-term tunnel vision for some principals, a major reason that the position is no longer as attractive as it once was and why there is a shortage of high quality school leaders seeking positions in challenging schools (Jacobson, 2005). In fact, Beteille et al. (2011) report principal turnover rates of almost 30 per cent per year in US schools with concentrations of poor, minority and low achieving students. Sustaining school success for the long term is quite different from just addressing short term, externally imposed goals. It requires the school's ability to self-renew by building capacity in the teacher workforce and school community, which in turn depends upon establishing trusting relationships, all of which takes time and stable leadership. Obviously, principal turnover can disrupt this process, which begs the question, How do leaders successfully sustain improvement, especially in high need schools in the USA?

Sustained success: trust and leadership stability

The next phase of the ISSPP was to examine whether and how principals sustained success over time in the successful high need schools we had already studied. To that end, the UB team returned to two of the seven schools studied in the initial round of data collection five years later. Of those original seven schools, only two had the same principal – four of the other principals had retired and one had been promoted to a central office position. We chose to focus only on those schools with leadership continuity in order to get a better sense of the successful practices these principals had employed over time. We found that remaining faithful to the commitment made by the principal to keep the collective focus on improving student performance was essential, even if it necessitated major refinements to the organization (converting from a traditional public school to a district charter school in one case and from a grades 6 through 8 middle school to grade 5–6 in the other). In order to maintain the continued development and capacity of the staff, principals had to find ways to promote organizational learning through personal and collective self-renewal and professional growth (Jacobson et al., 2009; Schoenfeld, 2013). In this regard, organizational learning was oriented towards building social capital rather than just accomplishing externally mandated tasks such as AYP. The principals consciously worked at creating supportive workplace conditions built on shared commitment and the building of relationships grounded in mutual support, care, trust and consensus, a continuation of the work begun years before (Giles et al., 2005). Structures for teacher self-renewal were put in place, with on-site collegial professional development through the leadership of the teachers themselves, particularly in the school that became a conversion charter (Minor-Ragan & Jacobson, 2014). The sustained academic success of that school has made it increasingly attractive to other parents across the district; parents who can now seek placements for their children since the school is a charter. In fact, improvements in the quality of this school have led to an increase in the real property value of homes in the surrounding neighbourhood (Jacobson & Szczesek, 2013). As a result, members of the community and student parents are unlikely to ever allow the school to return to the sorry state it was in before the principal arrived because it would not only diminish the academic opportunities of their children, but also reduce the market value of their homes, a finding that others have suggested school reformers and urban planners consider for the stabilization and revitalization of neighbourhoods in older core cities in the USA (Silverman, 2014).

The ability to sustain success was also evidenced through instructional leadership by curriculum innovations introduced by the principals to reinforce achievement gains already made. These innovations include summer programmes and 'Advanced Placement' (AP) courses in maths, language and science, but more importantly, teacher-led, job embedded professional development. In both schools, accountability was initially an externally driven force leveraged by the principals to galvanize a common objective, but over time it had become internalized by faculty, parents and students, so that they now hold themselves personally and collectively responsible for student performance. It was clear that both principals we studied were committed to making a difference for their school communities as revealed through their resilience, commitment, persistence and sense of optimism, even in the face of daunting challenges. Of these challenges, the most critical in one case was the need to change the governance structure in response to human resource cuts that threatened school performance (Jacobson et al., 2009), while in the other case it was a required response to a district mandated change in school configuration (Schoenfeld, 2013). Through our interviews with teachers, support staff, parents and other community members, it was clear that because of their positional longevity, over ten years in one case and seventeen in the other, these principals had been able to build the trust of their faculty and their parent community in support of the tough decisions and changes they had to make. Trust is predicated on several common facets: benevolence, competence, honesty, openness, reliability and vulnerability (Tschannen-Moran, 2004). Faculty trust was therefore dependent upon teachers' willingness to be vulnerable based on their belief that their principal was benevolent, competent, honest, open and reliable (Hoy & Miskel, 2013). Unfortunately, trust in high need schools is often a scarce commodity, with teachers feeling that the odds are stacked against them because principals are more concerned with meeting mandates than caring for people, and parents feeling that the school and its administration really does not care about their children as individuals. However, these two principals had chosen to stay in their positions in order to create and sustain the conditions that led to improved student academic performance for an extended period of time. They had slowly built the trust of their faculty and parent communities, and when difficult hurdles needed to be scaled, teachers and parents were willing to follow. From this, one might infer that a school's capacity for sustaining successful improvement may be affected by the relative stability of its leadership, with frequent turnovers leading to instability and potentially a lack of trust, while extremely long tenures can possibly lead to complacency and inertia. Mascall and Leithwood (2012: 146) wonder whether 'change theory suggests a "best by" date for principals beyond which they should move on – or be moved on'. Perhaps research will eventually produce an algorithm that connects school context to a leader's time in position to the development of faculty and community trust; thus providing a better understanding of these critical relationships. Generalizing from the two cases presented in this prensented here is clearly unwise, but the potential policy implications for successful and effective school leadership require further study, especially in those North American educational systems that have built principal turnover sanctions into accountability. This seems to be a research agenda ripe for further exploration.

Concluding thoughts

Over the past fifty years there has been a significant evolution in our understanding of effective and successful school leadership in North America, especially in terms of its effects on student learning. Prior to the Coleman Report, school leadership was *assumed* to influence student achievement, but only in so far as a principal managed his or her school well. Findings from Coleman suggested that this was not the case, and that whatever success a school had in terms of student academic performance, it had far more to do with the social and economic capital of its children's parents than the managerial skills of its principal. Yet there were some schools whose results challenged these findings, revealing correlates between high performing schools and effective principals.

While the emphasis of this earlier research was still on school leadership as a singular construct and the skills the principal had acquired, particularly those focused on instruction, it begged the question of how these skills were translated into actions that could actually improve student learning. Leadership at the school level slowly began to be viewed as a collective enterprise that distributed influence to others within the organization, especially teams of teachers. As research was aggregated, patterns in the findings revealed core practices necessary for successful improvement, not only in the short term, but fundamental to a school's ability to self-renew and sustain these gains over time. Building trust and collective capacity seem central to successful improvement in all school settings, while developing culturally responsive practices is increasingly important in a growing number of others. However, the mediating effect of leadership stability on all of these contributors to effectiveness and success is still in need of further study.

The good news appears to be that we now have a pretty good idea of what successful and effective leadership looks like in North America, especially at the building level and in our high need schools. More challenging, however, is developing a better understanding of successful and effective leadership at the district and system levels and how policies promulgated at those levels interact with practices on the ground.

12

Caribbean Perspectives

Disraeli M. Hutton

Introduction

The drive to improve the performance of schools rests, to a large extent, with the strength of the leadership that is provided by principals and other levels of leaders. As Stewart (2013: 48) pointed out, 'there is growing evidence that weak school leadership leads to poor school performance . . . and strong school leadership to significant school improvement'. In addition to Stewart's position, for countries such as those in the English speaking Caribbean, principals are also challenged when attempting to improve school performance because the education system remains centralized, and they are given limited powers to make meaningful change. In other words, the strength of the principal cannot be effectively demonstrated if the conditions for effective performance are not in place. In Jamaica, for example, there has been a process of decentralizing the education system which has resulted in the strengthening of school boards and the establishment of regional entities.[1] However, in countries such as Antigua and Barbuda, school boards are not established and activities such as the recruitment of teachers are still in the domain of the central Ministry for Education. In fact, for schools to achieve greater levels of success and effectiveness, the autonomy of the principals has to be significantly enhanced. As Hutton (2009) pointed out, the democratization and decentralization of the leadership system is a precondition for improving the overall performance of schools and students. Therefore, for schools to be effective, it is necessary for relevant and appropriate systems and structures to be successfully implemented. Borden (2002: 3) addressed the issue of school leadership in Latin America and the Caribbean and placed the issue of making structural changes squarely on the front burner, when he pointed out that:

Numerous reforms call for the decentralization of decision making to the school and the community, creating the potential for the principal to take action to lead efforts to improve teaching and learning at his school. But the possibility also exists that reforms may in fact do very little to change the principal's traditional roles long supported and maintained by centralized education systems.

Borden was highlighting a major limitation of education in Latin America which is also reflected in the Caribbean countries. Based on his stated position, the goal to achieve effective and successful leadership will be even more challenging, given the fact that leadership is constrained not only by the role being emphasized for principals but also by contextual factors such as culture, physical state of schools, systems and structures, and the economic challenges facing the region's states.

Approach to the chapter

The chapter first examines the characteristics of the successful and effective school leadership as defined by Luthans (2011), Leithwood (2005), Davis et al. (2005), the Wallace Foundation (2013), New Leaders for New Schools (2009) and New Leaders (2011). The vital area of students' performance, which is an important correlate of successful and effective leadership, preceded the presentation on the support systems being implemented to improve student performance. The chapter then explores both the practices and strategies being implemented to develop successful and effective leaders in a number of Caribbean countries. Finally, the chapter concludes by emphasizing the need to learn from the experiences of each other, deepen systems change to enhance leadership effectiveness, and increase collaboration of schools within and among the countries in order to address some of the pressing issues regarding the development of successful and effective leadership in schools.

Research questions

The following questions seek to focus the reader on the critical issues related to successful and effective leadership practice, the actual practices being employed and the strategies applied to improve performance.

1   What are the characteristics of successful and effective leadership and what is the relationship between both?

2 What is the state of students' academic performance and how are their support systems and learning practices being strengthened in the school system?

3 What are some of the practices and strategic interventions being implemented by regional governments to realize successful and effective school leadership?

This chapter on successful and effective leadership represents an attempt to examine the development of the public education system from a regional perspective. Specifically, focus is placed on the performances, practices and strategies being implemented to impact change. No attempt was made to examine all fifteen countries of the Caribbean Common Market (CARICOM), but those selected represented the mix of countries which best portray the focus of the chapter.

What are the characteristics of successful and effective leadership and what is the relationship between both?

Defining successful leadership

The difference between successful and effective leadership seems not to be emphasized generally by those who write on school performance and effectiveness. In fact, both terms have been used interchangeably by a number of authors to identify the factors related to the performance of leadership (Luthans, 2011). However, some authors seem to deliberately identify elements related to successful leadership while others focus on effective leadership.

An examination of the definition of successful leadership by three of the recognizable authors should assist in elucidating the meaning of the term. Leithwood (2005), for example, identified nine specific practices which are the drivers for accomplishing three general indicators of success: setting directions, developing people and redesigning the organization. For setting directions, the specific practices include developing a shared vision in order to create a sense of purpose, building consensus regarding the short-term goals to be pursued and demonstrating high expectations for the work done by staff members; developing people involves supporting the initiatives and ideas of colleagues, providing intellectual support and modelling those practices and values which are important for success; redesigning the organization includes developing the school culture using a collaborative approach, facilitating decision making that is participatory and building relationships with parents and the wider community. Davis et al. (2005) highlighted two factors when they advanced the view that 'successful school leaders influence student achievement through two important pathways – the support and development of effective teachers and the implementation of effective organizational processes' (p. 5). Luthans (2011) identified successful leaders as those who were able to achieve rapid progress or promotion in the organization. Identifying what they do to be named successful leaders, Luthans suggested that these leaders 'spend relatively more time and effort socializing, politicking, and interacting with outsiders' (p. 461). In all three definitions provided for the successful leader, the factors presented could be characterized as the base on which students' performance is anchored. The definition provided by Luthans revealed the personal quality of networking, which underpinned effective performance of schools and students.

Defining the effective leadership

Regarding effective leadership, the Wallace Foundation (2013), for example, identified five areas of responsibilities in which principals must be able to lead a team to achieve effective performance. The areas include the following: (a) shaping a vision of academic success for all students; (b) creating a climate hospitable to education; (c) cultivating leadership in others; (d) improving instruction; and (e) managing people, data and processes to foster school improvement. New Leaders for New Schools (2009) made reference to the Urban Excellence Framework[2] which identified the factors related to effective school leadership as 'ensuring rigorous, goal- and data-driven learning and teaching; building and managing a high-quality staff aligned to the school's vision of success for every student; developing an achievement- and belief-based school-wide culture; instituting operations and systems to support learning; and modelling the personal leadership' (p. 17). The emphasis on students' outcomes and the need to provide the necessary support for student learning has been underlined both by the use of data and also by providing the conditions for learning. The definition provided by New Leaders for New Schools for effective leadership also, in many ways, emphasized areas similar to those outlined by the Wallace Foundation. But it is instructive to note that culture was specifically targeted by New Leaders for New Schools.

Overall, what the definitions revealed is that there is a relationship between successful and effective leadership. Successful leadership is about implementing the basic structures and systems which provide the platform on which effective leadership performance is achieved. In other words, the performance factors related to effective leadership represent the proceeding steps arising from the platform established by the successful principal. Thus, successful leadership precedes effective leadership, which is more about the direct actions that are taken to impact students' achievement and overall performance. School leadership in the Caribbean public education system is not demonstrated in all those elements associated with successful and effective leadership. New Leaders (2011), however, identified three important factors which give rise to effective leadership – leadership actions, teacher effectiveness and student outcomes. This chapter examines the (a) state of students' performance and the steps being taken to address the constraints, and (b) practices of leadership and strategies being implemented to improve principals' success and effectiveness. The teacher effectiveness factor is addressed to some extent in both.

What is the state of students' academic performance and how are their support systems and learning practices being strengthened in the school system?

State of student academic performance

This chapter examines how a number of countries in the Caribbean have been performing, based on students' outcomes measured by academic performance. First of all, it should be stated that there is no doubt that strides have been made in improving student academic performance and their preparation for the world of work over the past twenty years, but the fact is that many of the countries remain behind, even if a few seem to be moving in the right direction. For example, literacy remains a basic challenge for most countries, but there are other problems including inequalities in countries such as Guyana, declining academic performance in the Organization of Eastern Caribbean States (OECS) countries and Trinidad and Tobago, and a failure to implement structures and systems to support effective leadership.

In Jamaica, the Task Force on Educational Reform (2005) showed that students at all levels of the public education system were performing outside the targeted levels of outcomes. The magnitude of the problem was highlighted by the Task Force report which showed that 'less than one-third of the children entering grade 1 were ready for the primary level, some 30% of primary school leavers were illiterate, and only about 20% of secondary graduates had the requisite qualification for meaningful employment' (p. 21). In 2014, illiteracy continued to be a problem in the school system and even though progress has been made following interventions for almost a decade since the publication of the Task Force report, pass rates in Caribbean Secondary School Certificate (CSEC) mathematics and English are 66 per cent and 56 per cent respectively.

For St Lucia, one of the OECS countries, Caesar (2013: 110), commenting on the poor performance of schools, said 'what is more alarming is that more than 50% of primary school cohorts perform below the national mean of the national common entrance examination (the qualifier examination to gain access to secondary school) and are unable to satisfy the entry requirements for secondary education'. The same performance is also evident in national examinations that are taken at grades 2 and 4.

The OECS (2012), in its education sector strategy plan for 2012–21, identified deficiencies which included students completing secondary school without achieving minimum standards for the next level of the education process. In relation to formal education, besides the literacy problem, performance in mathematics, science and technology has been at a low ebb. In fact, 'performance in mathematics continues to decline with pass rates reaching 40% for all States in 2011. In that year, a mere 23 per cent graduated with the basic qualifications of five passes, including mathematics and English' (p. 23). The situation is essentially the same at the lower grades where 50 and 40 per cent underperformed in mathematics and English respectively.

The reason for the weak academic performance is not easily discernible. Like Barbados, Guyana has achieved literacy of 95 per cent of the population (Beepat, 2013) but the academic performance by Barbados is assessed as better than Guyana. At the same time, Jamaica has a literacy rate of 85 per cent, which has not changed over the past two decades. However, the country continues to make strides in students' academic performance. Guyana, like a number of other Caribbean countries, has an education system that is fraught with inequalities. For example, based on the selection process obtaining in Guyana, the schools which are rated the best performers usually secure the students who demonstrate the most outstanding performances in the entrance examination. Of course those with the weakest performance are usually assigned to the worst performing schools (Beepat, 2013). This feature is reflected in most other countries mainly because of the disparities resulting from available financial resources, the quality of facilities, leadership and school history, among other factors.

But even in the case of Trinidad and Tobago where these factors leading to disparities have been addressed, there is a reported decline in the performance of students at the (CSEC) level in both English and mathematics because the school system is no longer responsive to the needs of the current learners. As the Ministry of Education Report (Trinidad and Tobago) (2008) indicated, between 2003 and 2007, 30 per cent of the students scored between 10.3 and 13.5 per cent in the Secondary Entrance Examination (SEA), even after millions of dollars had been spent to improve their performance. Additionally, CSEC results between 2002 and 2007 showed a decline from a 64 per cent pass rate in 2002 to a pass rate of 52 per cent in 2007. For mathematics the pass rate varied from 41.2 to 51.1 per cent over the same period.

For the Cayman Islands, the data showed that the performance in external examinations by students achieving Curriculum Level 4 or above in English moved from 33 per cent in 2011 to 50 per cent in 2012. In the case of mathematics, student achievement moved from 25 per cent in 2011 to 42 per cent in 2012. For external examinations for secondary school students which include the CSEC, students achieving five or more subjects at level 2 moved from 38 per cent in 2009 to 49 per cent in 2012. This would compare favourably with 27 per cent in 2007. It should be noted that in all three examples, achievement does not exceed 50 per cent, suggesting that much more must be done in order to claim effectiveness against reasonable standards (Ministry of Education, Cayman Government Island, 2013).

In Antigua and Barbuda, the situation is even worse. An examination of the 2010 results shows that students who attended private primary schools continue to outperform the government-owned and run schools, and girls continue to outperform boys in the common entrance examination in all four subjects tested. At the secondary level, Antigua performed 5 per cent below the average performance of students in the other Caribbean countries who sit the CSEC examination in mathematics (Ministry of Education, Antigua and Barbuda, 2012).

As established by the OECS (2012), the impact of the problems related to academic performance included: (a) insufficient preparation for the workforce and labour market; (b) reinforcing of social exclusion and inequalities; and (c) declining participation of male students at the upper secondary and tertiary level. These findings would be similarly demonstrated in many of the other states in the region. If leadership is second only to the quality of teaching and teachers, it can be concluded without hesitation that leadership must be one of the factors to be strengthened in order to improve students' academic performance in schools. In fact, the Jamaican experience shows that academic performance is trending up as systems are strengthened and focus on effective leadership receives greater attention. Of course, the quality of teaching and teachers must be treated as one of the factors affecting the academic performance of students and has to be examined.

Strengthening students' support systems and learning practices

This area has received significant attention in countries such as the Cayman Islands, Jamaica and Guyana. The report of the Cayman Islands Government

(2005) identified areas where student support is making a difference. These include promoting a nurturing attitude by schools towards students, providing dedicated transportation to and from school, and providing counsellors to deal with personal needs among others. The study of high performing principals in Jamaica shows that one of the factors which received attention was student support. What was also noticeable was the fact that student support extended beyond the provision of the basics such as breakfast, bus fare and transportation. Hutton (2013: 83) indicated that school leaders sought to help students to develop self-confidence by guiding them 'to believe that they can make a difference in their own lives, but they will have to demonstrate personal commitment and conviction in order to achieve success'. Trinidad and Tobago is implementing new strategies which are being employed to improve the process of teaching and learning with more emphasis being placed on student-centred teaching and learning. In other words, learner participation in the actual learning process is being emphasized. Overall, Trinidad and Tobago is taking steps to reform the curriculum at both the secondary and primary levels in order to better meet the needs of the school system and specifically the learners at all levels of the school system (Ministry of Education Report, Trinidad and Tobago, 2008).

Fox (2007) pointed to the fact that Guyana has introduced the concept of the 'new school', which is aimed at moving from the traditional approach of teacher-controlled lessons delivery to one which is more child-centred, where the teacher assumes the role of facilitator of the learning process and not just purveyor of knowledge. Among the strategies employed to facilitate the new thinking at that time were a 'student government', multi-grade teaching, learning corners, use of learning guides, child-friendly classrooms and a stronger relationship between school and community, with an emphasis on parental involvement. Further, the programme also actively promotes localization of the curriculum so that student education becomes relevant to the economic and social needs of the community and the individual learner.

Fox (2007), further elaborating on the changes being implemented in Guyana, said that a learning environment to facilitate inclusive learning at the school and classroom levels is to be instituted. This included celebrating cultural activities for the various ethnic groups so as to give everyone a chance to appreciate the culture of others, implementing projects to improve student achievement and ongoing teacher training, utilizing a more child-centred and interactive approach in the teaching and learning process, and increasing access to the use of school library facilities by both teachers and students. Teaching methodologies are now also focusing on differentiated child-centred instruction, and practical and authentic learning, among others. Further, academic programmes are being introduced which reflect current curriculum needs and the technological advances available to the education system (Fox, 2007).

Improving students' academic performance is tied to both teacher effectiveness and the need to have principals who are both successful and effective. The evidence presented shows that some progress is being made, but the remediation efforts must be intensified and expanded across the region. However, there are underlying problems external to the schools which must be addressed at the same time. The strategies and policies related to education, which are implemented by the central governments, must be focused on those factors critical to student performance. In fact, for developing countries such as these in the Caribbean, the role of central government is to assist in removing the obstacles which will impact the effectiveness of the school-related factors that are central to effective school performance.

What are some of the practices and strategic interventions being implemented by schools and regional governments to realize successful and effective school leadership?

Practices and strategies to improve principals' success and effectiveness

As established earlier, leadership performance should be both successful and effective. Jamaica is one of the countries which may have advanced the furthest in building the base for successful and effective leadership in the school system. The government has decentralized the system by establishing regional entities which will have legal authority to carry out some of the functions which were the responsibility of the central ministry. More importantly, the regional entities will have their dedicated budgets that will allow them to carry out functions such as the recruitment of teachers and principals, the employment and remuneration of support staff and the administration of planning functions. A number of these functions are currently being carried out by the schools and the regions, but they will now fall within a legal framework.

In relation to effective leadership practice, high performing principals are emerging from the traditional management role and responsibilities, partly because they have to be more inclusive in order to bring all constituents on board. However, a number of these leaders continue to rely on the traditional bureaucratic approach in order to get the desired results. For example, Hutton (2013: 89) made reference to one of the high performing principals who described her 'leadership style as mixed, which means democratic at times and autocratic at other times'. In regard to the more democratic and participative approach, Hutton (2011b: 59) pointed out that these principals 'practise situational and transformational leadership behaviour, which is visionary, engaging, passionate, visible and demanding'. This emphasizes the need to involve the academic staff and the school constituents in the decision making process, which includes consultation on academic matters (Hutton, 2011a). Williams and Fox (2013) also identified the more democratic side of leadership in the Jamaican school system. This they say is 'manifested in innovation and risk taking and the application of unconventional methods of achieving school goals, insistence on harmonized practices across classrooms and facilitating ongoing strategic interventions as agreed by parents, students and teachers' (p. 42). But leadership is also manifested in those management and administrative responsibilities which 'pay significant attention to the teacher accountability, the development and implementation of their "School Improvement Plans" (SIPs), observe classroom activities in their schools and provide support to staff for the achievement of goals and targets' (William & Fox, 2013: 42).

The government of Jamaica, along with the Ministry of Education, has embarked on an initiative to address the issue of leadership in the education system. First, the National Education Inspectorate (NEI) was established in 2009 to evaluate the performance of schools and make recommendations for improvement at all levels of the education system. Eight criteria were identified against which the performance of schools would be evaluated. The criterion addressing leadership seeks to determine how effectively schools are led and managed by the boards and the principals, the senior management team and middle leadership. Alongside the NEI, the government established the Jamaican Teaching Council (JTC), which has the basic responsibility to recognize, regulate and promote the teaching profession and maintain professional standards for educators, as well as to raise the character and status of the teaching profession. Specifically, the Jamaica Teaching Council (2009: 9) has established 'leadership standards for principals [which] are designed to provide the knowledge and skills necessary for proficiency in leadership'. The Jamaican government has also established the National College for Educational Leadership (NCEL) which has the primary responsibility of providing training for principals who are currently employed in the education system. In addition, all new principals are required to complete the certificate programme before they can be employed as principals in the school system.

The OECS (2012: 31), commenting on the challenges facing the education system, pointed out that 'the aspiration for a more professional approach to school management and leadership therefore remains a priority, with institutional leaders in the OECS still requiring greater access to leadership training and continuous professional development'. Some of the options shared by the strategic plan to train principals included online and blended training, setting up a community of practice using both online and face-to-face modalities. It is expected that this approach will assist in preparing principals who will make a difference in students' performance.

For Trinidad and Tobago, the decline in performance of students, especially in the area of mathematics and English, has resulted in a comprehensive overhauling of what is done in schools. This has included the institution of professional development programmes for principals and other school administrators. Providing an explanation for the inability of school leaders to maintain and improve students' performance, Brown and Lavia (2013) citing Brown and Conrod, said that the bureaucratic system which has existed since colonialism continues even today and restricts school leaders in making decisions to improve the effectiveness of schools. Brown and Lavia concluded that even though concerted attempts were made to strengthen school leadership resulting from the 'comprehensive structural changes proposed by the authors of the Education Policy Paper 1993–2003 . . . and the Strategic Plan 2002–2006 . . . the inherent challenges in overcoming the tenacious effects of colonial history' (p. 57) remain a formidable task.

For Guyana, Beepat (2013) said that the limited importance placed on leadership is a reflection of the worth being placed on the competencies that leaders bring to the job. This again is consistent with the view expressed by Borden (2002) that management routinely takes clear precedence over leadership. Beepat bemoaned the fact that there is a lack of emphasis placed on leadership in education and school leadership in particular. He made reference to the 'current strategic plan which has highlighted priority issues and areas, but the present list fails to highlight the development of the leadership capacity of the sector' (p. 70). Beepat described the nature of management practice in Guyana's secondary school system as focusing on 'what the principal ought to be on functions, tasks, and behaviours and that if these functions are carried out competently, the work of others in the organization will be facilitated' (p. 71). There is clearly an elevation of the management function and seemingly a de-emphasizing of the leadership role in Guyana's school system, a challenge which must be addressed in order to improve student outcomes.

The Ministry of Education (Cayman Government Inland) (2013) recognized that for schools at all levels of the education system to perform more effectively, the leadership issue has to be addressed. Some methods to bring about improvement include introducing a professional development programme for senior leadership and those who are aspiring to become leaders, implementing strategies to improve middle and subject leadership in the school system, reviewing the inspection framework and implementing a new quality assurance system. It should be noted that this call is not new for the Cayman school system. The Cayman Islands Government (2005) in a conference report outlined the areas that the education system should address in order to improve educational performance and output. Among the recommendations was for 'school leaders to develop the professional judgement, confidence and competence to commit their schools to the pursuit of excellence' (p. 18).

What is evident so far from the territories in the Caribbean is that much work is needed to develop the capacity for both successful and effective leadership. The experience of Trinidad and Tobago should be instructive. The reversal in students' performance in that country at the secondary level in both mathematics and English suggests that capacity building is necessary in order to maintain student performance. This supports the notion that the development of successful leadership is necessary to sustain effective leadership. Generally, the thrust by Caribbean states to address all aspects of the teaching and learning process (including leadership, teacher effectiveness and students outcomes) seems to be the correct approach. And this is consistent with the position articulated by New Leaders (2011). But while steps are being taken to strengthen personal leadership, Beepat (2013) has envisioned that a more systemic approach to leadership, which does not depend on the individual school principals, is necessary at this time. What is being suggested is that the education system should rethink leadership which relies on the effective principal and move to a shared leadership which includes senior teachers, classroom teachers and the other critical constituents in the school. In other words, a distributed leadership approach is being proposed which is reflected in some of the changes being implemented in the Jamaican education system. This approach at first seems to be a step in the right direction, but can it be implemented?

Conclusion

For the practice of successful and effective school leadership to be fully realized in the Caribbean, greater use has to be made of the lessons learned (both at the country as well as at the regional levels) from the actual practice and experience of getting schools to improve their performance. What is clear is that successful and effective leadership cannot be realized if schools continue to be run based on bureaucratic principles. The decentralization of the education system in order to empower principals and other school leaders is a central requirement at this time. For a number of the countries, the establishment of school boards became a major concern no more than fifteen years ago. In other words, vital systems which are related to successful leadership must be instituted. The implementation of programmes to support pre-service and in-service training for teachers and principals and strengthening of the support systems for students are areas of focus geared to achieve successful and effective school leadership in the Caribbean.

13

European Perspectives

Stefan Brauckmann and Petros Pashiardis

The policy making and shaping of high quality leadership in school systems across Europe – expectation setting

In Europe, education systems are deeply rooted in national traditions and are characterized by specific national features (Hörner & Döbert, 2007: 1). The latest economic crisis in Europe has once more demonstrated the need for policy makers, business leaders and scholars to learn more about the characteristics of national education systems in order to calculate better chances and limitations within standardized reference frameworks of quality in education as well as in order to identify measures of quality assurance and development across different education systems. This is true not only for the areas of higher education and continuing education, but also for the school sector. For Hörner and Döbert (2007: 1), for example, the growing interest of almost all European states in European educational policy making can be explained by several factors, such as:

- the enlargement of the European Union (EU);

- the increasing relevance of international school and student assessment studies;

- the growing internationalization of education and educational studies within the overall process of globalization.

More and more countries in the EU participate in large-scale surveys such as TIMSS and PISA, which is meant to provide an opportunity to evaluate the outcomes of the educational system in comparison to other countries, to detect strong and weak points, and to make appropriate monitoring decisions (Döbert et al., 2004; Woessmann et al., 2007). However, sometimes results are still not as well-known among the general public and those involved in school life as such. The focus on student assessment outcomes as measurable, hard variables leaves out, like it or not, essential information on institutional and pedagogical contexts within which schools and their leaders are operating. It rather gives the impression that factors of success in schooling can be linked to school organization as part of the legal framework and the structures in place in each education system. Although quality assurance (QA) might take different forms and different names and can be found in some countries at a rather early conceptualization and implementation phase, nevertheless promising trends of school quality measures are becoming more and more visible across Europe. In general, recent years have seen the launch of a whole range of developments, some of which may be seen as long-term and sustainable reform and innovation strategies which have revealed that the countries have taken a number of evaluation measures combining various quality assurance and quality development procedures (Daley and Kim, 2010; Danielson, 2011; Marshall, 2012; Papay, 2012). These measures, which are embedded in more output-driven overall strategies of European countries for quality evaluation and QA, include:

- System monitoring, through regular measurement of learning outcomes in crucial subject areas of the curriculum, and of the attitudes of pupils, parents, teachers and school leaders towards schooling (Sammons, 2009).

- Enlarging the scope for autonomous decisions and independent actions at the individual school level, this being placed mainly in the hands of the school principals.

- The use of standards as an improved way of defining given objectives and as a basis for measuring learning results across schools. The introduction of the State School Inspectorate as a professional system of external supervision performs the practical task of applying educational standards and quality control in schools. The school inspection process can be followed by measures corresponding to the seriousness of any identified shortcomings, including recommendations to change the school principal or even to shut down the school entirely (Faubert, 2009; Rosenthal, 2004; Ryan et al., 2007).

- The school programme concept, as a comprehensive internal strategy for school development. The programme outlines how work has been carried out on improving quality, and the results achieved.

The development of an output steering approach has rendered the school management business more complex, due to the increase in the number of external and internal agents interacting with the school leader, and has moreover caused a considerable diversification of the duties of school leaders, leading to increased demands on their knowledge, skills and professional versatility. The school leader has been considered as an important indicator of an education system's functioning. Among the current issues in the educational debate on school leadership is the attainment of the right balance between centralization and decentralization (Hanushek et al., 2012). Competition and profiling have made the atmosphere more antagonistic between schools and their leaders, and this has also resulted in increased evaluation practices. As a consequence, comparisons between schools have increased, creating a certain informal ranking among them. Schools are also increasingly seeking to attract private money to augment public funding due to the drastic reduction of the latter in recent years (Levacic, 2008). In summary, some critics of the new output-steering paradigm stress that accountability, as the flipside of decentralization, has brought a continuous and controlling system of evaluation that may render obsolete the advantages achieved through curriculum design at the local or even at the single school level (OECD, 2010a; Woessmann et al., 2009).

Many school leaders and teachers are, as a consequence, concerned about the extent to which school leaders are able to acquire and maintain the special competences required for leading, managing and monitoring their schools at the same time. Therefore the introduction of these quality assurance and development measures is (in most countries) accompanied by measures to strengthen the professionalism of school principals and teachers (Brauckmann & Pashiardis, 2011). This is done by developing and improving the quality of the basic and ongoing training of teaching staff and school leaders. Another aspect that should be mentioned concerns the fact that, first and foremost, school leaders at autonomous schools should be concerned with the improvement of instruction and school life to promote the personal development of children and youth (Hallinger, 2000, 2011; Seashore Louis et al., 2010). School leadership in autonomous schools must therefore be characterized by a leadership concept that increasingly focuses on self-governance, QA and quality development of school work. This responsibility for QA and quality development incorporates tasks concerning school and lesson development, as well as targeting the improvement of instruction, including guidance to students. School leadership in autonomous schools needs to make sure that learning and academic work become more targeted and subject to shared responsibility.

Having said all that, it is still the particular organizational context of the single school within the broader systemic frame which highlights the conceptual and implementation challenges of standardized measures of quality assurance and development ('one size fits all') and their political and practical implications across different education systems. Numerous schools in Europe are characterized by structural environments that are unsuitable even for basic educational purposes; heating systems, water supply and sanitary facilities are in poor condition and in some cases even pose a health hazard. Against these social realities how can one be sure that those measures of meeting the expected educational outcomes can serve as realistic reference points for the day-to-day management of school principals in their own schools? And how can those measures really ensure that these standards are actually attained by all students coming from different socioeconomic backgrounds (OECD 2010a, 2010b)? The (also contextually bound) agreement on what actually characterizes a school's success provides therefore an opportunity to better understand the activities performed by individual school leaders or leadership teams and constitutes a starting point to develop them further in a meaningful way.

Shaping school quality – the role of school leaders

Although school effectiveness seems to have been primarily characterized by student, class and school outcomes, usually stemming from external evaluation measures (*output*), it does not only comprise outcomes and is therefore not uni-dimensional. On the contrary, the term 'school quality' comprises a field covering different kinds of objectives, both enabling intermediate objectives as well as final objectives. Moreover, quality development and QA as well as the introduction of continuous system monitoring can be understood as ongoing processes. The school leadership impact can therefore take place at the input, process and output levels of a school and not just at the output level, as it oftentimes happens in school systems around the world.

Against this background the following framework combines both the multi-level structure (system-, organization, interaction and individual level) as well as the sequential process character (context, input, process and output-dimension) in education. This constitutes a comprehensive frame of reference for monitoring the status and progress of the education system in different domains, for heterogeneous units of analysis, from various perspectives, and for all the school leaders involved. It therefore allows for a precise and intelligible assignment of education indicators following the system modelling approach to describe the highly complex conditions, continuous dynamics and effects of education processes (Kühne, 2009) and can therefore describe in a

TABLE 13.1 Framework for the classification and systematization of education indicators (translated and adapted from Kühne, 2009)

Level of intervention	Dimensions of school quality			
	Context	Input	Process	Output
System	*Societal conditions* (e.g. demographics, institutional structures)	*Investments* (e.g. resource allocation, curricula, recruiting and training programmes)	*Instruments of regulation and deregulation* (e.g. QA and development, school autonomy)	*Social and fiscal returns* (e.g. economic growth, migration movement)
Organization	*Institutional environment* (e.g. other educational institutions, sociodemographic surroundings)	*Resources* (e.g. school buildings and equipment, material and personal situation)	*Organizational development* (e.g. cooperation and coordination, evaluation)	*Institutional outcomes* (e.g. school leavers/dropouts, large-scale results, central exams)
Interaction	*Surrounding circumstances* (e.g. rooms and interior, class sizes)	*Preconditions* (e.g. appointed staff, time budget, learning material)	*Procedures and activities* (e.g. pedagogical methods, learning rate)	*Quality of instruction and learning* (e.g. cognitive activation, supportive behaviour of teaching staff)
School leader (individual)	*Personal background* (e.g. migration status, sex, age)	*Professional stage* (e.g. skill set, attitudes, value system)	*Professional development* (e.g. leadership behaviour, sensitiveness, openness, training)	*Personal gains* (e.g. motivation, work satisfaction, experience, routines)

more differentiated and structured way the influence of leadership practices on school quality across Europe.

Within this conceptual framework, which guides the systematic literature review, different kinds of system-related problem analysis can be undertaken, such as potentials of conflicts and integration of personality systems in their interplay with social entities as well as an interplay with the structure and functions of the education system as a whole. In this way, school leadership-related interactions can be visualized as diagonals – not as one-way streets with clear monocausal impact factors but mutual effects which need to be investigated.

At this point, the authors of this chapter want to stress that they are aware of the fact that the variance *within* an education system can often turn out to be much greater than the variance *between* education systems. Therefore the authors integrate that perspective into their conceptual framework as it takes into account the coordination of the person, the schools as a single pedagogical unit, and the overall regulations and functions of the education system itself.

Thus, as can be inferred from the above, this chapter is organized around the systemic modelling approach of inputs, processes and outputs through which school leaders are operating during the execution of their daily duties, inside as well as outside their organization. As they are opting for this criteria-based systematic literature review of successful practices in Europe, the authors are aware of the fact that, against this background, they offer a snapshot of successful and effective leadership practices across Europe at a given point in time. It is not possible to cover all European educational systems within the scope of this chapter alone.

Input

Due to continuing changes in organizational and structural conditions, quality assurance and development processes are constantly threatened. The creation of a reliable mid-term framework and the expansion of room for manoeuvre (input) can release positive energies and power among all those seeking common ground. Quality development requires participation of the entire school community. School quality and quality development via a specific school vision contribute to fostering all participants' involvement, sharing in decision making and even holding people responsible. Teachers, parents and students are invited to take on responsibility with respect to developing and supporting concepts for sustainable thoughts and actions which might result in better outcomes. More concretely, recent research on successful and effective school leaders around Europe has established that successful school principals create a clear vision about where their schools are heading in the long term, and especially after these principals are no longer there (Pashiardis et al., 2012). In fact, their vision can be summarized as to 'How do I want my school to look like after I am gone?' Additionally, in successful schools, the school vision is clearly communicated to teachers, students and parents while the teachers are actively supported by the principals in fulfilling the school's vision. Furthermore, once this vision is identified, school leaders try to implement it based on a certain set of values such as: honesty; trust in people and for people; passion for excellence; a hard working ethos; decisiveness; and risk-taking behaviour. Passion and commitment were actively demonstrated and communicated in order to promote modelling of these expectations by the students and teachers in several research programmes with regards to school leaders' practices around Europe. These are very important inputs which contribute greatly towards success and effectiveness at the individual school level and should be part of the equation when assessing success.

For example, a school principal in Cyprus had a strong focus on building human relations and social networks, as she firmly believed that through these actions she would enhance student achievement. She was committed to improving students' learning outcomes and behaviour through this vision which she shared with all stakeholders in the school. As a result, she developed and communicated a clear vision to all internal and external stakeholders as well as clear rules and regulations that should be adhered to by all in order to achieve that vision (Brauckmann & Pashiardis, 2011). In short, she clearly showed the way forward in order to focus all resources on the desired goals.

Further, successful principals in Europe have actively demonstrated their commitment to their schools through consistent and hard work. They set high standards in their schools and effectively motivate the children and teachers to strive for excellence. This feature of successful leadership is also corroborated by previous research (e.g. Day et al., 2000; Gold et al., 2003) which advocates that successful school leaders are driven by a personal value system and communicate a clear sense of purpose and direction. These inputs, which stem primarily from the school leader's sense of moral purpose, seem to be one of the most important inputs in the education process at the school level and should not be discarded during the assessment process in order to make value judgements about merit, worth, success and effectiveness at the individual school level.

Process

We often forget that process-oriented action structures are at the foreground of school quality development as well as experiences concerning school development processes in the areas of instruction, organizational and human resource management and development. Team development, joint quality conceptualization, stocktaking and orientation discussions, open discussions and reference to a culture of debate that favours quality, activation of the current relevant school actors, awareness of jointly seeking to pursue quality endeavours and shared responsibility – these are just a few positive parameters of a quality discussion that affect a change in the self-knowledge of school leaders' professional understanding and actions. In this sense school quality is achieved by the correct use of school development instruments and procedures by leaders and leadership teams in schools. In a sense, successful school leaders become the best teacher and the best student in the school by exhibiting strong instructional/pedagogical leadership.

This pedagogical leadership is manifested at the school level by setting high goals and expectations for all in the school. This is a very important message that a school leader can transmit to both teachers and students in order to steer the process towards success (Borich, 2015). Additionally, the principals' instructional/pedagogical leadership actions, such as advising teachers after going over their lesson planning and praising them for something positive they have done, are some of the pedagogical strategies that successful school leaders employ. Another aspect of pedagogical leadership is when school leaders take extra care in organizing, coordinating and evaluating the teaching and learning process and the curriculum, and they are actively involved in problem solving regarding teachers' issues related to problems within the profession and students' problems related to issues within the school setting (Thoonen et al., 2011). Pedagogical dialogue after classroom observations, in order to help teachers to become reflective about their teaching, is another way that school leaders can create the right instructional atmosphere for students and teachers to flourish (Sullivan & Glanz, 2009).

Another process-oriented mechanism that successful school leaders in Europe use is to create teams, sustain them, nurture them and provide solutions to problems and conflicts arising, thus creating a group school climate which is conducive to teaching and learning. Many of the successful principals researched in Europe exhibited these democratic characteristics, providing a sense of shared ownership in their schools combined with high transparency. The specific behaviour was introduced by some principals in order to set high standards of satisfaction and trust between themselves and members of the school community, such as teachers, students and secretaries. This action can be linked with the tenth strong claim about successful school leadership, as mentioned in a recent report of the National College of School Leadership (2010), and made reference to the establishment of trust as one of the most important elements that successful leadership depends on. Trust was further reinforced by encouraging teachers' participation in decision making (creating collegial cultures).

In particular, some of the school principals researched in Cyprus, England and the Nordic countries were instrumental in promoting the creation of a collaborative learning organization by equally distributing powers and responsibilities regarding all school matters as well as by promoting team spirit among not only the teachers and the pupils but also the secretaries and other support staff. Thus, inclusive leadership was used in order to increase ownership of the school goals. When appropriate, effort was also made to include the children in decision making. The creation of a positive and inclusive learning environment not only for students but also for teachers is supported by other research in Australia and the USA (Gurr et al., 2003; Jacobson et al., 2005; Leithwood & Jantzi, 2006).

Another process that successful school leaders utilize is when they create alliances with stakeholders outside and around the schools they lead so that they can improve their schools on the inside. Most European principals in various research projects gave great attention to the creation of a strong relationship between themselves and all external stakeholders. Specifically, by cooperating with parents and the community at large, they established close contacts and communication, and managed to maintain good relationships with parents' associations, school boards and the local community, thus exhibiting a strong entrepreneurial leadership style (Brauckmann & Pashiardis, 2011). This establishment of networks with parents and the wider community seems to form an important element of successful principalship, not only in Europe but also globally (Day et al., 2000). In a paper by Pashiardis and Savvides (2011), it was stressed that successful principals gave particular attention to the relations of the school with the local community. All principals created interactive networks with the local community whereby community members and parents were regularly invited to either attend or actively take part in school events. The students for their part initiated community projects, demonstrating their commitment to the local community. In addition, the principals personally made an active effort to involve themselves in community life, which made parents and members of the local community feel respected.

Consistently, successful principals around Europe seem to be able to communicate with everybody who may affect the school from the outside, thus bringing more help into the school. In an economic era of constantly shrinking resources, the need to look outside for assistance on the inside becomes increasingly more important and it seems that school leaders need to exhibit more awareness and ability to exercise this entrepreneurial leadership style. Assessing how successful school leaders are in implementing this type of leadership style should be made an important part of the exercise, mainly because the ability to secure extra resources (human as well as material) greatly contributes towards the creation of the necessary prerequisites on which schools can further build and enhance their success.

Output

What are we measuring and/or counting as outputs for the school and various educational systems around the world? How about citizenship results? Should these count and, if so, in what order of significance (Stronge et al., 2007)? The fallacy is that, even though we live in democracies, we do not have ways to identify whether our schools and our educational systems can prepare democratic citizens who respect freedoms and abide by the law. The questions of what school is all about and what kind of learning is important are very much contested issues at this time, and there is no broad agreement or understanding around these concepts in different parts of the world. How about measuring impact as the school's effect on student well-being? Should that become a priority and should we therefore assess whether our education systems prepare citizens who are physically active and live healthy lifestyles, protecting their environment and being aware of climate change and the destruction of our natural environment (European Commission, 2012)? We should always remember that what gets measured gets taught. Thus, what we assess as output is what will be considered as important to be taught in our schools.

At the same time, what is measured as success and effectiveness in one education system in Europe may not be good enough in another, due to contextual influences. The phase of development in which a society finds itself is a very important determinant in terms of what counts as success. Furthermore, a feeling of satisfaction and belonging for students and teachers could equally well be counted as a measure of success in a school. The feeling of being wanted and valued is an important output for some societies, especially for special populations within the school system. The traditions of country/society/population and family structures play an equally important role in terms of what is considered as an important output. Even more critically, instead of the uni-dimensional examination of just exam scores in final assessments, schools should probably be assessed on all of the inputs and processes, as described above. In short, what should count as success and effectiveness is 'pp' at the individual school level: process and product.

High quality leadership across Europe in an era of output oriented governance – why should it work?

In continuation of the previous discussion, we know that school leaders play an important role in the overall responsibility for schools by framing the conditions for teaching and learning. Moreover, leaders administer the budget allocated to a school and decide on seeking funding for securing lessons. On the one hand, schools use pedagogical freedom of instruction, for example, by variation in timetables, additional forms of assessment of achievement and school internal curricula. On the other hand, they are committed to subjecting outcomes to internal evaluation processes and being held accountable. Altogether, these aspects raise the question of which school leadership actions are particularly promising in governing the central task of assuring good lesson/instructional quality, and what obstacles are encountered.

To this end, the introduction of new governance approaches in the school system has not proceeded without friction. In particular, school administration has not yet succeeded in reducing legal regulations and directives and focusing on a small number of core regulations. Instead, school leaders face comprehensive directives with which they are meant to deal and act on accordingly. But, in many cases school quality as well as effective conceptual work are made impossible because schools' internal resources are used for 'patching up' interim solutions, further increasing pressure on time. Depending on school structural characteristics and various experiences, schools differ greatly in school QA and improvement concerning the scope and priorities of conceptual work. Adequate conditions need to be provided for the autonomy of a school and increased conceptual work. At the same time, it is evident that, for all schools, fundamental prerequisites are lacking, particularly time resources that would be needed for the school leaders' stronger commitment to conceptual tasks.

School leaders can only conditionally influence the development of instructional quality. At an operative level, school leaders as well as individual teachers assure instructional quality. Even despite the existence of evaluation counsellors, some schools are inappropriately prepared for permanent internal and external evaluation and subsequent problems – for example, implementation issues, data assessment and transfer of findings from the evaluations into concrete school improvement targets and measures. For example, are we certain that, when a school receives its evaluation report, teachers and school leaders are able to make sense of the data presented, in order to improve the core process of teaching and learning? There is sometimes too little external support for quality assurance measures and for the implementation of a quality assurance system.

High quality leadership across different school contexts in Europe – how could it work?

Davis et al. (2005) point out that the same set of management and organization competencies will not produce the same effects for different schools and different social contexts. Hence, the question is whether and to what extent schools actually use their newly gained freedom – and why some schools use this freedom more intensively and are more innovative than others (Rolff, 2009). To find out whether and to what extent school leaders can trigger or influence the creation of an effective teaching and learning environment, it is necessary to look at their position within a school as an organization, and their contextual nesting in the entire system. Factors and procedures are thus placed in the foreground that might enable new forms of school leadership action. Remaining administrative limitations or expansions of (given and feasible) actions are based on intra-organizational requirements and the individual predispositions of a school leader. These pertain to individual-internal dispositions and situational requirements. The latter, for instance, might serve to explicate the ways and means of how individual school leaders interpret their remit and act accordingly (Warwas, 2009: 477). This contributes to answering the question of whether and to what extent there actually exists a correspondence of tasks, capacities, responsibilities and skills which school leaders ought to perform.

In view of mostly output-oriented school systems governance across Europe, the question of school leadership effectiveness, differentiated by different types of school leadership, their success, possibilities and limits, has so far not been resolved and convincing research is still scarce. However, to sum up, it seems that the following are the most important practices for successful and effective school leaders around Europe. They:

- create a vision which is value-driven and can be shared with all stakeholders inside and outside the school in order to commit everybody to its achievement;

- become the best teacher and the best student in the school, exercise pedagogical/instructional leadership and lead by example; they understand that we are all eternal students who constantly fight for professional growth;

- create teams, sustain them, nurture them, and provide solutions to problems and conflicts in a school climate which is conducive to teaching and learning;

- form alliances with other stakeholders outside and around the schools they lead, that is, they make the education of our children everybody's work and responsibility, remembering the African proverb that it takes a whole village to educate a child.

It should be kept in mind that institutional and organizational structural arrangements still have to be seen as prerequisites that need to be addressed before any more ambitious improvement efforts can be initiated. As a consequence, school quality management does not mean that all decisions are made at the school level by the school leadership team; both local and central government play a significant role in managing education. Schools should focus on issues that they define in consultation with local policy makers. They should decide on what decisions belong at each administrative level and also on respective responsibilities for each steering level. It should therefore be stressed that the absence of an efficient and supportive broader policy environment is risky, not only for individual schools, but also for the system as a whole, which will be threatened by disintegration and disparity. The danger is that leaders of schools, as with leaders of any other open social system, will lose their ability to interact with their environments through the feedback they receive and thus lose their ability to adjust to contextual challenges.

In other words, successful practice-oriented school leaders have to constantly search for a balanced and effective interplay between input, process and output variables. Thus, system leadership becomes more and more a prerequisite for carrying out successful leadership practices more effectively. It is not about successful leadership practices effected at the individual school level by principals, but about leadership practices carried out by leadership teams across different levels of intervention in order to become more sustainable.

PART THREE

The Impact of Successful and Effective School Leadership

14

Understanding the Impact of Successful and Effective School Leadership as Practised

Petros Pashiardis, Georgia Pashiardi and Olof Johansson

Introduction

Research worldwide has so far produced mixed results about the impact that school leaders can have on student outcomes. In fact, previous research on the effects of school leadership on students' academic achievement has (sometimes) produced contradictory findings. However, a number of studies have found the effects of school leadership (Cheng, 1994; Edmonds, 1979; Fuller, 1987; Kythreotis et al., 2010; Leithwood et al., 2010; Levine & Lezotte, 1990; Mortimore et al., 1988; Mulford and Silins, 2011; Pashiardis, 1995, 1998, 2004, 2014; Reynolds & Cuttance, 1992; Sammons et al., 2011). More recently, Heck and Hallinger (2014) have indicated in their research that the faculty of a school has a collectively positive effect on student learning – i.e. what they called a 'compounding benefit', which could be the collective effect of school leadership that takes place in the school. In sum, Heck and Hallinger argue that effective school leaders should try to increase the quality of instruction in their schools, not just for individual teachers, but collectively as well. In our view, what is important to understand and accept is that, whatever the research method or context in which leadership research has been carried out, leadership is only second to teaching in order to produce effective schools (Seashore Louis et al., 2010). Thus, education systems and schools need to understand that in order to have schools which teach well and students who learn best, we need to provide them with leaders who can lead and guide these processes. At the same time, the importance of context should be taken into consideration. Cultural, and indeed local, values are an essential prerequisite to bear in mind when investigating and creating new policies with regard to school leadership. The context from one country to the other plays an important role because, to a great extent, school leaders' actions and behaviours greatly depend on their perceptions of the particular context in which they work – that is, how they (the school leaders) interpret the external environment and legal framework which relate to their practices (Brauckmann & Schwarz, 2014). In particular, the local context is of great importance here. This means that how the different agents at this level (i.e. school boards, superintendents, assistant superintendents as well as principals and teachers) act in the enactment process of policy is of great importance for the implementation results (Bredeson et al., 2011).

The main purpose of this chapter is to present successful and effective school leadership practices in seven regions around the world and to identify any commonalities that might exist. However, a note of caution is appropriate here, in that we do understand the difficulties and limitations of trying to generalize from a few case studies in one or two countries in the various regions covered in this book. Thus, we acknowledge and understand that when there is an intent to generalize beyond the specifics studied, it is incumbent on us to indicate the contexts, activities, data collection methods and so forth (the domains) to which the generalization is intended to apply and (at least implicitly) those to which it may *not* apply.

It is a well-accepted assumption that school leaders employ different practices in their schools and exhibit certain personality traits/characteristics that seem to influence students' performance. At the same time, it is increasingly recognized that the concept of *leadership* is a complex mixture of styles, modes and approaches. An example of leadership styles is the one explored in the LISA (Leadership Improvement for Student Achievement) research project, which may be distinguished as follows: (1) instructional style; (2) structuring style; (3) participative style; (4) entrepreneurial style; and (5) personnel development style (Brauckmann & Pashiardis, 2011; Pashiardis, 2014). Each leadership style consists of specific behaviours, actions or practices which are likely to be exhibited by school principals. As the authors mention, the *leadership radius* is the epicentre of the Pashiardis–Brauckmann Holistic Leadership Framework. However, it should be noted that the sum of the five styles does not equal the leadership radius; this concept is more than the sum of its parts and it points to the often under-researched as well as under-theorized leader's personality and moral purpose in order to make this complex concept operational. Moreover, the five styles partially overlap and are congenial to each other when in full motion and operation. This leadership radius is what came to be called the 'leadership cocktail mix' (Pashiardis, 2014). The main question is then: Through which behaviours and actions do school leaders impact the day-to-day operations of the schools they lead in order to have successful and effective schools in the various regions of the world? One answer to this question is that school leaders must act as the prime learners and in that capacity work as stewards, communicators, experts and models of learning (Bredeson & Johansson, 2000).

The impact of successful and effective school leadership within the African context

Within the African context 'successful' has recently acquired a new meaning and it may require a principal who balances between task (what needs to be done) and person orientation (how it is to be operationalized with a human touch). In order for this to materialize, *trust* is increasingly recognized as a key element in encouraging collaboration. Individuals are more likely to trust those with whom they have established good relationships, as the authors from the African region inform us. Some ways in which the principals operationalize this effort is through the creation of common planning times for teachers and the establishment of teams and group structures within their schools in order to foster more collaboration and trust among staff.

At the same time, the authors stress the fact that monitoring and adjusting the structural organization of the school, including how tasks are assigned and performed, and the use of time and space, are important elements in these reorganization efforts. Thus, the aim is to enhance the performance of their schools by providing opportunities for staff to participate in decision making about issues that affect them and for which their knowledge is crucial.

Another practice used by African school leaders is the provision of regular positive feedback which helps to motivate and inspire staff. Acknowledging and celebrating individual and collective successes as teachers and the senior management team is another important characteristic of successful leadership, as exercised within this region. In this way, principals are responsible for creating a positive culture within their schools. This can be further enhanced by working closely with other community structures such as non-governmental organizations (NGOs) and community-based organizations (CBOs). Therefore, another feature of the practices of successful school leaders is to ensure continuous communication with parents, students, staff and the school governing body.

Moreover, besides all of the above, there was consensus among African school leaders that their personal qualities made a very significant contribution to their success as leaders. Some of these personal attributes include being trustworthy and honest, dealing with everybody with a sense of integrity and a sense of humour, being friendly yet firm, being exemplary, exhibiting commitment, being hardworking and transparent, being a good communicator, showing a sense of self-discipline, and possessing strong moral and ethical values and a sense of responsibility. Other attributes included decisiveness, being a fast learner, 'thinking on your feet', being patient, always striving for continuous improvement, and being fair and consistent, as the authors of the African chapters underline. But, above all, successful school leaders in this context stressed the fact that a leader should always remember to say 'thank you', to acknowledge good work, effort, and commitment.

The impact of successful and effective school leadership within the South Asian context

Some of the most important principal leadership practices within the Asian context included building a shared vision as a positive driving force, within an environment which supports all-round student development, thus motivating teachers and students to perform at higher levels. The school leaders further practised *distributed leadership* in order to set in motion change with a core team of teachers who would follow and show the necessary resilience. At the same time, support and professional development would be provided for teachers who did not have the necessary characteristics and knowledge to follow through the many changes that school leaders wanted to initiate.

Thus, in one of the schools described in the Asian chapters, the new concept of *invitational education* was initiated by the school principal as a successful practice. As the authors inform us, invitational education is an approach to creating, sustaining and enhancing an authentic and truly welcoming learning environment based on trust, respect, optimism and care, that facilitates better learning outcomes and enables students to realize their full potential. The school leader himself exercised instructional leadership to improve both teachers' practices and the overall quality of the school; as a result, many of his teachers had the impression that their school principal behaved more like a teacher educator than a principal.

Moreover, one of the most important practices of successful principalship exhibited in schools in Hong Kong was the capability of school leaders to lead change. Principals presented in the relevant Asian chapters were able to cope with the changing face of the communities in which their schools were located and the students lived. As the authors inform us, both school leaders demonstrated distributed leadership as well as instructional leadership, focusing on whole-school teaching and a school-wide learning programme. Their actions were influenced by the context in which they operated, and certainly as they perceived it, but, at the same time, their practices provided a broader understanding of successful school leadership which is capable of seizing new opportunities. Furthermore, the leaders were able to raise awareness of the cultural, social and pedagogical changes needed for the diversity of the population their schools were serving as a result of changing demographics in the area in which the schools were situated.

At the same time, the school leaders realized that they could not do everything by themselves or with the teaching staff within their schools. They realized early on that they needed the help of the wider community, and thus collaborated with social workers from NGOs, helping the children to build a new school culture. Additionally, they collected parents' opinions in surveys to support mutual understanding of the school's development and they built partnerships with parents and other organizations in the community for active communal participation, thus creating the necessary space for participation in various communal activities. Thus, the authors make it quite obvious how local contextual characteristics shaped principals' leadership practices, especially when the principals were able to seize new opportunities and had the strength and tenacity to develop these into actions at the school site. This outward-looking style, which came to be called the entrepreneurial style, is often combined with thinking about the future and trying to develop and improve old thinking through thinking outside the box. In short, what this style is all about is doing more with less in an era of economic austerity and other challenges.

The impact of successful and effective school leadership within the Australian/Pacific context

In the Australian/New Zealand context, the authors of the relevant chapters stress the fact that common features of successful school principals centred on: values and beliefs; personal qualities and skills; interventions/practices that lead to success; and capacity building. As the authors further point out, their studies show that successful school leaders interact within a particular school context to deliver strategic interventions aimed at improving student outcomes.

The leaders' values were perceived on several levels, such as the professional level and the core values about human interaction and behaviour, but at the same time principals' actions centred around universal values, such as social justice, dignity and freedom, empathy for the less well off, compassion and tolerance. Moreover, principals in that part of the world exhibited another kind of value, that of companionship and doing things together, that is, they exercised the distributed notion of leadership. Thus, the leaders were people-centred, good at developing relationships and modelling appropriate behaviour, and good at establishing relational trust.

It is interesting to note that one of the principals described in the relevant chapter built a clear sense of shared direction for a non-privileged school, named '2 for 1' – i.e. for the school to be truly successful and provide students with the best opportunities, the teachers had to try to get two years' worth of learning gain into one year. In this way students had the opportunity to catch up with their learning and, consequently, that particular school would be elevated to the level of the rest of the schools in the state.

At the same time, just as for school leaders in other regions of the world, the principals in this area tried to provide support and advice to parents and often influenced the community at large. They did not just see themselves as school leaders, but as community leaders, as social workers, as motivators, as cultural initiators and many more roles that they undertook in order to have the greatest possible impact in their communities. Finally, the authors conclude that, 'more than ever before we need school leaders who are learners. And because school leaders are, at heart, educators they should exemplify the power of learning upon their leadership development.'

The impact of successful and effective school leadership within the Caribbean context

As the authors of the chapters in this region of the world inform us, the practice of school leadership in the Caribbean is not uniform; at the same time, they stress the fact that within and between countries there are many perspectives that can be considered to be similar. Career progression within the various education systems is considered to be problematic as it is not so much a meritorious process, it is rather a process based on national political, religious and social connections. Therefore, the process of progression and advancement to the principalship seems to be a political process based on seniority.

With the above comments in mind, it seems that some of the practices exhibited by high performing principals in the region include having a personal philosophy along with personal abilities which operate as the guiding force to successful leadership behaviour. This philosophy revolves around instructional leadership which is considered an important aspect of school leadership and has been highlighted in a number of the countries in the region, including

Trinidad and Tobago and Guyana. If we define *instructional* or *pedagogical* leadership as all the actions that refer to the interventions that school leaders employ in their schools in order to improve the process of teaching and learning, then the key word here is *intervention*, which means it must be an action with a core purpose to improve teaching and learning. We find many different ways of expressing these interventions in the various countries of the Caribbean region. The school leaders themselves exercise instructional leadership in order to improve both teachers' practices and the overall quality of the school. For example, an important aspect of instructional school leadership is when the school leaders exercise pedagogical leadership and lead by example, emphasizing the fact that we are all 'students' constantly fighting for professional growth.

The impact of successful and effective school leadership within the European context

The authors from this part of the world stress the fact that although school quality seems to have been primarily characterized by student, class and school outcomes, usually stemming from external evaluation measures, it does not only comprise outcomes and is therefore not uni-dimensional. On the contrary, school quality comprises a field covering different kinds of objectives, both enabling/intermediate objectives as well as final objectives. Thus, it is emphasized that school leadership impact and successful practices can take place at the input, process and output levels of the school and not just at the final output level, as often happens in school systems around the world. In some parts of the world, these variables are called 'intermediary variables' or 'school climate variables' and they are treated as the means towards desired student outcomes. On the other hand, in some contexts, these very same variables may be treated as measures of success and effectiveness. For instance, if a school is able to attract resources in order to make its premises more attractive and conducive to learning, this is considered as a measure of effectiveness. Or if there is a great deal of job satisfaction among teachers, this is considered a good measure of effectiveness, as the assumption is that the more satisfied a teacher is, the more productive he/she will be at the school.

Thus, the expected student outcomes seem to become quite subjective and indicate what is most important for a particular school system. That is, did we have an influence on what kind of citizens they become and with what kind of academic achievements they have made? Are these the kinds of persons that society needs and wants from its schools? It seems that the message stemming from the European perspective about the most important practices for successful and effective school leaders around Europe revolves around some of the following aspects.

School leaders in Europe create a vision which is value-driven and can be shared with all stakeholders. This vision then becomes the driving force and the area of focus for intense action towards improvement at all levels within the school. The vision deals also with the necessary structures, rules and regulations in place in order to fulfil this vision. Moreover, the implementation of all of the above takes place in a uniform and consistent way so that there is a feeling of fairness among school leadership, teachers and students.

Moreover, European school leaders exercise pedagogical leadership and lead by example, emphasizing the fact that we are all eternal students constantly fighting for professional growth. In fact, they provide the necessary atmosphere for the core function of the school, which is teaching and learning. This becomes the primary focus for all involved and pedagogical dialogues among colleagues promote the idea of excellence in teaching.

Finally, school leaders within the European context create alliances with other stakeholders outside and around the schools they lead. In essence they go the extra mile in developing strategic alliances with the municipality, parents' associations, the police, civil society and other perceived stakeholders in order to bring the 'outsiders' into their schools. In this way, they are reinforcing, informing and creating collaborators who will increase their effectiveness inside the school but from an 'outsider's' perspective.

The impact of successful and effective school leadership within the North American context

In the chapters for this region, particular attention is paid to how principals sustained improvement under very challenging circumstances by setting a direction for their school; developing their teachers, staff, and parents; refining and aligning their schools to build collaborative structures and removing potential obstacles to success; and improving the instructional programme. The authors claim that effective principals and teachers could make enough of a difference in academic performance to overcome the negative consequences of poverty. The centrepiece of their behaviour for increasing academic performance was 'instructional leadership'. Even more so, the authors attribute the successes of these principals to their ability to build trust between themselves and their staff and among the staff themselves. In this way, there is a 'reconceptualization of leadership from being a narrow, individual construct based upon the skills a principal possesses to a broader, collective construct that is critically dependent upon the relationships leaders cultivate'.

Therefore, these principals' leadership practices revolve around empowerment, transformation and community building, thus capitalizing on teacher leadership which seems to play an important role in understanding school success as distributed leadership expands and the principal's role is somehow converted from manager to facilitator and orchestrator. Moreover, the authors stress that principals in this region of the world are committed to making a difference for their school communities, as revealed through their resilience, commitment, persistence and sense of optimism, even in the face of very difficult challenges.

Longevity of service in their positions was another clear factor as to why these principals were so influential. Over several years of serving at the same school, these principals were able to build the trust of their faculty and their parent community in order to support the tough decisions and changes they had to make. Trust was evident throughout the schools in various different forms, such as benevolence, competence, honesty, openness, reliability and vulnerability. Based on what the authors say, it may be concluded that the relative stability of leadership at a school is indeed an important factor contributing towards success and effectiveness, with 'frequent turnovers leading to instability and potentially a lack of trust, while extremely long tenures can possibly lead to complacency and inertia'.

The impact of successful and effective school leadership within the South American context

The authors for the chapters on this region begin by acknowledging the fact that socioeconomic and cultural status are the most important factors influencing student performance, especially in a continent with marked social inequalities. Thus, the challenge for school leaders in the region is to raise the quality of basic education with the objective of improving social equity and reducing the regional differences both between countries and within the countries themselves.

What is considered very important for the schools in the region is stability of personnel and the leadership shown by the principal and the teachers, indicated by respect for the opinions of the teachers, and the sharing of responsibilities, thus exercising distributed and shared forms of leadership. School leaders are considered a very important factor within the schools of the region and local research corroborates this. The emphasis is primarily on being, again, the instructional leader of the school as well as exercising this leadership through a good working environment, and relying on a close working relationship with the school community which encourages a two-way relationship and communication between students and teachers, in a climate which is conducive to learning. More concretely, in Brazil, some studies showed that higher school performance is associated with principals having the following particular characteristics: a firm, objective and participative leadership style; good relations within the community; motivation to win over the teachers; and a desire to help students in difficulty, in a joint effort with parents and teachers.

At the same time however, school principals in South America need to be able to combat the very limited tradition of participation of 'outsiders' in the school system. As the chapter authors inform us, the history of the continent with its colonial past and succession of oligarchies and dictatorships has led to school leaders in the field seeing themselves as experts in education, and as a result the opinions of other ordinary citizens and students, the 'subjects of the educational process', are not welcome.

Another aspect of school leadership that is stressed for the region is that schools which have a flexible organization, which are participative, relatively autonomous and with high levels of consensus among the various stakeholders, are more successful and have a stronger impact on the performance of students from lower income groups. Moreover, it is stressed that responsibility should be taken to train teachers as leaders, and probably this responsibility falls on the shoulders of school principals. Perhaps this kind of professional staff development is one of the major practices that needs to be undertaken by school leaders in that part of the world in order to enhance the distribution of leadership among all participants in the teaching and learning process in the school, and therefore enhance the quality of learning that takes place in the classroom.

Understanding the impact of successful and effective school leadership: concluding remarks and reflection

Around the world the pressure to perform successfully, and doing so efficiently, is increasing among the various stakeholders in education, with a focus on international and comparative large-scale assessments. In fact, it cannot be considered as a coincidence that in recent years we have seen a proliferation of large-scale international assessments such as: the Programme for International Student Assessment (PISA); the Teaching and Learning International Survey (TALIS); the Third International Mathematics and Science Study (TIMSS); the

Progress in International Reading Literacy Study (PIRLS); the Programme for the International Assessment of Adult Competencies (PIAAC); the CIVic Education programme (CIVED); the International Civic and Citizenship Education Study (ICCS); and the Second Information Technology Education Study (SITES). These evaluation studies are one reason why we concentrate on comparing school success and drafting up league tables between countries. There is also another reason, which is linked to school results and, more importantly, has a greater impact on modern societies, that can be described as a changing labour market with much higher educational demands on the workforce. Young people need to have at least a high-school certificate to be seen as candidates for future employment.

These several studies have compared educational systems across the globe on a number of variables regarding students' academic achievement, adult literacy, quality of teachers and many more that are still being developed. The tendency is to increasingly compare and try to discover the 'best' practices and interventions and to identify common features that help to build success in the different regions around the world.

But, is there a best practice and best achievement suitable for all? What is valued as 'best' education and what is valued *within* education is politically and value driven. However, politics and values are society driven and there are vast differences from one society to another. Education systems are micro-political, and in this regard they represent the culture and values of real people on the ground. Thus, it is possible that what is successful and effective in one part of the world may be only 'good enough' in another part of the world. Depending on the level of development of a society and its educational system, what is successful and what is effective suddenly becomes very relative. It really depends on the local 'state of affairs'. At the same time, it seems that the world has some commonalities that should be stressed and singled out in order to better understand the debate about successful and effective schools and school leaders. Again, readers are reminded at this point that our 'commonalities' should be viewed with caution, due to the smallness of our sample from the different regions around the world, and thus our ability to generalize. In any case, the following tendencies become quite obvious.

The first common point that can be made, based on the above descriptions and analyses of the regions of the world, is that context and the interplay between context and the various actors at the school level is an important factor to reckon with. Successful and effective school leaders are aware of the broader context in the internal and external environment in which they operate as well as of the international trends in education, allowing them to be adaptive and learn in order to lead. In other words, school leaders are contextually literate, have a deep knowledge and understanding of their school's demographic situation, and they act accordingly in order to meet their students' needs. In fact, different leadership styles and qualities are expected in a school whose ethnic composition is very diverse – different sets of behaviours and actions are probably required of an elementary, middle or a high school. Further, depending on where the school is situated (urban, suburban or rural) different constituents may make different demands on school leaders as well as different sets of expectations. It could be stressed here that this area is quite under-researched and needs further refinement and development.

Second, the role of the principal as a leader of leaders is a prominent one and enhances, mostly indirectly, students' performance. This leadership role, which seems to be evident in most studies in the international literature, is called *instructional leadership* in the US context or *pedagogical leadership* in other contexts, and has an impact on the quality of teaching and learning that takes place at the school level. Instructional or pedagogical leadership refers to all the interventions that school leaders employ in their schools in order to improve the process of teaching and learning. Thus, defining instructional objectives, setting high expectations, monitoring and evaluating students and teachers, enabling achievement of instructional objectives, stimulating instructional innovation and carrying out pedagogical dialogues with teachers about the quality of their teaching and the kind of expectations that school leaders have of their teachers, become their everyday commitment. Usually, these kinds of actions and behaviours have the effect of enhancing teacher self-reflection, increasing their innovation and creativity, their risk-taking behaviour, their motivation and satisfaction as well as their sense of security and self-efficacy. This leadership style improves the quality of teaching and enhances the school climate, which should be conducive to teaching and learning, and instruction becomes the leader's priority and a measure of success and effectiveness. This research topic could be further investigated, especially in those education systems where school principals, besides being leaders, also have considerable teaching duties, in order to find out how they can combine the two 'instructional' and 'leadership' roles at different levels in a productive way.

At the same time, *distributed leadership* seems to be another commonality irrespective of context. School leaders around the globe have probably realized the need to build collaborative structures within as well as outside their schools. Within the school, school leaders empower their teachers and the school's leadership team, and embrace shared decision making. This leadership style highlights the importance of positive and productive relationships among school participants based on trust and mutual support. Similarly, they work closely with other stakeholders, such as parents and community members, in order to build coalitions and form alliances that will help in pursuing common school goals. Thus, they exhibit an *entrepreneurial* style of leadership, which is an essential component of the leadership cocktail mix irrespective of context (Brauckmann & Pashiardis, 2011). In a sense, the argument could be made that what came to be called the entrepreneurial style of leadership has two axes on which it operates: an internal and an external one. Thus, school leaders who exercise this style of leadership try to build coalitions and alliances both inside and outside the school, creating in this way distributed and efficient ways in which to exercise power both with others as well as among others.

Finally, school leaders seem to be *value-driven* and especially *trust-driven*. Successful principals share a set of values (professional, social and political) that they believe in and communicate to others. This can be seen as their *personal philosophy* and it is a common characteristic of leaders in different parts of the world. These values exist at both the personal and the professional level and include a humane understanding of what it means to be a leader who is honest and real. It seems that everywhere around the world leaders need to be able to build a common trust which they can use as a platform for everything else they do in their schools. *Building a shared vision* of what we want our schools to look like is another manifestation of this value-driven and trust-building aspect of school leadership that can make the difference at the school level and motivate students to realize and reach their full potential in education. Perhaps more research is needed in this area as well, specifically which personality types are more prone to and capable of building this trust base on which school leaders can operate more successfully and effectively.

Notes

Chapter 3

1 ISPP, http://www.ucalgary.ca/cwebber/ISPP/index.htm.

Chapter 7

1 PISA – The Programme for International Student Assessment conducted by OECD, and TIMMS – Trends in International Mathematics and Science Study conducted by IEA – are large international surveys.

2 http://europa.eu/pol/pdf/flipbook/en/education_training_youth_and_sport_en.pdf. Retrieved 18 January 2015.

3 TALIS – Teaching and Learning International Survey, http://www.oecd.org/edu/school/talis.htm. Retrieved 19 January 2015.

Chapter 9

1 There are four basic types of primary school in Hong Kong: government, aided, Direct Subsidy Scheme schools (DSS) and private schools. The first type is fully operated and funded by the government, while the second type is fully subsidized by the government but operated by charitable/religious/voluntary bodies (Education Bureau, 2014a). DSS schools (Education Bureau, 2014b) receive government subvention and are also permitted to charge fees. Private schools receive no government funding. See Hong Kong: The facts – Education (GovHK, 2014: http://www.gov.hk/en/about/abouthk/factsheets/docs/education.pdf) for an overview of the school types.

2 Low-income households refer to those domestic households with monthly household income less than 50 per cent of the median monthly domestic household income (news.gov.hk: /en/record/html/2014/01/20140117_ 114921.shtm). 'This corresponds to a poverty rate of about 17.6%. This means one in every six people in Hong Kong is living under the poverty line' (Oxfam Hong Kong: http://www.oxfam.org.hk/en/news_1972.aspx).

3 The CSSA scheme provides a basic safety net to those who cannot support themselves financially. It is designed to bring their income up to a prescribed level deemed sufficient to meet their basic needs.

4   In Hong Kong's mainstream Chinese-medium primary schools, the traditional
    Chinese written language is used for relevant subject learning materials and
    Cantonese for teaching all subjects except English language, although the
    EDB has recently encouraged schools to use Mandarin (Putonghua) rather
    than Cantonese to teach Chinese language.

5   The HKICT Awards acknowledge projects that have contributed to promoting
    digital inclusion and building a just and caring information society for
    underprivileged groups (HKICT Awards 2014: http://www.hkictawards.hk/
    news.asp?menuid=22681&supmenuid=9960).

6   International Alliance for Invitational Education, http://www.
    invitationaleducation.net/.

Chapter 12

1   Regional entities. Schools in Jamaica are divided into five regions, and each
    region is aligned to groups of parishes. Jamaica has fourteen parishes. The
    regional entities perform tasks related to staffing, recruitment and
    performance evaluation, among others.

2   The Urban Excellence Framework was developed by New Leaders 'to
    understand exactly what schools achieving dramatic gains are doing and to
    share that knowledge throughout our community of leaders' (New Leaders,
    2011).

References

Introduction

Brauckmann, S. & Pashiardis, P. (2011). Contextual framing for school leadership training: empirical findings from the Commonwealth Project on Leadership Assessment and Development (Co-LEAD). *Journal of Management Development*, 31(1): 18–33.

Bredeson, P.V., Klar, H. & Johansson, O. (2011). Context-responsive leadership: examining superintendent leadership in context. *Education Policy Analysis Archives*, 19(18): 1–28.

Coleman, J.S., Campbell, E.Q. & Hobson, C.J. et al. (1966). *Equality of Educational Opportunity*. Washington, DC: US Government Printing Office.

Hallinger, P. & Heck, R. (1998). Exploring the Principals' Contribution to School Effectiveness: 1980–1995. *School Effectiveness and School Improvement*, 9(2), 157–91.

Holmgren, M., Johansson, O. & Nihlfors, E. (2013). Sweden: centralisation and decentralisation as implementation strategies, in L. Moos (ed.) *Transnational Influences on Values and Practice in Nordic Educational Leadership*. Dordrecht: Springer, 73–85.

Hoy, W. (2012) School characteristics that make a difference for the achievement of all students: a 40-year odyssey. *Journal of Educational Administration*, 50(1): 76–97.

Johansson, O. (2015) *Rektorn och Styrkedjan* [The Principal and the Governing Chain] Statens offentliga utredningar SOU 2015:22. The Swedish Government's Public Investigations, SOU 2015:22/. Stockholm: Fritzes Publisher.

Kythreotis, A., Pashiardis, P. & Kyriakides, L. (2010). The influence of school leadership styles and school culture on students' achievement in Cyprus primary schools. *Journal of Educational Administration,* 48(2): 218–40.

Marzano, R.J., Waters, T. & McNulty, B.A. (2005). *School Leadership that Works. From Research to Results*. USA: ASCD and MCREL.

Merchant, B. et al. (2012). Successful school leadership in Sweden and the US: context of social responsibility and individualism. *International Journal of Educational Management*, 26(5): 428–41.

Moos, L., Johansson, O. & Day, C. (2011). *How School Principals Sustain Success: International Perspectives*. London: Springer.

Nihlfors, E. & Johansson, O. (2013). *Rektor – en stark länk I styrningen av skolan*. Stockholm: SNS Förlag.

OECD (Organization for Economic Cooperation and Development) (2008). *Improving School Leadership Policy and Practice*. Paris: OECD.

Pashiardis, P. (ed.) (2014). *Modeling School Leadership Across Europe: In Search of New Frontiers.* Dordrecht: Springer.

Pashiardis, P. & Brauckmann, S. (2008). Introduction to the LISA Framework from a social system's perspective. Paper presented during the LISA Conference, 13–15 November 2008, Budapest, Hungary.

Chapter 1

Amagoh, F. (2009). Leadership development and leadership effectiveness. *Management Decision*, 47(6): 989–99.

Asuga, G.N. & Eacott, S. (2012). The learning needs of secondary school principals: an investigation in Nakuru district, Kenya. *International Journal of Education Administration and Policy Studies*, 4(5), 133–40.

Bolden, R. & Kirk, P. (2009). African leadership surfacing new understandings through leadership development. *International Journal of Cross Cultural Management*, 9(1): 69–86.

Bush, T. (2007). Educational leadership and management: theory, policy, and practice. *South African Journal of Education*, 27(3): 391–406.

Bush, T. (2009). Leadership development and school improvement: contemporary issues in leadership development. *Educational Review*, 61(4): 375–89.

Bush, T. & Oduro, G.K.T. (2006). New principals in Africa: preparation, induction and practice. *Journal of Educational Administration*, 44(4): 359–75.

Bush, T., Kiggundu, E. & Moorosi, P. (2011). Preparing new principals in South Africa: the ACE: School Leadership Programme. *South African Journal of Education*, 31: 31–43.

Chapman, D.W., Burton, L. & Werner J. (2010). Universal secondary education in Uganda: the head teachers' dilemma. *International Journal of Educational Development*, 3: 77–82.

City Press (2013). Motshekga: Only 36% of school principals are women, 23 August. Retrieved from http://www.citypress.co.za/news/motshekga-only-36-of-school-principals-are-women/. Accessed October 2014.

DeJaeghere, J.G., Williams, R. & Kyeyune, R. (2009). Ugandan secondary school headteachers' efficacy: what kind of training for whom? *International Journal of Educational Development*, 29: 312–20.

Department of Education (2008). *Course Outline for Advanced Certificate: Education (School Management and Leadership)*. Pretoria: Government Printers

Eacott, S. & Asuga, G.N. (2014). School leadership preparation and development in Africa: a critical insight. *Educational Management Administration & Leadership*, 1–16.

Ghana (2014). Literacy rate in Ghana. http://www.unicef.org/infobycountry/ghana_statistics.html, accessed 2 February 2015.

Grant, C. (2014). Postgraduate research learning communities and their contribution to the field of educational leadership and management. *International Studies in Educational Administration*, 42(1): 89–100.

Handford, V. & Leithwood, K. (2013). Why teachers trust school leaders. *Journal of Educational Administration*, 51(2): 194–212.

Heystek, J. (2007). Leaders or moulded managers in managerialistic schools? *South African Journal of Education*, 27(3): 491–505.

Heystek, J. (2014). Principals' perceptions about performance agreements as motivational action. *Educational Management Administration & Leadership*, 42(6): 889–902.

Heystek, J. & Terhoven, R. (2015). Motivation as critical factor for teacher development in contextually challenging underperforming schools in South Africa. *Journal of Professional Development*, 41(4): 624–39.

Hoadley, U., Christie, P. & Ward, C.L. (2009). Managing to learn: instructional leadership in South African secondary schools. *School Leadership and Management*, 29(4): 373–89.

Huber, S.G. (2004a). School leadership and leadership development. Adjusting leadership theories and development programs to values and the core purpose of school. *Journal of Educational Administration*, 42(6): 669–84.

Huber, S.G. (2004b). *Preparing School Leaders for the 21st Century. An international comparison of development programs in 15 countries*. London: Routledge Falmer.

Jooste, H. (2008). Management and leadership in rural secondary Schools in Mpumalanga (doctoral thesis). Pretoria: Tshwane University of Technology.

Jull, S., Swaffield, S. & MacBeath, J. (2014). Changing perceptions is one thing: barriers to transforming leadership and learning in Ghanaian basic schools. *School Leadership & Management*, 34(1): 69–84.

Kenya (2014). Literacy rate in Kenya. http://www.unicef.org/infobycountry/kenya_statistics.html, accessed 2 February 2015.

Kiggundu, E. & Moorosi, P. (2012). Networking for school leadership in South Africa: perceptions and realities. *School Leadership & Management*, 32(3): 215–32.

Kitavi, M.W. & Van Der Westhuizen, P.C. (1997). Problems facing beginning principals in developing countries: a study of beginning principals in Kenya. *International Journal of Educational Development*, 17(3): 251–63.

LEAD-Link (2009). *Leadership Role Models in Africa*. Johannesburg: Matthew Goniwe School of Leadership and Governance.

Lessem, R. & Nussbuam, B. (1996). *Sawubona Africa. Embracing Four Worlds in South African Management*. Sandton: Zebra.

Lumby, J., Crow, G. & Pashiardis, P. (2008). *International Handbook on the Preparation and Development of School Leaders*. New York: Routledge.

Mncube, V. & Harber, C. (2010). Chronicling educator practices and experiences in the context of democratic schooling and quality education in South Africa. *International Journal of Educational Development*, 30: 614–24.

Moloi, K.C. (2010). How can schools build learning organisations in difficult education contexts? *South African Journal of Education*, 30: 621–33.

Moorosi, P. (2012). Mentoring for school leadership in South Africa: diversity, dissimilarity and disadvantage. *Professional Development in Education*, 38(3): 487–503.

Moyo, G. (2004). Re-inventing educational leadership for school and community transformation: learning from the educational leadership management and development programme of the University of Fort Hare. Unpublished PhD, Rhodes University.

Mulford, B. & Silins, H. (2011). Revised models and conceptualisation of successful school principalship for improved student outcomes. *International Journal of Educational Management*, 25(1): 61–82.

Naidoo, S.V. (2011). Leadership development of school principals through communities of practice: a case study of one leadership practice community. Master of Education (MEd) degree in the discipline Educational Leadership, Management and Policy, School of Education and Development, Faculty of Education, University of KwaZulu-Natal.

Onguko, B.B., Abdalla, M. & Webber, C.F. (2012). Walking in unfamiliar territory: headteachers' preparation and first-year experiences in Tanzania. *Educational Administration Quarterly*, 48(1): 86–115.

Pashiardis, P. & Heystek, J. (2007). School improvement – it is achievable: a case study from a South African school. In C.S. Sunal and K. Mutua (eds), *The Enterprise of Education, Research on Education in Africa, the Caribbean, and the Middle East*. Book IV, Charlotte, NC: Information Age Publishing, 41–61 (http://www.infoagepub.com/products/content/p46434bae6c7d7.php)

Piggot-Irvine, E., Howse, J. & Richard, V. (2013). South Africa: principal role and development needs. *International Studies in Educational Administration*, 41(3): 55–72.

Scott, J.M. (2010). An investigation into the nature of leadership development programmes for South African principals in Gauteng schools. Retrieved from http://wiredspace.wits.ac.za/handle/10539/7608. Accessed October 2014.

Snook, S., Nohria, N. & Khurana, R. (2012). *The Handbook for Teaching Leadership. Knowing, doing and being*. Los Angeles: Sage.

South Africa Department of Basic Education (2009). *External Evaluation Research Report of the Advanced Certificate in Education: School leadership and management*. Pretoria: Department of Basic Education.

South Africa Department of Basic Education (2011a). *Report on the National Senior Certificate Examination 2011 School Performance Analysis*. Pretoria: Government Printers, http://www.education.gov.za. Accessed October 2014.

South Africa Department of Basic Education. (2011b). *Report on Dropout and Learner Retention Strategy to Portfolio Committee on Education*. Retrieved from http://www.education.gov.za/LinkClick.aspx?fileticket=jcSsY0rHcME%3 D&tabid=358&mid=1261. Accessed October 2014.

South Africa Department of Basic Education (2013). *Report on the National Senior Certificate Results*. Pretoria: Department of Basic Education.

South Africa. Department of Basic Education (2014). Annual report 2013–2014. Retrieved from http://www.education.gov.za/DocumentsLibrary/Reports/tabid/358/Default.aspx. Accessed October 2014.

South Africa Department of Education (2008). *Course outline for Advanced Certificate: Education (school management and leadership)*. Pretoria: Government printers. Accessed October 2014.

Statistics South Africa (2014). *Work & Labour Force*. Retrieved from http://beta2.statssa.gov.za/?page_id=737&id=1. Accessed October 2014.

Tanzania (2014). Literacy rate in Tanzania. http://www.unicef.org/infobycountry/tanzania_statistics.html, accessed 2 February 2015.

Thom, D. (2014). Business Leadership Continuing Professional Development of Education Management Teams in a South African School Group. *International Studies in Educational Administration*, 42(1): 31–44.

Uganda (2014). Literacy rate in Uganda. http://www.unicef.org/infobycountry/uganda_statistics.html, accessed 2 February 2015.

Walker, A. Hu, R., & Qian, H. (2012). Principal leadership in China: an initial review. *School Effectiveness and School Improvement*, 23(4): 369–99.

Wood, L. & Govender, B. (2013). 'You learn from going through the process': the perceptions of South African school leaders about action research. *Action Research*, 11(2): 176–93.

Young, M.D., Crow, G.M., Murphy, J. & Ogawa, R. (2009). *Handbook of Research on the Education of School Leaders*. New York, Routledge.

Chapter 2

Cheng, Y.C. & Tam, W.M. (2007). School effectiveness and improvement in Asia: three waves, nine trends and challenges, in T. Townsend, B. Avalos, B. Caldwell, Y.C. Cheng, B. Fleisch, L. Moos, L. Stoll, S. Stringfield, W.M. Tam, N. Taylor & C. Teddlie (eds), *International Handbook of School Effectiveness and School Improvement*. Dordrecht, Netherlands: Springer, 245–68.

Cheng, Y.C. & Walker, A. (2008). When reform hits reality: the bottleneck effect in Hong Kong primary schools. *School Leadership and Management*, 28(5): 505–21.

Cheng, K.M. & Wong, K.C. (1996). School effectiveness in East Asia: concepts, origins and implications. *Journal of Educational Administration*, 34(5): 32–49.

Cheung, M.B. (2000). Securing a better future: a Hong Kong school principal's perception of leadership in times of change, in C. Dimmock & A. Walker (eds), *Future School Administration: Western and Asian Perspectives*. Hong Kong: Chinese University Hong Kong Press, 225–48.

Cheung, R.M.B. & Walker, A. (2006). Inner worlds and outer limits: the formation of beginning school principals in Hong Kong. *Journal of Educational Administration*, 44(4): 389–407.

Chu, H. & Cravens, X.C. (2012). Principal professional development in China: challenges, opportunities, and strategies. *Peabody Journal of Education*, 87(2): 178–99.

Day, C. & Leithwood, K. (eds) (2007). *Successful Principal Leadership in Time of Change*. Dordrecht: Springer.

Dimmock, C. & Walker, A. (1998). Transforming Hong Kong's schools: trends and emerging issues. *Journal of Educational Administration*, 36(5): 476–91.

Dimmock, C. & Walker, A. (2000). Globalisation and societal culture: redefining schooling and school leadership in the twenty-first century. *Compare: A Journal of Comparative Education*, 30(3): 303–12.

Dimmock, C. & Walker, A. (2005). School leadership in context: societal and organisational cultures, in T. Bush (ed.), *The Principles and Practice of Educational Management*. London: Paul Chapman, 70–85.

Education Commission (1996). *Quality School Education (EC report No.7)*. Hong Kong: Government Printer.

Fry, G.W. & Bi, H. (2013). The evolution of educational reform in Thailand: the Thai educational paradox. *Journal of Educational Administration*, 51(3): 290–319.

Hallinger, P. (2001). Leading educational change in Southeast Asia: the challenge of creating learning systems, in C. Dimmock & A. Walker (eds), *Future School Administration: Western and Asian Perspectives*. Hong Kong: Chinese University Press, 169–90.

Hallinger, P. (2003a). The emergence of school leadership development in an era of globalization: 1980–2000, in P. Hallinger (ed.), *Reshaping the Landscape of School Leadership Development: A Global Perspective*. Lisse: Swets & Zeitlinger, 3–22.

Hallinger, P. (2003b). School leadership development in the Asia Pacific region: trends and directions for future research and development, in J. Keeves & R. Watanabe (eds), *The Handbook of Educational Research in the Asia Pacific Region*. New York: Kluwer Academic Press, 1001–14.

Hallinger, P. (2004). Meeting the challenges of cultural leadership: the changing role of principals in Thailand. *Discourse: Studies in the Cultural Politics of Education*, 25(1): 61–73.

Hallinger, P. (2010). Making education reform happen: Is there an 'Asian' way? *School Leadership and Management*, 30(5): 401–8.

Hallinger, P. (2011a). Developing a knowledge base for educational leadership and management in East Asia, *School Leadership and Management*, 31(4): 305–20.

Hallinger, P. (2011b). Leadership for learning: lessons from 40 years of empirical research. *Journal of Educational Administration*, 49(2): 125–42.

Hallinger, P. & Bryant, D.A. (2013a). Mapping the terrain of research on educational leadership and management in East Asia. *Journal of Educational Administration*, 51(5): 618–37.

Hallinger, P. & Bryant, D.A. (2013b). Synthesis of findings from 15 years of educational reform in Thailand: lessons on leading educational change in East Asia. *International Journal of Leadership in Education: Theory and Practice*, 16(4): 399–418.

Hallinger, P. & Heck, R.H. (1996). Reassessing the principal's role in school effectiveness: a review of empirical research, 1980–1995. *Educational Administration Quarterly*, 32(1): 5–44.

Hallinger, P. & Lee, M.S. (2011). Assessing a decade of education reform in Thailand: broken promise or impossible dream? *Cambridge Journal of Education*, 41(2): 139–58.

Hallinger, P. & Lee, M.S. (2013). Exploring principal capacity to lead reform of teaching and learning quality in Thailand. *International Journal of Educational Development*, 33: 305–15.

Hallinger, P., Chantarapanya, P., Sriboonma, U. & Kantamara, P. (2000). The challenge of educational reform in Thailand: Jing Jai, Jing Jung, Nae Norn, in T. Townsend & Y.C. Cheng (eds), *Educational Change and Development i n the Asia-Pacific Region: Challenges for the Future*. Lisse: Swets & Zeitsinger, 207–26.

Hallinger, P., Walker, A. & Bajunid, I.A. (2005). Educational leadership in East Asia: implications for education in global society. *UCEA Review*, 45(1): 1–4.

Hampden-Turner, C. & Trompenaars, F. (1997). *Mastering the Infinite Game: How Asian Values are Transforming Business Practice*. Oxford: Capstone Press.

Hofstede, G. (1983). The cultural relativity of organizational practices and theories. *Journal of International Business Studies*, 14(2): 75–89.

Hofstede, G. (1991). *Cultures and Organizations: Software of the Mind*. Maidenhead: McGraw-Hill.

Holmes, H. & Tangtongtavy, S. (1996). *Working with Thais: A Guide to Managing in Thailand*. Bangkok: White Lotus.

Hussein, H.A. (2014). Implementation of strategic education policy plan at micro-level contexts: management and leadership challenges. *Malaysian Online Journal of Educational Management*, 2(2): 1–21.

Lam, J. (2003). Balancing stability and change: implications for professional preparation and development of principals in Hong Kong, in P. Hallinger (ed.), *Reshaping the Landscape of School Leadership Development: A Global Perspective*. Lisse: Swets & Zeitlinger, 175–90.

Lee, M. & Hallinger, P. (2012). National contexts influencing principals' time use and allocation: economic development, societal culture, and educational system. *School Effectiveness and School Improvement*, 23: 461–82.

Lee, M., Hallinger, P. & Walker, A. (2012). Leadership challenges in international schools in the Asia Pacific region: evidence from programme implementation of the International Baccalaureate. *International Journal of Leadership in Education: Theory and Practice*, 15(3): 289–310.

Leithwood, K., Day, C., Sammons, P., Harris, A. & Hopkins, D. (2006). *Successful School Leadership: What it is and how it influences pupil learning*. Nottingham: University of Nottingham.

Leithwood, K., Harris, A. and Hopkins, D. (2008). Seven strong claims about successful school leadership. *School Leadership and Management*, 28(1): 27–42.

Lin, M.D. (2003). Professional development for principals in Taiwan: the status quo and future needs, in P. Hallinger (ed.), *Reshaping the Landscape of School Leadership Development: A Global Perspective*. Lisse: Swets & Zeitlinger, 191–204.

McLaughlin, M. (1990). The Rand change agent study revisited. *Educational Researcher*, 5: 11–16.

Ministry of Education Malaysia (2013). *Malaysia Education Blueprint 2013–2015*. Putrajaya: Kementerian Pendidikan Malaysia.

Ministry of Education Malaysia (2014). *Malaysia Education Blueprint Annual Report 2013*. Putrajaya: Kementerian Pendidikan Malaysia.

Mok, M.M.C. (2007). Quality assurance and school monitoring in Hong Kong. *Educational Research for Policy and Practice*, 6(3): 187–204.

OECD (Organization for Economic Cooperation and Development) (2011). *Lessons from PISA for the United States: Strong performers and successful reformers in education*. Paris: OECD Publishing, http://dx.doi.org/10.1787/9789264096660-en. Accessed October 2014.

Qian, H.Y. & Walker, A. (2011). Leadership for learning in China: the political and policy context, in T. Townsend & J. Macbeath (eds), *The International Handbook of Leadership for Learning*. Netherlands: Springer, 209–25.

Tang, S.B., Lu, J.F. & Hallinger, P. (2014). Leading school change in China: a review of related literature and preliminary investigation. *International Journal of Education Management*, 28(6): 655–75.

Thang, D.T. (2013). *Confucian Values and School Leadership in Vietnam*. Unpublished PhD dissertation, Victoria University of Wellington, Wellington, New Zealand.

Varavarn, K. (2008). Personal communication at a meeting at the Office of the Basic Education Commission, Bangkok, Thailand, June.

Walker, A. (2003). School leadership and management, in J. Keeves & R. Watanabe (eds), *The Handbook on Educational Research in the Asia-Pacific Region*. Netherlands: Kluwer, 973–86.

Walker, A. (2004). Constitution and culture: exploring the deep leadership structures of Hong Kong. *Discourse: Studies in the Cultural Politics of Education*, 25(1): 75–94.

Walker, A. (2007). Leading authentically at the cross-roads of culture and context. *Journal of Educational Change*, 8(3): 257–73.

Walker, A. (2012). *Gateways to Leading and Learning: School Leadership as Connective Activity*. Hong Kong: The Joseph Lau Luen Hung Charitable Trust Asia Pacific Centre for Leadership and Change, Hong Kong Institute of Education.

Walker, A. & Chen, S.Y. (2007). Leader authenticity in intercultural school contexts. *Educational Management Administration & Leadership*, 35: 185–204.

Walker, A. & Dimmock, C. (2000). Leadership dilemmas of Hong Kong principals: sources, perceptions and outcomes. *Australian Journal of Education*, 44(1): 5–25.

Walker, A. & Hallinger, P. (2007). Navigating culture and context: the principalship in East and Southeast Asia, in R. Maclean (ed.), *Learning and Teaching for the Twenty-First Century: Festschrift for Professor Phillip Hughes*. Dordrecht: Springer, 255–73.

Walker, A. & Hallinger, P. (2013). International perspectives on leader development: definition and design. *Educational Management, Administration and Leadership*, 41(4), 401–4.

Walker, A. & Ko, J. (2011). Principal leadership in an era of accountability: a perspective from the Hong Kong context. *School Leadership and Management*, 31(4): 369–92.

Walker, A. & Qian, H.Y. (2006). Beginning principals: balancing at the top of the greasy pole. *Journal of Educational Administration*, 44(4): 297–309.

Walker, A. & Qian, H.Y. (2011). Successful school leadership in China, in C. Day (ed.), *International Handbook of Teacher and School Development*. Oxford: Routledge, 446–57.

Walker, A. & Qian, H.Y. (2012). Reform disconnection in China. *Peabody Journal of Education*, 87(2): 162–77.

Walker, A. & Stott, K. (1993). Preparing for leadership in schools: the mentoring contribution, in B. Caldwell & E. Carter (eds), *The Return of the Mentor*. London: Falmer Press, 77–90.

Walker, A. & Wang, X.J. (2011). Same mother, different lives: the social organization of leadership for learning across three Chinese societies, in T. Townsend & J. MacBeath (eds), *The International Handbook of Leadership for Learning*. Dordrecht: Springer, 1083–1106.

Walker, A., Hallinger, P. & Qian, H.Y. (2007). Leadership development for school effectiveness and improvement in East Asia, in T. Townsend (ed.), *International Handbook of School Effectiveness and School Improvement*. Dordrecht: Springer.

Walker, A., Chen, S.Y. & Qian, H.Y. (2008). Leader development across three Chinese societies, in J. Lumby, G. Crow & P. Pashiardis (eds), *International Handbook of the Preparation and Development of School Leaders*. New York: Routledge, 410–34.

Walker, A., Hu, R. & Qian, H.Y. (2012). Principal leadership in China: an initial review. *School Effectiveness and School Improvement: An International Journal of Research, Policy and Practice*, 23(4): 369–99.

Chapter 3

Begley, P. (2008). The nature and specialized purpose of educational leadership, in J. Lumby, G. Crow & P. Pashiardis (eds), *International Handbook on the Preparation and Development of School Leaders*. New York: Routledge, 21–4.

Browne-Ferrigno, T. (2003). Becoming a principal: role conception, initial socialization, role identity transformation, purposeful engagement. *Educational Administration Quarterly*, 39(4): 468–503.

Bush, T. & Jackson, D. (2002). A preparation for school leadership: international perspectives. *Educational Management and Administration*, 30(4): 417–29.

Caldwell, B., Calnin, T. & Cahill, W.P. (2003). Mission possible? An international analysis of headteacher/principal training, in N. Bennett, M. Crawford & M. Cartwright (eds), *Effective Educational Leadership*. London: Open University, 111–30.

Clarke, S. & Wildy, H. (2004). Context counts: viewing small school leadership from the inside out. *Journal of Educational Administration*, 42(5): 555–72.

Clarke, S. and Wildy, H. (2010). Preparing for principalship from the crucible of experience: reflecting on theory, practice and research. *Journal of Educational Administration and History*, 41(1): 1–16.

Clarke, S. & Wildy, H. (2011). Providing professional sustenance for leaders of learning – the glass half full?, in T. Townsend & J. MacBeath (eds), *International Handbook of Leadership for Learning*. Dordrecht: Springer, 673–90.

Clarke, S., Wildy, H. & Pepper, C. (2007). Connecting preparation with reality: primary principals' experiences of their first year out in Western Australia. *Leading & Managing*, 13(1): 81–90.

Cowie, M. & Crawford, M. (2009). Headteacher preparation programme in England and Scotland: do they make a difference for the first-year head? *School Leadership & Management*, 29(1): 5–21.

Cranston, N.C. (2007). Through the eyes of potential aspirants: another view of principalship. *School Leadership & Management*, 27(2): 109–28.

Crow, G.M. (2007). The professional and organizational socialization of new English headteachers in school reform contexts. *Educational Management Administration & Leadership*, 35(1): 51–71.

Darling-Hammond, L., LaPointe, M., Meyerson, D., Orr. M.T. & Cohen, C. (2007). *Preparing School Leaders for a Changing World: Lessons from Exemplary Leadership Development Programs*. Stanford, CA: Stanford University, Stanford Educational Leadership Institute.

Dempster, N. (2001). *The Professional Development of School Principals: A Fine Balance*. Professorial Lecture, Griffith Public Lecture Series, 24 May, Griffith University.

Dempster, N. (2009). *Leadership for Learning: A Framework Synthesising Recent Research*. Paper 13. Deakin West, Australia: Australian College of Educators.

Dempster, N. (2011). Leadership and learning: making connections down under, in T. Townsend & J. MacBeath (eds), *International Handbook of Leadership for Learning*. Dordrecht: Springer, 89–102.

Dempster, N., Lovett, S. & Flückiger, B. (2011). *Strategies to Develop School Leadership. A Select Literature Review*. Melbourne: Australian Institute for Teaching and School Leadership (AITSL).

Dempster, N., Fluckiger, B. & Lovett, S. (2012). *Principals Reflecting on their Leadership Learning with an Heuristic: A Pilot Study.* Sydney: University of Sydney, Joint Australian Association Research in Education and Asia Pacific Educational Research Association Conference (AARE & APERA), 2–6 December.

DeRue, D. & Ashford, S.J. (2010). Power to the people: where has personal agency gone in leadership development? *Industrial and Organizational Psychology,* 3: 24–17.

Duignan, P. (2006). *Educational Leadership. Key Challenges and Ethical Tensions.* Port Melbourne: Cambridge University Press.

Earl, L., Watson, N. and Torrance, N. (2002). Front row seats: what we've learned from the national literacy and numeracy strategies in England. *Journal of Educational Change,* 3: 35–53.

Fink, D. (2011). The succession challenge: warm bodies or leaders for learning, in T. Townsend & J. MacBeath (eds), *International Handbook of Leadership for Learning.* Dordrecht: Springer, 589–602.

Higgs, M. (2009). The good, the bad and the ugly: leadership and narcissism. *Journal of Change Management,* 9(2): 165–78.

Huber, S. (2008). School development and school leaders' development: new learning opportunities for school leaders and their schools, in J. Lumby, G. Crow & P. Pashiardis (eds), *International Handbook on the Preparation and Development of School Leaders.* New York: Routledge, 163–75.

Loader, D. (1997). *The Inner Principal.* London: Falmer Press.

Loader, D. (2010). Developing inner leadership, in B. Davies & M. Brundrett (eds), *Developing Successful Leadership.* London: Springer, 195–206.

Lovett, S., Dempster, N. & Flückiger B. (2014). Personal agency in leadership learning using an Australian heuristic. *Professional Development in Education,* DOI: 10.1080/19415257.2014.891532.

McCall, M.W. (2010). Recasting leadership development. *Industrial and Organizational Psychology,* 3: 3–19.

Masters, G. (2008). *Understanding and Leading Learning. Principals' Big Day Out.* Melbourne, available at: http://works.bepress.com/geoff_masters/118, accessed 11 November 2009.

NCSL (National College for School Leadership) (2007). What we know about school leadership. www.ncsl.org.uk/publications., retrieved 25 January 2008.

Robertson, J. (2011). Partnership in leadership and learning, in J. Robertson & H. Timperley (eds), *Leadership and Learning.* London: Sage, 213–26.

Southworth, G. (2010). Developing leadership development, in B. Davies & M. Brundrett (eds), *Developing Successful Leadership.* London: Springer, 177–94.

Starratt, R.J. (2011). *Refocusing School Leadership. Foregrounding Human Development Throughout the Work of the School.* New York: Routledge.

Stoll, L. & Fink, D. (1996). *Changing our Schools.* Buckingham: Open University Press.

Swaffield, S. & Dempster, N. (2009). A learning dialogue (principle 3), in J. MacBeath & N. Dempster (eds), *Connecting Leadership and Learning: Principles for Practice.* London: Routledge, 106–20.

Wildy, H. & Clarke, S. (2005). Leading the small rural school: the case of the novice principal. *Leading & Managing,* 11(1): 43–56.

Wildy, H. & Clarke, S. (2008). Charting an arid landscape: the preparation of novice primary principals in Western Australia. *School Leadership & Management*, 28(5): 469–87.

Chapter 4

Adams, J.E. & Copland, M.A. (2005). *When Learning Counts: Rethinking licenses for school leaders*. Seattle, WA: Center on Reinventing Public Education.

Ann-Lumsden, M., Bore, M., Millar, K., Jack, R. & Powis, D. (2005). Assessment of personal qualities in relation to admission to medical school. *Medical Education*, 39(3): 258–65.

Browne-Ferrigno, T. & Shoho, A. (2002). An exploratory analysis of leadership preparation selection criteria. Paper prepared for the Interactive Symposium on 'How Will We Know Whether Cohorts and Other Delivery Strategies Produce Effective School Leaders?' Annual conference of the University Council for Educational Administration, Pittsburgh, Pennsylvania, November 2002.

Cai, O. (2011). Can principals' emotional intelligence matter to school turnarounds? *International Journal of Leadership in Education*, 14(2): 151–79.

Canole, M. & Young, M. (2013). Standards for educational leaders: an analysis. ISSLC Analysis Report. Washington, DC: Council of Chief State School Officers.

Capper, C.A., Theoharis, G. & Sebastian, J. (2006). Toward a framework for preparing leaders for social justice. *Journal of Educational Administration*, 44(3): 209–24, DOI 10.1108/09578230610664814.

CCSSO (2008). *Educational Leadership Policy Standards: ISLLC 2008*. As adopted by the National Policy Board for Educational Administration. Washington, DC. Retrieved 21 May 2014 from http://www.ccsso.org/Documents/2008/Educational_Leadership_Policy_ Standards_2008.pdf.

CCSSO (2011). *In TASC Model Core Teaching Standards: A Resource for State Dialogue*. Retrieved 13 June 2014 from http://www.ccsso.org/Resources/Publications/InTASC_Model_Core_Teaching_Standards_A_Resource_for_State_Dialogue_(April_2011).html.

CCSSO (2012). *Our Responsibility, Our Promise: Transforming educator preparation and entry into the profession*. Washington, DC. Retrieved 21 May 2014, from http://www.ccsso.org/Documents/2012/Our%20Responsibility%20Our%20Promise_2012.pdf.

Creighton, T., & Jones, G. (2001). Selection or self-selection? How rigorous are our selection criteria for education administration preparation programs? Paper presented at the 2001 conference of the National Council of Professors of Educational Administration, Houston, Texas, 7–11 August 2001.

Darling-Hammond, L., Meyerson, D., La Pointe, M. & Orr, M.T. (2010). *Preparing Principals for a Changing World: Lessons from effective school leadership programs*. San Francisco: Jossey-Bass.

Day, C. & Leithwood, K. (2007). *Successful School Principalship in Times of Change: An international perspective*. Dordrecht: Springer.

Dufour, R., Dufour, R., Eaker, R. & Karhanek, G. (2004). *Whatever it Takes: How professional learning communities respond when kids don't learn*. Bloomington, IN: National Educational Service.

Educational Research Service (1998). *Enhancing Student Engagement in Learning*. Bethesda, MD: Education Week.

Flessa, J. (2007). The trouble with the Ed.D. *Leadership & Policy in Schools*, 6(2): 197–208.

Gale, J.J. & Bishop, P.A. (2014). The work of effective middle grade principals: responsiveness and relationship. *Research in Middle Level Education*, 37(9): 1–23.

Gurr, D., Drysdale, L., Ylimaki, R. & Jacobson, S. (2011). Preparation for sustainable leadership, in L. Moos, O. Johansson & C. Day (eds), *How School Principals Sustain Success Over Time: International perspectives*. Dordrecht: Springer, 183–97.

Hess, F.M. & Kelly, A.P. (2007). Learning to lead: what gets taught in principal-preparation programs. *Teachers College Record*, 109(1): 244–74.

Hollingsworth, L. (2009). Innovative programs: The University of Texas at San Antonio preparing leaders for social justice and leadership in diverse communities. *UCEA Review*, 50(2): 22–3.

Hopson, L.M. & Lee, E. (2011). Mitigating the effect of family poverty on academic and behavioral outcomes: the role of school climate in middle and high school. *Children and Youth Services Review*, 33(11): 2221–9.

Hoy, W.K., Gage, Q. & Tarter, C.J. (2006). School mindfulness and faculty trust: necessary conditions for each other. *Educational Administration Quarterly*, 4: 236–55.

Jackson, B.L. & Kelley, C. (2002). Exceptional and innovative programs in educational leadership. *Educational Administration Quarterly*, 38, 192–212.

Kearney, W.S. & Herrington, D.E. (2013). The role of inquiry in closing the gap between university experience and assistant principal career transition through simulated realistic job preview. *Educational Leadership Review*, 14(1): 69–82.

Kearney, W.S., Kelsey, C. & Sinkfield, C. (2014). Can emotionally intelligent leadership skills be taught to aspiring school leaders? *Journal of Planning and Changing*, 45(1&2): 31–47.

Klein, A. (2007). Joining forces. *Education Week*, 27(3): S16–19.

Kobe, L.M., Reiter-Palmon, R. & Rickers, J.D. (2001). Self-reported leadership experiences in relation to inventoried social and emotional intelligence. *Current Psychology: Developmental Learning, Personality, Social*, 20(2): 154–63.

Lashway, L. (2003). Transforming principal preparation. *Eric Digest*, 165, 1–8.

Levine, A. (2005). Educating school leaders. The Education Schools Project. Retrieved from ERIC archives, US Department of Education, 20 October 2014, http://files.eric.ed.gov/fulltext/ED504142.pdf.

Louis, K.S. & Wahlstrom, K. (2011). Principals as cultural leaders. *Phi Delta Kappan*, 92(5): 52–6.

Moore, B. (2009). Emotional intelligence for school administrators: a priority for school reform? *American Secondary Education*, 37(3): 20–8.

Moos, L., Johansson, O. & Day, C. (2011). *How School Principals Sustain Success Over Time: International perspectives*. Dordrecht: Springer.

Murakami, E., Törnsén, M. & Pollock, K. (2014). School principals' standards and expectations in three educational contexts. *Canadian and International Education Journal*, 43(1): Article 6, available at: http://ir.lib.uwo.ca/cie-eci/vol43/iss1/6.

Murakami-Ramalho, E., Garza, E. & Merchant, B. (2010a). Successful school leadership in socio-economically challenging contexts: school principals creating and sustaining successful school improvement. *International Studies in Educational Administration*, 38(3): 35–56.

Murakami-Ramalho, E., Byng, J.M., Garza, E. & Thompson, D. (2010b). Reforming preparation programs for leadership improvement: the case of Texas. *Journal of School Leadership*, 20(4): 404–24, DOI: 201018212809002.

NAESP (2008). *Leading Learning Communities: Standards for what principals should know and be able to do.* Alexandria, VA: National Association of Elementary School Principals and Collaborative Communications Group.

NASSP (2012). Breaking Ranks Framework: a comprehensive framework for school improvement, https://www.principals.org/SchoolImprovement/ BreakingRanksPublications/BreakingRanksComprehensiveFramework.aspx, accessed 3 July 2014.

NCATE (2011). *Educational Leadership Program Standards.* Retrieved 22 June 2014 from http://www.ncate.org/LinkClick.aspx?fileticket=zRZI73R0nOQ%3D &tabid=676.

NCES (2013). Characteristics of public and private elementary and secondary school principals in the United States: results from the 2011–2012 schools and staffing survey. Retrieved 29 June 2014 from http://nces.ed.gov/pubs2013/ 2013313.pdf.

NCES (2014). *The Condition of Education 2014.* Institute of Education Sciences, National Center for Education Statistics, US Department of Education. Retrieved 29 June 2014 from http://nces.ed.gov/pubs2014/2014083.pdf.

Nelson, D.B. & Low, G.R. (2011). *Emotional Intelligence*, 2nd edn. Boston, MA: Prentice Hall.

Normore, A.H. & Jean-Marie, G. (2010). *Educational Leadership Preparation: Innovation and interdisciplinary approaches to the Ed.D. and graduate education.* New York: Palgrave.

Orr, M.T. (2006). Mapping innovation in leadership preparation in our nation's schools of education. *Phi Delta Kappan*, 87: 492–9.

Orr, M. & Orphanos, S. (2011). How graduate-level preparation influences the effectiveness of school leaders: a comparison of the outcomes of exemplary and conventional leadership preparation programs for principals. *Educational Administration Quarterly*, 47(1): 18–70.

Pashiardis, P. & Brauckmann, S. (2009). Professional development needs of school principals. *Commonwealth Education Partnerships*, 120–4.

Sadri, G. (2012). Emotional intelligence and leadership development. *Public Personnel Management*, 41(3): 535–48.

Southern Regional Education Board (2002). *Are SREB States Making Progress? Tapping, preparing and licensing school leaders who can influence student performance.* Atlanta, GA: Southern Regional Education Board. Retrieved 3 July 2014 from http://www.wallacefoundation.org/knowledge-center/ school-leadership/state-policy/Pages/Are-SREB-States-Making-Progress.aspx.

Wallace, J. (2010). Facing 'reality': including the emotional in school leadership programmes. *Journal of Educational Administration*, 48(5): 595–610.

Ylimaki, R.M. & Jacobson, S.L. (2011). *US and Cross-national Policies, Practices, and Preparation: Implications for successful instructional leadership, organizational learning, and culturally responsive practices.* New York: Springer.

Young, M. (2005). Letters. *Chronicle of Higher Education*, 51(34): A47.
Young, M., Tucker, P. & Orr, M.T. (2012). *University Council for Educational Administration (UCEA) Institutional and Program Quality Criteria*. UCEA Preparation Tool Kit series. Charlottesville, VA: University of Virginia Curry School of Education.

Chapter 5

Aguerrondo, I. & Vezub, L. (2011). Las instituciones terciarias de formación docente en Argentina. Condiciones institucionales para el liderazgo pedagógico. *Educar*, 47(2): 211–35.
Brazil Ministério da Educação (2011). Fundação Instituto Nacional de Estudos e Pesquisas Educacionais Anísio Teixeira. *Perfil do dirigente municipal de educação*, 2010. Brasília: INEP.
Casassus, J. (2007). *A escola e a desigualdade*. Brasília: Liber, UNESCO.
Cury, C.R.J. (2002). Gestão democrática da educação: exigências e desafios. *Revista Brasileira de Política e Administração da Educação*, 18(2): 163–74.
Donoso, S. (2011). El financiamiento de la educación pública chilena vía subsidio: consecuencias críticas sobre el rol del estado en educación. *FINEDUCA. Revista de Financiamento da Educação*, 1(1): 1–11.
Donoso, S., Benavides, N., Cancino, V., Castro, M. & López, L. (2012). Análisis crítico de las políticas de formación de directivos escolares en Chile: 1980–2010. *Revista Brasileira de Educação*, 17(49): 133–58.
Fernández Aguerre, T. (2004). De las 'escuelas eficaces' a las reformas educativas de 'segunda generación'. *Estudios Sociológicos*, 22(65): 377–408.
Galdames-Poblete, S. & Rodríguez-Espinosa, S. (2010). Líderes educativos previos a cargos directivos. Una nueva etapa de formación. *Revista Iberoamericana sobre Calidad, Eficacia y Cambio em Educación*, 8(4): 51–64.
Garostiaga, J.M. (2011). Participación y gestión escolar en Argentina y Brasil: una comparación de políticas subnacionales. *Revista Brasileira de Política e Administração da Educação*, 27(2): 249–64.
Gomes, C.A. (2005). *A educação em novas perspectivas sociológicas*, 4th edn. São Paulo: EPU.
Horn, A. & Marfán, J. (2010). Relación entre liderazgo educativo y desempeño escolar: revisión de la investigación en Chile. *Psicoperspectivas*, 9(2): 82–104.
Kracwczyk, N.R. & Vieira, V.L. (2008). *A reforma educacional na América Latina nos anos 1990: uma perspectiva histórico-sociológica*. São Paulo: Xamã.
Libâneo, J.C. (2007). Concepciones y prácticas de organización y gestión de la escuela: consideraciones introductorias para un examen crítico de la discusión actual en Brasil. *Revista Española de Educación Comparada*, 13: 155–91.
LLECE (Laboratório Latinoamericamo de Evaluación de la Calidad de la Educación) (2010). *Factores asociados al logro de los estudiantes de América Latina y el Caribe*. Santiago de Chile: UNESCO.
Machado, M. de F.E. (2013). *A escola e seus processos de humanização: implicações da gestão escolar e da docência na superação do desafio de ensinar a todos e a cada um dos estudantes*. Brasília: Líber, UNESCO.
Mella, O. (ed.) (2002). *Qualitative Study of Schools with Outstanding Results in Seven Latin American Countries*. Santiago de Chile: UNESCO.

Miranda M., Juan Carlos (2011). La eficacia en el contexto de las reformas educativas en América Latina y Colombia. *Revista Pensamiento Americano*, 2(6): 9–12.

Mizala, A. & Torche, F. (2010). Bringing the school back in: the stratification of educational achievement in the Chilean voucher system. *International Journal of Educational Development*, 32(1): 132–44.

OECD (Organization for Economic Cooperation and Development) (2009). *Teaching and Learning International Survey: TALIS 2009*. Available at: www.oecd.org/edu, accessed 2 May 2014.

OECD (Organization for Economic Cooperation and Development) (2011). School autonomy and accountability: are they related to student performance? *Pisa in Focus*, 9.

Parra Osorio, J.C. & Wodon, Q. (eds) (2011). *Escuelas religiosas en América Latina: estudios de caso sobre Fe y Alegría*. Washington, DC: The World Bank.

Sander, B. (1995). *Gestão da educação na América Latina: construção e reconstrução do conhecimento*. Campinas/SP: Autores Associados.

Soares, T.M., Fernandes, N.S., Nóbrega, M.C.M. & Melo, M.F.P.C. (2011). A gestão escolar e o Ideb da escola. *Revista Pesquisa e Debate em Educação*, 1(1): 38–56.

Souza, D.B. de (ed.) (2013). *Mapa dos conselhos municipais de educação no Brasil*. São Paulo: Loyola.

Torrecilla, F.J.M. & Carrasco, M.R. (2013). La distribución del tiempo de los directores de escuelas de educación primaria en América Latina. *Revista de Educación*, 361: 141–70.

Trojan, R.M. (2010). Estudo comparado sobre políticas educacionais na América Latina e a influência dos organismos multilaterais. *Revista Brasileira de Política e Administração da Educação*, 26(1): 55–74.

Velloso, J. (2000). Universidade na América Latina: rumos do financiamento. *Cadernos de Pesquisa*, 110: 39–66.

World Bank (2006). *Empréstimos para América Latina e Caribe – 2001–2006*. Previously available online.

Zibas, D. (2008). A revolta dos pingüins e o novo pacto educacional chileno. *Revista Brasileira de Educação*, 13(38): 199–220.

Chapter 6

Ambrosini, V. & Bowman, C. (2001). Tacit knowledge: some suggestions for operationalization. *Journal of Management Studies*, 38(6): 811–29.

Barber, M., Mourshed, M. & Chijioke, C. (2010). *Capturing the Leadership Premium: How the world's top school systems are building leadership capacity for the future*. London: McKinsey.

Beepat, R. (2013). From management to leadership: the case for reforming the practice of secondary education in Guyana, in P. Miller (ed.), *School Leadership in the Caribbean: Perceptions, practices and paradigms*. Didcot: Symposium Books.

Bissessar, C. (2013). Teacher professional development: a tool kit for Caribbean principals, in P. Miller (ed.), *School Leadership in the Caribbean: Perceptions, practices and paradigms*. Didcot: Symposium Books.

Brown, L. & Lavia, J. (2013). School leadership and inclusive education in Trinidad and Tobago: dilemmas and opportunities for practice, in P. Miller (ed.), *School Leadership in the Caribbean: Perceptions, practices and paradigms*. Didcot: Symposium Books.

Day, C. & Leithwood, K. (eds) (2007). *Successful School Principal Leadership in Times of Change: International Perspectives*. Dordrecht: Springer.

Day, C., Sammons, P., Hopkins, D. et al. (2009). *The Impact of School Leadership on Pupil Outcomes*. Research Summary Number DCSF-RS108. Nottingham: DCSF/NCSL.

Day, C., Sammons, P., Leithwood, K. et al. (2011). *Successful School Leadership: Linking with learning*. Buckingham: Open University Press.

Department for Education and Skills (2004) *School Leadership: End to end review of school-leadership policy and delivery*. London: DfES.

Earley, P. (2013). Foreword, in P. Miller (ed.), *School Leadership in the Caribbean: Perceptions, practices and paradigms*. Didcot: Symposium Books.

Fodor, J.A. (1968). The appeal to tacit knowledge in psychological explanation. *The Journal of Philosophy*, 65(20): 627–40.

Hallinger, P. & Heck, R.H. (2010). Leadership & student outcomes, in J. Robertson & H. Timperley (eds), *Leadership and Learning*. Thousand Oaks, CA: Sage.

Hallinger, P., & Lee, M. (2013). Mapping instructional leadership in Thailand: has education reform impacted principal practice? *Educational Management, Administration and Leadership*, 42(1): 6–29.

Harris, A (2006). Leading change in schools in difficulty, *Journal of Educational Change*, 7(1–2): 9–18.

Hildreth, P.M. & Kimble, C. (2002). The duality of knowledge. *Information Research*, 8(1): 27–39.

Hutton, D. (2013). High-performing Jamaican principals: understanding their passion, commitment and abilities, in P. Miller (ed.), *School Leadership in the Caribbean: Perceptions, practices and paradigms*. Didcot: Symposium Books.

James, T. (1980). Can the mountains speak for themselves? *Scisco Conscientia*, 3.

Kirk, D. & Jones, T (2004). *Effective Schools: Assessment Report*. London: Pearson Education.

Knight, V. (2014). The policy of universal secondary education: its influence on secondary schooling in Grenada. *Research in Comparative & International Education*, 9(1): 16–35.

Kolb, D.A. (1984). *Experiential Learning: Experience as the source of learning and development*. Englewood Cliffs, NJ: Prentice Hall.

Kowalski, T.J. (1995). Preparing teachers to be leaders: barriers in the workplace, in M.J. O'Hair & S.J. O'Dell (eds), *Educating Teachers for Leadership Change*. Thousand Oaks, CA: Sage.

Kruger, M. & Scheerens, J. (2012). Conceptual perspectives on school leadership, in J. Scheerens (ed.), *Leadership Effects Revisited: Review and meta-analysis of empirical studies*. Springer Education Briefs. London: Springer.

Leithwood, K. & Seashore-Louis, K. (2012). *Linking Leadership to Student Learning*. San Francisco: Jossey-Bass.

Leithwood, K., Day, C., Sammons, P., Harris, A. & Hopkins, D. (2006). *Successful School Leadership: What is it and how it influences pupil learning.* Research Report 800. Nottingham: Department for Education and Skills.

Lezotte, L. (2001). *Revolutionary and Evolutionary: The effective schools movement.* Okemos, MI: Effective Schools Products, Ltd.

McCallum, D. (2013). Teachers as leaders: building the middle leadership base in Jamaican schools, in P. Miller (ed.), *School Leadership in the Caribbean: perceptions, practices and paradigms.* Didcot: Symposium Books.

Mendels, P. (2012). *The Effective Principal: Five pivotal practices that shape instructional leadership.* New York: Wallace Foundation.

Miller, P. (2012). Editorial: The changing nature of educational leadership in the Caribbean and beyond. *Journal of the University College of the Cayman Islands*, 6: 1–3.

Miller, P. (ed.) (2013a). *School Leadership in the Caribbean: Perceptions, practices and paradigms.* Didcot: Symposium Books.

Miller, P. (2013b). *The Politics of Progression: Primary teachers' perceived barriers to gaining a principalship in Jamaica.* Research Report. Kingston: University of Technology, Jamaica and The Institute for Educational Administration & Leadership, Jamaica.

Miller, P. (2014). Editorial: Education for all in the Caribbean: promise, paradox and possibility. *Research in Comparative and International Education*, 9(1): 1–3.

Miller, P. & Hutton, D. (2014). Leading from 'within': towards a comparative view of how school leaders' personal values and beliefs influence how they lead in England and Jamaica, in S. Harris and J. Mixon (eds), *Building Cultural Community through Global Educational Leadership.* Ypsilanti, MI: NCPEA Publications.

NCSL (National College for School Leadership) (2001). *Leadership in Schools.* Available at: http://www.ncsl.org.uk/media/ECE/65/leadership-in-schools.pdf. Accessed 12 August 2014.

Pashiardis, P., Savvides, V., Lytra, E. & Angelidou, K. (2011). Successful school leadership in rural contexts: the case of Cyprus. *Educational Management Administration & Leadership*, 39(5): 536–54.

Polanyi, M. (1958). *Personal Knowledge: Towards a post-critical philosophy.* Chicago: University of Chicago Press.

Polanyi, M. (1966). *The Tacit Dimension.* Chicago: University of Chicago Press.

PricewaterhouseCoopers (2007). *Independent Study into School Leadership: A report for the DfES.* Research Report 818A. Nottingham: Department for Education and Skills.

Robinson, V., Hohepa, M. & Lloyd, C. (2009). *School Leadership and Student Outcomes: Identifying what works and why. Best Evidence Synthesis Iteration (BES).* Wellington: Ministry of Education.

Roofe, C. (2014). One size fits all: perceptions of the revised primary curriculum at grades one to three in Jamaica. *Research in Comparative & International Education*, 9(1): 4–15.

Shotte, G. (2013). School leadership for sustainable education: reflections on Montserrat, in P. Miller (ed.), *School Leadership in the Caribbean: Perceptions, practices and paradigms.* Didcot: Symposium Books.

Wallace Foundation (2012). *The School Principal as Leader: Guiding schools to better teaching and learning.* New York: The Wallace Foundation.

Chapter 7

Ärlestig, H., Johansson, O. & Day, C. (2015). *Research on Principals and Their Work – Cross Cultural Perspectives*. Dordrecht: Springer.

Ball, S.J. (2003). The teacher's soul and the terrors of performativity. *Journal of Educational Policy*, 18(2): 215–28.

Brauckmann, S. & Schwarz, A. (2014). Autonomous leadership and a centralised school system – an odd couple? Empirical insights from Cyprus. *International Journal of Educational Management*, 28(7): 823–41.

Day, C. & Armstrong, P. (2015). School leadership research in England, in H. Ärlestig, O. Johansson & C. Day (eds) *Research on Principals and Their Work – Cross Cultural Perspectives*. Dordrecht: Springer.

Day, C. & Leithwood, K. (2007). *Successful Principal Leadership in Times of Change*. Dordrecht: Springer.

EU Official Journal (2009). *The Professional Development of Teachers and School Leaders*, C 302/04.

Gu, Q. & Johansson, O. (2013). Sustaining school performance: school contexts matter. *International Journal of Leadership in Education*, 16(3): 301–26.

Halász, G. (2012). Policy cultures and education policy: a Central and Eastern European perspective, in K. Seashore Louis & B. van Velzen (eds) *Educational Policy in an International Context*. New York: Palgrave.

Hall, D. (2013). Drawing a veil over managerialism: leadership and the discursive disguise of the new public management. *Journal of Educational Administration and History*, 45(3): 267–82.

Hallinger, P., Lee, T.H.T. & Szeto, E. (2013). Review of research on educational leadership and management in Hong Kong, 1995–2012: Topographical analysis of an emergent knowledge base. *Leadership and Policy in Schools*, 12(3): 256–81.

Harris, A. (2008). *Distributed School Leadership: Developing tomorrow's leaders*. London: Routledge.

Höög, J. & Johansson, O. (2011). *Struktur, Kultur, Ledarskap förutsättningar för framgångsrika skolor*. [Structure, culture, leadership, prerequisites for successful schools]. Lund: Studentlitteratur.

Höög, J. & Johansson, O. (2014). *Framgångsrika skolor, mer om struktur, kultur, ledarskap* [Successful schools, more about structure, culture and leadership] Lund: Studentlitteratur.

Huber, S.G. (2010). *School Leadership – International Perspectives*. Dordrecht: Springer.

Huber, S.G. (2015). School leadership: research base in Switzerland, in H. Ärlestig, O. Johansson & C. Day (eds) *Research on Principals and Their Work – Cross Cultural Perspectives*. Dordrecht: Springer.

Huber, S.G. & Hiltmann, M. (2010). The recruitment and selection of school leaders – first findings of an international comparison, in S.G. Huber (ed.) *School Leadership – International Perspectives*. Dordrecht: Springer.

Koren, A. (2013). Accountabilities for equity and learning. Keynote article for European Policy Network on School Leadership, http://www.schoolleadership.eu/portal. Retrieved 10 July 2015.

Kukemelk, H. & Ginter, J. (2015). School leadership in Estonia 2001–2013, in H. Ärlestig, O. Johansson & C. Day (eds), *Research on Principals and Their Work – Cross Cultural Perspectives*. Dordrecht: Springer.

Lawn, M. & Grek, S. (2012). *Europeanizing Education: Governing a new policy space*. Southampton: Symposium Books.

Leithwood, K. & Seashore Louis, K. (2012). *Linking Leadership to Student Learning*. San Fransisco: Jossey-Bass.

Lumby, J. (2013). Longstanding challenges, new contexts: leadership for equality. *International Studies in Educational Administration*, 40(3).

Mac Ruaric, G. (2013). *Including Inclusion – Exploring inclusive education for school leadership*. Keynote article for European Policy Network on School Leadership, http://www.schoolleadership.eu/portal. Retrieved 10 July 2015.

Möller, J. (2011) Research on principals in Norway, in O. Johansson (ed.), *Rektor, en forskningsöversikt*. Stockholm: Vetenskapsrådet.

Nordin, A. & Sundberg, D. (2014). *Transnational Policy Flows in European Education: The making and governing of knowledge in the education policy field*. Oxford: Symposium Nooks.

Norman, R. (2015). Between civil service and republican ethics: the statist vision of leadership among French principals, in H. Ärlestig, O. Johansson & C. Day (eds) *Research on Principals and Their Work – Cross Cultural Perspectives*. Dordrecht: Springer.

Pashiardis, P. (2014). *Modeling School Leadership Across Europe*. Dordrecht: Springer.

Schratz, M. (2015). Overcoming a bureaucratic heritage as a trigger for research on leadership in Austria, in H. Ärlestig, O. Johansson & C. Day (eds) *Research on Principals and Their Work – Cross Cultural Perspectives*. Dordrecht: Springer.

Seashore Louis, K. & van Velzen, B. (2012). *Educational Policy in an International Context*. New York: Palgrave.

Uljens, M., Möller, J., Ärlestig, H. & Fredriksen, L.F. (2012). The professionalization of Nordic School Leadership, in L. Moos, (Ed.) *Transnational Influences on Values and Practice in Nordic Educational Leadership*. Dordrecht: Springer.

Chapter 8

Ayiro, L.P. (2014). Transformational leadership and school outcomes in Kenya: does emotional intelligence matter? *FIRE – Forum for International Research in Education,* 1(1): 26–49.

Bekker, C.J. (2007). Ubuntu leadership, http://www.regent.edu/acad/global/leadershiptalks/home.htm. Retrieved 12 January 2015.

Blasé, J., Blasé, J. & Philips, D. (2010). *Handbook of School Improvement*. Thousand Oaks, CA: Sage.

Bloch, G. (2009). *The Toxic Mix*. Cape Town: Tafelberg.

Bryk, A.S. & Schneider, B. (2002). *Trust in Schools: A core resource for improvement*. New York: Russell Sage Foundation.

Bush, T. & Glover, D. (2003). *School Leadership: Concepts and evidence*. Nottingham: National College for School Leadership.

Connole, H. (1998). The research enterprise, in *Research Methodologies in Education*. Study guide. Geelong: Deakin University.

Creswell, J.W. (2009). *Research Design: Qualitative, quantitative, and mixed methods approaches*. Thousand Oaks, CA: Sage.

Crow, M.G., Matthews, L.J. & McCleary, L.E. (1996). *Leadership: A relevant and realistic role for principals*. Larchmont: Eye on Education.

Davies, B. (ed.) (2005). *The Essentials of School Leadership*. London: Paul Chapman Publishing.

Day, C. & Schmidt, M. (2007). *Resilient Leadership*, in B. Davies (ed.), *Developing Sustainable Leadership*. London: Paul Chapman Publishing.

Derue, D.S., Nahrgang, J.D., Wellman, N. & Humphrey, S.E. (2011). Trait and behavioral theories of leadership: an integration and meta-analytic test of the irrelative validity. *Personnel Psychology*, 4(1): 7–52.

Drucker, P.E. (2001). *Management Challenges for the 21st Century*. New York: Harper Business.

Fleisch, B. (2008). *Primary Education in Crisis: Why South African schoolchildren underachieve in reading and mathematics*. Cape Town: Juta.

Glanz, J. (2006). *What Every Principal Should Know About Instructional Leadership*. Thousand Oaks, CA: Sage.

Goslin, K.G. (2009). How instructional leadership is conveyed by high school principals: the findings of three case studies. Paper presented at the International Congress for School Effectiveness and Improvement, Rotterdam, 6 January 2009.

Gunter, H.M. (2001). *Leaders and Leadership in Education*. London: Paul Chapman Publishing.

Harris, A. & Chapman, C. (2002). *Effective Leadership in Schools Facing Challenging Circumstances*. Nottingham: National College for School Leadership (NCSL).

Ibukun, W.O., Oyewole, B.K. & Abe, T.O. (2011). Personality characteristics and principal leadership effectiveness in Ekiti State, Nigeria. *International Journal of Leadership Studies*, 6(2): 247–60.

Joseph, M. (2011). ANAs: no surprise. Naptosa notes. *Gauteng Newsletter*, 4(1): 1–2.

Khoza, R.J. (2012). *Attuned Leadership: African Humanism as a Compass*. Johannesburg: Penguin Books.

Leithwood, K. & Riehl, C. (2003). *What We Know About Successful School Leadership*. Nottingham: National College for School Leadership, http://dcbsimpson.com/randd-leithwood-successful-leadership.pdf. Retrieved 31 July 2014.

Leithwood, K., Seashore, K., Anderson, S. & Wahlstrom, K. (2004). *How Leadership Influences Student Learning*. Minneapolis, MN: University of Minnesota.

Leithwood, K., Day, C., Sammons, P., Harris, A. & Hopkins, D. (2006). *Successful School Leadership: What it is and how it influences pupil learning*. Nottingham: National College for School Leadership, http://webarchive.nationalarchives.gov.uk/20130401151715/http://www.education.gov.uk/publications/eOrderingDownload/RR800.pdf. Retrieved 1 August 2014.

Luthans, F. (1988). Successful vs. effective managers. *The Academy of Management Executive*, 11(2): 127–32.

Masango, M. (2002). Leadership in the African context. *Verbum et Ecclesia* JRG, 23(3): 707–18.

McEwan, E.K. (2003). *10 Traits of Highly Effective Principals: From good to great performers*. Thousand Oaks, CA: SAGE Publishing.

McKechnie, J.L. (ed.) (1983). *Webster's New Universal Unabridged Dictionary*, 2nd edn. New York: Simon & Schuster.

McMillan, J.H. & Schumacher, S. (2006). *Research in Education: Evidence-based inquiry*. Boston, MA: Pearson/Allyn & Bacon.

Merriam, S.B. (1998). *Qualitative Research and Case Study Applications in Education*. San Francisco: Jossey-Bass.

Mestry, R. & Singh, P. (2007). Continuing professional development for principals: a South African perspective. *South African Journal of Education*, 27(3): 477–90.

Nahavandi, A. (2000). *The Art and Science of Leadership*. Upper Saddle River, NJ: Prentice Hall.

Podsakoff, P.M., MacKenzie, S.B., Moorman, R.H. & Fetter, R. (1990). Transformational leader behaviors and the effects on followers' trust in leader, satisfaction and organizational citizenship behaviors. *The Leadership Quarterly*, 1(2): 107–42.

Roe, W.H. & Drake, T.J. (1980). *The Principalship*, 2nd edn. New York: Macmillan.

Sergiovanni, T.J. (1984). Leadership and excellence in schooling. *The Education Digest*, October: 6–9.

Shenton, A.K. (2004). Strategies for ensuring trustworthiness in qualitative research projects. *Education for Information*, 22: 63–75.

Soanes, C. & Stevenson, A. (2004). *The Concise Oxford Dictionary*. Oxford: Oxford University Press.

Spillane, J.P. (2001). Investigating school leadership practice: a distributed perspective. *Educational Researcher*, 30(3): 23–8.

Tutu, A.D. (2004). *God Has a Dream*. New York: Doubleday.

Zaccaro, S.J., Kemp, C. & Bader, P. (2004). *Leader Traits and Attributes. The nature of leadership*. Thousand Oaks, CA: Sage.

Chapter 9

Bloom, D.E., Canning, D. & Finlay, J.E. (2010). Population aging and economic growth in Asia, in *The Economic Consequences of Demographic Change in East Asia, NBER-EASE, Volume 19*. Chicago: University of Chicago Press, 61–89.

Bryk, A.S. (2010). Organizing schools for improvement. *The Phi Delta Kappan*, 91(7): 23–30.

Bush, T. & Glover, D. (2012). Distributed leadership in action: leading high-performing leadership teams in English schools. *School Leadership and Management*, 32(1): 21–36.

Cheng, K.M. (1998). Can education values be borrowed? Looking into cultural differences. *Peabody Journal of Education*, 73(2): 11–30.

Cohen, L., Manion, L. & Morrison, K. (2007). *Research Methods in Education*, 6th edn. New York: Routledge.

Creswell, J.W. (2012). *Educational Research: Planning, conducting, and evaluating quantitative and qualitative research*. Boston, MA: Pearson.

Day, C. & Sammons, P. (2013). *Successful Leadership: A review of the international literature*. Reading: CFBT Education Trust.

Dimmock, C. & Walker, A. (2000). Introduction – justifying a cross-cultural comparative approach to school leadership and management. *School Leadership & Management*, 20(2): 137–41.

Drysdale, L. & Gurr, D. (2011). Theory and practice of successful school leadership in Australia. *School Leadership & Management*, 31(4): 355–68.

Education Bureau (2014a). *Education System and Policy*. Retrieved from http://www.edb.gov.hk/en/edu-system/list-page.html.

Education Bureau (2014b). *Direct Subsidy Scheme*. Retrieved from http://www.edb.gov.hk/ en/edu-system/primary-secondary/applicable-to-primary-secondary/direct-subsidy-scheme/featurearticle.html.

Goldring, E., Huff, J., May, H. & Camburn, E. (2008). School context and individual characteristics: what influences principal practice? *Journal of Educational Administration*, 46(3): 332–52.

Hallinger, P. (2011). Developing a knowledge base for educational leadership and management in East Asia. *School Leadership & Management*, 31(4): 305–20.

Hallinger, P. & Bryant, D.A. (2013a). Accelerating knowledge production on educational leadership and management in East Asia: a strategic analysis. *School Leadership & Management*, 33(3): 202–23.

Hallinger, P. & Bryant, D. (2013b). Mapping the terrain of educational leadership and management in East Asia. *Journal of Educational Administration*, 51(5): 618–37.

Hallinger, P. & Bryant, D. (2013c). Review of research publication on educational leadership and management in Asia: a comparative analysis of three regions. *Oxford Review of Education*, 39(3): 307–28.

Hallinger, P. & Chen, J. (2015). Review of research on educational leadership and management in Asia. A comparative analysis of research topics and methods, 1995–2012. *Educational Management Administration & Leadership*, 43(1): 5–27.

Hornby, G. & Lafaele, R. (2011). Barriers to parental involvement in education: an explanatory model. *Educational Review*, 63(1): 37–52.

Larocque, M., Kleiman, I. & Darling, S.M. (2011). Parental involvement: the missing link in school achievement. *Preventing School Failure: Alternative Education for Children and Youth*, 55(3): 115–22.

Lee, W.O. (1996). The cultural context for Chinese learners: conceptions of learning in the Confucian tradition, in D. Watkins & J.B. Biggs (eds), *The Chinese Learner: Cultural, psychological and contextual influences*. Melbourne and Hong Kong: Australian Council for Educational Research and the Comparative Education Research Centre, University of Hong Kong, 63–7.

Leithwood, K., Day, C., Sammons, P., Hopkins, D. & Harris, A. (2006). The nature of successful leadership practices, in *Successful School Leadership: What It Is and How It Influences Pupil Learning*. Nottingham: University of Nottingham, 18–44.

Marginson, S. (2011). Higher education in East Asia and Singapore: rise of the Confucian model. *Higher Education*, 61(5): 587–611.

Muijs, D., Ainscow, M., Dyson, A., Raffo, C., Goldrick, S. & Kerr, K. (2010). Leading under pressure: leadership for social inclusion. *School Leadership and Management*, 30(2): 143–57.

Ngcobo, T. & Tikly, L.P. (2010). Key dimensions of effective leadership for change: a focus on township and rural schools in South Africa. *Educational Management Administration and Leadership*, 38(2): 202–28.

Pashiardis, P. (2012). Guest editorial. *International Journal of Educational Management*, 26(5).

Pont, B., Nusche, D. & Moorman, H. (2008). *Improving School Leadership (Vol. 1: Policy and Practice)*. France: Organization for Economic Cooperation and Development.

Ross, J.A. & Berger, M.J. (2009). Equity and leadership: research-based strategies for school leaders. *School Leadership and Management*, 29(5): 463–76.

Szeto, E. (2014). From recipient to contributor: the story of a social justice leader in a Hong Kong primary school. *Management in Education*, 28(3): 116–19.

Tam, F.W.M. (2007). Rethinking school and community relations in Hong Kong. *The International Journal of Educational Management*, 21(4): 350–66.

Walker, A.D. & Dimmock, C. (2002). Moving school leadership beyond its narrow boundaries: developing a cross-cultural approach, in K. Leithwood & P. Hallinger (eds), *Second International Handbook of Educational Leadership and Administration*. Dordrecht: Springer, 67–204.

Walker, A., Hu, R. & Qian, H. (2012). Principal leadership in China: an initial review. *School Effectiveness and School Improvement*, 23(4): 369–99.

Yin, R.K. (2014). *Case Study Research: Design and Methods*, 5th edn. Los Angeles: Sage.

Yukl, G. (1989). *Leadership in Organizations*, 2nd edn. Englewood Cliffs, NJ: Prentice Hall.

Chapter 10

Anderson, M. & Cawsey, C. (2008). *Learning for Leadership* (Camberwell: ACER Press).

Bassett, G.W., Crane, A.R. & Walker, W.G. (1967). *Headmasters for Better Schools*, 2nd edn. St Lucia, Queensland: University of Queensland Press.

Beare, H., Caldwell B.J. & Millikan, R.H. (1989). *Creating an Excellent School*. London: Routledge.

Belchetz, D. & Leithwood, K. (2007). Does context matter and if so, how?, in K. Leithwood & C. Day (eds) *Successful School Leadership in Times of Change*. Dordrecht: Springer-Kluwer, 117–38.

Caldwell, B.J. and Harris, J. (2008). *Why Not the Best Schools?* Camberwell: ACER Press.

Caldwell, B.J. & Spinks J.M. (1992). *Leading the Self-Managing School*. London: Falmer Press.

Cotter, M. (2011). Examination of the Leadership Expectations of Curriculum Coordinators in the Archdiocese of Melbourne – A Case Study Approach. Doctoral thesis, University of Melbourne.

Cranston, N. (2009), Middle-level school leaders: understanding their roles and aspirations, in N. Cranston & L. Ehrich (eds), *Australian Educational Leadership Today*. Brisbane: Australian Academic Press, 217–41.

Crowther, F., Ferguson, M. & Hann, L. (2009). *Developing Teacher Leaders*, 2nd edn. Thousand Oaks, CA: Corwin Press.

Day, C. & Gurr, D. (eds) (2014). *Leading Schools Successfully: Stories from the field*. London: Routledge.

Dimmock, C. & O'Donoghue, T. (1997). Innovative school principals and restructuring, in *Life History Portraits of Successful Managers of Change*. London: Routledge.

Dinham, S. (2005). Principal leadership for outstanding educational outcomes. *Journal of Educational Administration*, 43(4): 338–56.

Dinham, S. (2007). The secondary head of department and the achievement of exceptional student outcomes. *Journal of Educational Administration*, 45(1): 62–79.

Dinham, S. (2008). *How to Get Your School Moving and Improving*. Camberwell: ACER Press.

Drysdale, L. (2001). Towards a model of market centred leadership. *Leading and Managing*, 7(1): 76–89.

Drysdale, L. (2002). A Study of Marketing and Market Orientation in Selected Victorian Schools of the Future. Unpublished doctor of philosophy thesis, University of Melbourne.

Drysdale. L. (2011). Evidence from the new cases in the International Successful School Principalship Project (ISSPP). *Leadership and Policy in Schools*, 10(4): 444–65.

Drysdale, L. & Gurr, D. (2011). The theory and practice of successful school leadership in Australia. *School Leadership and Management*, 31(4): 355–68.

Drysdale, L., Goode, H. & Gurr, D. (2011) Sustaining school and leadership success in two Australian schools, in L. Moos, O. Johansson & C. Day (eds), *How School Principals Sustain Success Over Time: International Perspectives*. Dordrecht: Springer-Kluwer, 25–38.

Duignan, P. & Gurr, D. (eds) (2007a). *Leading Australia's Schools*. Sydney: ACEL and DEST.

Duignan, P. & Gurr, D. (2007b). Hope for a better future, in P. Duignan & D. Gurr, (eds), *Leading Australia's Schools*. Sydney: ACEL and DEST, 157–64.

Duignan, P., Marshall, A.R., Harrold, R.I., Phillipps, D.M., Thomas, E.B. & Lane, T.J. (1985). *The Australian School Principal: A summary report*. Canberra: Commonwealth Schools Commission.

Fleming, J. & Kleinhenz, E. (2007). *Towards a Moving School*. Camberwell: ACER Press.

Gurr, D. (2008). Principal leadership: what does it do, what does it look like, and how might it evolve? *Monograph*, 42. Melbourne: Australian Council for Educational Leaders.

Gurr, D. (2009). Successful school leadership in Australia, in N. Cranston & L. Erlich (eds), *Australian Educational Leadership Today: Issues and trends*. Brisbane: Australian Academic Press, 369–94.

Gurr, D. (2012). Successful schools, successful leaders: the Australian case, in C. Day (ed.), *The Routledge International Handbook on Teacher and School Development*. London: Routledge, 458–67.

Gurr, D. & Drysdale, L. (2007). Models of successful school leadership: victorian case studies, in K. Leithwood & C. Day (eds), *Successful School Leadership in Times of Change*. Toronto: Springer, 39–58.

Gurr, D. & Drysdale, L. (2013). Middle-level school leaders: potential, constraints and implications for leadership preparation. *Journal of Educational Administration*, 51(1): 55–71.

Gurr, D. & Duignan, P. (2007). Leading Australia's schools, in P. Duignan & D. Gurr (eds), *Leading Australia's Schools*. Sydney: ACEL and DEST, 5–12.

Gurr, D., Drysdale, L. & Mulford, B. (2005). Successful principal leadership: Australian case studies, *Journal of Educational Administration*, 43(6): 539–51.

Gurr, D., Drysdale, L. & Mulford, B. (2006). Models of successful principal leadership. *School Leadership and Management*, 26(4): 371–95.

Gurr, D., Drysdale, L. & Goode, H. (2010). Successful school leadership in Australia: a research agenda, *The International Journal of Learning*, 17(4): 113–29.

Gurr, D., Drysdale, L., Clarke, S. & Wildy, H. (2014). High needs schools in Australia. *Management in Education*, 28(3): 86–90.

James, S. (ed.) (2012). *An Extraordinary School: Re-modelling special education*. Melbourne: ACER.

Keane, W. (2010). Case Studies in Learning Area Leadership in Catholic Secondary Schools in Melbourne, Australia. Doctoral thesis, University of Melbourne.

Leithwood, K. & Riehl, C. (2005). What we know about successful school leadership, in W. Firestone & C. Riehl (eds), *A New Agenda: Directions for Research on Educational Leadership*. New York: Teachers College Press, 22–47.

Leithwood, K., Day, C., Sammons, P., Harris, A. & Hopkins, D. (2006). *Seven Strong Claims about Successful School Leadership*. Nottingham: National College of School Leadership.

Lewis, M. & Andrews, D. (2007). The dance of influence: professional relationships evolve as teachers and administrators engage in whole school renewal, *Leading and Managing*, 13(1): 91–107.

Mulford, B. & Edmunds, B. (2009). *Successful School Principalship in Tasmania*. Launceston: Faculty of Education, University of Tasmania.

Mulford, B. & Silins, H. (2003). Leadership for organisational learning and improved student outcomes. *Cambridge Journal of Education*, 33(2): 175–95.

Mulford, W., Silins, H. & Leithwood, K. (2004). *Educational Leadership for Organisational Learning and Improved Student Outcomes*. Dordrecht: Kluwer Academic.

Mulford, B., Johns, S. & Edmunds, B. (2009). *Successful School Principalship in Tasmania: Case studies*. Launceston: Faculty of Education, University of Tasmania.

Notman, R. (ed.) (2011a). *Successful Educational Leadership in New Zealand: Case studies of schools and an early childhood centre*. Wellington: NZCER Press.

Notman, R. (2011b). Building leadership success in a New Zealand context, in R. Notman (ed.) (2011) *Successful Educational Leadership in New Zealand: Case studies of schools and an early childhood centre*. Wellington: NZCER Press, 135–52.

Notman, R. (2012). Intrapersonal factors in New Zealand school leadership success. *International Journal of Educational Management,* 26(5): 470–9.

Notman, R. (2014) A values-led principalship: the person within the professional, in C. Day & D. Gurr (eds), *Leading Schools Successfully: Stories from the field*. London: Routledge, 117–28.

Notman, R. & Henry, A. (2009). The human face of principalship: a synthesis of case study findings. *Journal of Educational Leadership, Policy and Practice*, 24(1): 37–52.

Notman, R. & Henry, A. (2011). Building and sustaining successful school leadership in New Zealand, *Leadership and Policy in Schools*, 10(4): 375–94.

Sergiovanni, T.J. (1991). *The Principalship – A Reflective Practice Perspective*, 3rd edn. Boston, MA: Allyn & Bacon.

Simpkins, W.S., Thomas, A.R, & Thomas, E.B. (eds) (1987). *Principal and Change: The Australian experience.* Armidale, NSW: University of New England.

Twelves, J.B. (2005). Putting Them in the Hands of God: A successful Christian School in Australia. Unpublished doctor of philosophy thesis, University of Melbourne.

White, P. (2000). The Leadership of Curriculum Area Middle Managers in Selected Victorian Government Secondary Schools. Doctoral thesis, University of Melbourne.

Chapter 11

Beteille, T., Kalogrides, D. & Loeb, S. (2011). *Stepping Stones: Principal career paths and student outcomes.* CALDER working paper 58. Washington, DC: Urban Institute.

Brookover, W. & Lezotte, L. (1979). *Changes in School Characteristics Coincident with Changes in Student Achievement.* East Lansing, MI: Institute for Research on Teaching.

Coleman, J., Campbell, E. Hobson, C., McPartland, J., Mood, A., Weinfeld, F. & York, R. (1966). *Equality of Educational Opportunity.* Washington, DC: US Government Printing Office.

Crowther, F., Kaagan, S., Ferguson, M. & Hann, L. (2002). *Developing Teacher Leaders: How teacher leadership enhances school success.* Thousand Oaks, CA: Corwin Press.

Day, C., Jacobson, S. & Johansson, O. (2011). Leading organisational learning and capacity building, in R. Ylimaki & S. Jacobson (eds), *U.S. and Cross-national Policies Practices and Preparation: Implications for successful instructional leadership, organizational learning, and culturally responsive practices.* Dordrecht: Springer-Kluwer, 29–49.

Edmonds, R. (1982). Programs of school improvement: an overview. *Educational Leadership*, 40(3): 4–11.

Fullan, M. (2001). *Leading in a Culture of Change.* San Francisco: Jossey-Bass.

Giles, C., Johnson, L., Brooks, S. & Jacobson, S. (2005). Building bridges, building community: transformational leadership in a challenging urban context. *Journal of School Leadership*, 15(5): 519–45.

Gronn, P. & Hamilton, A. (2004). A bit more life in the leadership: co-principalship as distributed leadership practice. *Leadership and Policy in Schools*, 3(1): 3–35.

Hallinger, P. (2003). Leading educational change: reflections on the practice of instructional and transformational leadership. *Cambridge Journal of Education*, 33(3): 329–51.

Hallinger, P. & Heck, R. (1996). Reassessing the principal's role in school effectiveness: a review of empirical research, 1980–1995. *Educational Administration Quarterly*, 32(1): 5–44.

Harris, A. (2002) *School Improvement – What's in it for schools?* London: Routledge Falmer.

Hopkins, D., Ainscow, M. & West, M. (1994) *School Improvement in an Era of Change.* London: Cassell.

Hoy, W. & Miskel, C. (2013). *Educational Administration: Theory, research and practice*, 9th edn. New York: McGraw-Hill.

Jacobson, S. (2005). The recruitment and retention of school leaders: understanding administrator supply and demand, in N. Bascia, A. Cumming, A. Datnow, K. Leithwood & D. Livingstone (eds), *International Handbook of Educational Policy*. London: Kluwer Press, 457–70.

Jacobson, S. (2011). School leadership and its effects on student achievement. *International Journal of Educational Management*, 25(1): 33–44.

Jacobson, S. & Battaglia, C. (2001). Authentic forms of teacher assessment and staff development in the US, in D. Middlewood & C. Cardno (eds), *Managing Teacher Appraisal and Performance: A comparative approach*. London: Routledge Falmer, 75–89.

Jacobson, S. & Bezzina, C. (2008). The effects of leadership on student academic/affective achievement, in G. Crow, J. Lumby & P. Pashiardis (eds), *The International Handbook on the Preparation and Development of School Leaders*. Thousand Oaks, CA: Sage, 80–102.

Jacobson, S. & Day, C. (2007). The International Successful School Principalship Project (ISSPP): an overview of the project, the case studies and their contexts. *International Studies in Educational Administration*, 35(3): 3–10.

Jacobson, S. & Schoenfeld, R. (2014). Leadership practices for sustained improvement in two high-need schools: understanding the importance of positional longevity and trust. Paper presented at the Commonwealth Council for Educational Administration and Management Conference, Fredericton New Brunswick, Canada.

Jacobson, S. & Szczesek, J. (2013). School improvement and urban renewal: the impact of a turn-around school's performance on real property values in its surrounding community. *Leadership and Policy in Schools*, 12(1): 1–11.

Jacobson, S., Brooks, S., Giles, C., Johnson, L. & Ylimaki, R. (2007). Successful leadership in three high poverty urban elementary schools, *Leadership and Policy in Schools*, 6(4): 1–27.

Jacobson, S., Johnson, L., Ylimaki, R. & Giles, C. (2009). Sustaining school success: A case for governance change. *Journal of Educational Administration*, 47(6): 753–64.

Johnson, L., Møller, J., Jacobson, S. & Wong, K.C. (2008). Cross-national comparisons in the International Successful School Principalship Project: the United States, Norway, and China. *Scandinavian Journal of Educational Research*, 52(4): 407–22.

Johnson, L., Møller, J., Pashiardis, P., Vedoy, G. & Savvides, V. (2011). Culturally responsive practices, in R. Ylimaki & S. Jacobson (eds), *U.S. and Cross-national Policies, Practices and Preparation: Implications for successful instructional leadership, organizational learning, and culturally responsive practices*. Dordrecht: Springer-Kluwer, 75–102.

Leithwood, K. (2005). Understanding successful principal leadership: progress on a broken front. *Journal of Educational Administration*, 43(6): 619–29.

Leithwood, K. (2012). Core practices: the four essential components of the leader's repertoire, in K. Leithwood & L. Louis (eds), *Linking Leadership to Student Learning*. San Francisco: Jossey-Bass, 57–67.

Leithwood, K. & Louis, K. (2012). *Linking Leadership to Student Learning*. San Francisco: Jossey-Bass.

Leithwood, K. & Riehl, C. (2005), What we know about successful school leadership, in W. Firestone & C. Riehl (eds), *A New Agenda: Directions for research on educational leadership*, New York: Teachers College Press.

Leithwood, K., Jacobson, S. & Ylimaki, R. (2011). Converging policy trends, in R. Ylimaki & S. Jacobson (eds), *U.S. and Cross-national Policies, Practices and Preparation: Implications for successful instructional leadership, organizational learning, and culturally responsive practices.* Dordrecht: Springer-Kluwer, 17–28.

Mascall, B. & Leithwood, K. (2012). Succession: a coordinated approach to leadership distribution, in K. Leithwood & K. Louis (eds), *Linking Leadership to Student Learning.* San Francisco: Jossey-Bass, 142–57.

Marzano, R., Waters, T. & McNulty, B. (2005). *School Leadership that Works: From research to results,* Alexandria, VA: Association for Supervision and Curriculum Development.

Minor-Ragan, Y. & Jacobson, S. (2014). In her own words: turning around an under-performing school, in C. Day & D. Gurr (eds), *Leading Schools Successfully: Stories from the field.* London: Routledge, 9–18.

Potter, D., Reynolds, D. & Chapman, C. (2002) School improvement for schools facing challenging circumstances: a review of research and practice. *School Leadership & Management,* 22(1): 243–26.

Rutter, M., Maughan, B., Mortimore, P. & Ouston, J. (1979) *Fifteen Thousand Hours.* London: Open Books.

Schoenfeld, R. (2013). Leadership and sustainability: continually making a difference as an educational leader over time, within challenging contexts, and changing times. Unpublished doctor of education thesis, University at Buffalo, State University of New York.

Silns, H. & Mulford, B. (2002) *Leadership and School Results: Second international handbook of educational leadership and administration.* Dordrect: Kluwer Press.

Silverman, R. (2014) Urban, suburban and rural contexts of school districts and neighborhood revitalization strategies: rediscovering equity in education policy and urban planning. *Leadership and Policy in Schools,* 13(1): 3–27.

Spillane, J., Camburn, E. & Pareja, A. (2007). Taking a distributed perspective to the school principal's workday. *Leadership and Policy in Schools,* 6(1): 103–25.

Tschannen-Moran, M. (2004). *Trust Matters: Leadership for successful schools.* San Francisco: Jossey-Bass.

Ylimaki, R., & Jacobson, S. (2013). School leadership practice and preparation: comparative perspectives on organizational learning (OL), instructional leadership (IL) and culturally responsive practices (CRP). *Journal of Educational Administration,* 51(1): 6–23.

Ylimaki, R., Jacobson, S. & Drysdale, L. (2007). Making a difference in challenging, high-poverty schools: successful principals in the US, England and Australia. *School Effectiveness and School Improvement,* 18(4): 361–81.

Ylimaki, R., Gurr, D., Moos, L., Kofod, K. & Drysdale, L. (2011). Democratic instructional leadership in Australia, Denmark and the United States, in R. Ylimaki & S. Jacobson (eds), *U.S. and Cross-national Policies, Practices and Preparation: Implications for successful instructional leadership, organizational learning, and culturally responsive practices.* Dordrecht: Springer-Kluwer, 51–74.

Chapter 12

Beepat, R. (2013). From management to leadership: the case for reforming the practice of secondary education in Guyana, in P. Miller & A. Minott (eds),

School Leadership in the Caribbean: Perceptions, Practices and Paradigms. Oxford: Symposium Books, 63–78.

Borden, M. (2002). School principals in Latin America and the Caribbean: leaders for change or subjects of change? Retrieved from http://www.iadb.org/wmsfiles/products/publications/documents/646204.pdf.

Brown, L. & Lavia, J. (2013). School leadership and inclusive education in Trinidad and Tobago: dilemmas and opportunities for practice, in P. Miller & A. Minott (eds), *School Leadership in the Caribbean: Perceptions, Practices and Paradigms*. Oxford: Symposium Books, 45–62.

Caesar, C. (2013). Leading in context: a review of leadership styles to inform school effectiveness in small island states. *European Journal of Sustainable Development*, 2(1): 1–18.

Cayman Islands Government (2005). National consensus on the future of education in the Cayman Islands. Retrieved from http://www.gov.ky/pls/portal/docs/Page/cighome/find/organisations/azagencies/meh/documents/edreport.pdf.

Davis, S., Darling-Hammond, L., LaPointe, M. & Meyerson, D. (2005). School leadership study: developing successful principals. Retrieved from https://edpolicy.stanford.edu/sites/default/files/publications/school-leadership-study-developing-successful-principals.pdf.

Fox, D.C. (2007). Inclusive education: approaches, scope and content. UNESCO International Bureau of Education Caribbean Symposium on Inclusive Education in Guyana, 5–7 December 2007, Kingston, Jamaica, http://www.ibe.unesco.org/fileadmin/user_upload/Inclusive_Education/Reports/kingston_07/guyana_inclusion_07.pdf.

Hutton, D. (2009). Decentralization of the public education system in Jamaica: learning from the experiences of local government and the public health sector. *Caribbean Journal of Education*, 31(2): 281–307.

Hutton, D. (2011a). Revealing the essential characteristics, qualities and behaviours of high performing principals: experiences of the Jamaican school system. Retrieved from file:///C:/Users/Disraeli%20Hutton/Downloads/m34881-1.4%20(3).pdf.

Hutton, D. (2011b). Profile of high-performing principals: some revelations of the Jamaican school system. *Journal of the University College of the Cayman Islands*, 5: 48–89.

Hutton, D.M. (2013). Leadership in practice: high performing principals in the Jamaican school system, in P. Miller & A. Minott (eds), *School Leadership in the Caribbean: Perceptions, Practices and Paradigms*. Oxford: Symposium Books, 79–103.

Jamaica Teaching Council (2009). *Professional Standards for the Education System in Jamaica*. Kingston: Ministry of Education.

Leithwood, K. (2005). Understanding successful principal leadership: progress on a broken front. *Journal of Educational Administration*, 43(6): 619–29. Retrieved from http://gse.buffalo.edu/gsefiles/documents/alumni/Fall08_Leithwood_Summary_Case_Studies.pdf.

Luthans, F. (2011). *Organizational Behaviour: An Evidence-based Approach*, 12th edn. New York: McGraw-Hill/Irwin.

Ministry of Education, Antigua and Barbuda (2012). *Draft Education Sector Plan 2013–2018*. Antigua: Ministry of Education.

Ministry of Education, Cayman Government Island (2013). *Cayman Islands Strategic Plan for Education 2012–2017*. Retrieved from http://www. education.gov.ky/pls/portal/docs/page/mehhome/education/strategicplan/ cayman%20islands%20strategic%20plan%20for%20education%202012- 2017%20-%20final_31.01.13.pdf.

Ministry of Education Report, Trinidad and Tobago (2008). *Forty-eighth Session of the International Conference on Education (ICE). National Report on the Development of Education in Trinidad and Tobago*. Trinidad and Tobago: Ministry of Education.

New Leaders (2011). New leaders urban excellence framework. Retrieved from http://www.newleaders.org/wp-content/uploads/2011/08/UEF-ConceptMaps1. pdf.

New Leaders for New Schools (2009). Principal effectiveness: a new principalship to drive student achievement, teacher effectiveness and school turnarounds. Retrieved from http://files.eric.ed.gov/fulltext/ED532065.pdf.

OECS (Organization of Eastern Caribbean States) (2012). *Education Sector Strategy 2012–2021*. Retrieved from http://www.oecs.org/uploads/ edmu/OECS-Education-Sector-Strategy-2012-21_web.pdf.

Stewart, V. (2013). School leadership around the world. *Educational Leadership*, 70(7): 48–54.

Task Force on Educational Reform (2005). *A Transformed Education System: Report,* revised edn. Kingston: Jamaica Information Service.

Wallace Foundation (2013). *The School Principal as Leader: Guiding Schools to Better Teaching and Learning*. Retrieved from http://www.wallacefoundation. org/knowledge-center/school-leadership/effective-principal-leadership/ Documents/The-School-Principal-as-Leader-Guiding-Schools-to-Better-Teaching- and-Learning-2nd-Ed.pdf.

Williams, C.W. & Fox, K. (2013). *Successful Schools in Jamaica: What do Successful Schools Look Like?* Kingston: Ministry of Education.

Chapter 13

Borich, G.D. (2015). *Observation Skills for Effective Teaching*, 7th edn. Boulder, CO: Paradigm.

Brauckmann, S. & Pashiardis, P. (2011). A validation study of the leadership styles of a holistic leadership theoretical framework. *International Journal of Educational Management*, 25(2): 11–32.

Daley, G. & Kim, L. (2010). *A Teacher Evaluation System that Works*. Working paper, National Institute for Excellence in Education, August 2010.

Danielson, C. (2011). Evaluations that help teachers learn. *Educational Leadership*, December 2010/January 2011: 35–9.

Davis, S., Darling-Hammond, L., LaPointe, M. & Meyerson, D. (2005). *School Leadership Study. Developing Successful Principals (Review of Research)*. Stanford, CA: Stanford Educational Leadership Institute.

Day, C., Harris, A., Hadfield, M., Tolley, H. & Beresfird, J. (2000). *Leading Schools in Times of Change*. Buckingham: Open University Press.

Döbert, H., Klieme, E. & Sroka, W. (eds) (2004). *Conditions of School Performance in Seven Countries*. Münster: Waxmann.

European Commission (2012). *Citizenship Education in Europe.* Brussels: Eurydice.

Faubert, V. (2009). *School Evaluation: Current practices in OECD countries and a literature review.* OECD Education Working Papers, No. 42. Paris: OECD Publishing.

Gold A., Evans, J., Earley, P., Halpin, D. & Collarbone, P. (2003). Principled principals? Values-driven leadership: evidence from ten case studies of 'outstanding' school leaders. *Educational Management & Administration,* 31(2): 127–38.

Gurr, D., Drysdale, L., Di Natale, E., Ford, O., Hardy, R, & Swann, R. (2003). Successful school leadership in Victoria: three case studies. *Leading and Managing,* 9(1): 18–37.

Hallinger, P. (2000). A review of two decades of research on the principalship using the Principal Instructional Management Rating Scale. Paper presented at the annual meeting of the American Educational Research Association, Seattle, WA.

Hallinger, P. (2011). Leadership for learning: lessons from 40 years of empirical research. *Journal of Educational Administration,* 49(2): 125–42.

Hanushek, E., Link, S. & Woessmann, L. (2012). *Does School Autonomy Make Sense Everywhere? Panel Estimates from PISA.* Retrieved from: http://www.adb.org/sites/default/files/economics-wp-296.pdf.

Hörner, W. & Döbert, H. (2007). The education systems of Europe – introductory methodological remarks, in W. Hörner (ed.), *The Education Systems of Europe.* Dordrecht: Süronger, 1–10.

Jacobson, S., Johnson, L., Ylimaki, R. & Giles, C. (2005). Successful leadership in challenging U.S. schools: enabling principles, enabling schools. *Journal of Educational Administration,* 43(6): 607–18.

Kühne, S. (2009). Conceptual principles in educational reporting. Keynote presentation at the fourth conference of the German Länder on 'Educational reporting – conception and realization'. 19 March 2009, Saechsisches Staatsministerium für Kultus.

Leithwood, K. & Jantzi, D. (2006). Transformational school leadership for large-scale reform: effects on students, teachers, and their classroom practices. *School Effectiveness and School Improvement,* 17(2): 201–27.

Levacic, R. (2008). Financing schools: evolving patterns of autonomy and control. *Educational Management Administration & Leadership,* 36(2): 221–34.

Marshall, K. (2012). Let's cancel the dog-and-pony show. *Phi Delta Kappan,* 94(3): 19–3.

National College for School Leadership (2010), 10 Strong Claims About Successful School Leadership. UK: National College for School Leadership.

OECD (Organization for Economic Cooperation and Development) (2010a). *Trends Shaping Education 2010.* Paris: OECD Publishing.

OECD (Organization for Economic Cooperation and Development) (2010b). *The High Cost of Low Educational Performance: The Long-run Economic Impact of Improving PISA Outcomes.* Retrieved from http://www.oecd.org.

Papay, J.P. (2012). Refocusing the debate: assessing the purposes and tools of teacher evaluation. *Harvard Educational Review,* 82(1): 123–41.

Pashiardis, P. & Savvides, V. (2011). The Interplay between instructional and entrepreneurial leadership styles in Cyprus rural primary schools. *Leadership and Policy in Schools,* 10(4): 412–27.

Pashiardis, P., Kafa, A. & Marmara, C. (2012). Successful secondary principalship in Cyprus: what have 'Thucydides' and 'Plato' revealed to us? *International Journal of Educational Management*, 26(5): 480–93.

Rolff, H.-G. (2009). Führung als Gestaltung und ihre Bedeutung für die Schulreform. In: *Die Deutsche Schule*, 101(3): S. 253–65.

Rosenthal, L. (2004). Do school inspections improve school quality? OFSTED inspections and school examination results in the UK. *Economics of Education Review*, 23(1): 143–51.

Ryan, K.E., Chandler, M. & Samuels, M. (2007). What should school-based evaluation look like? *Studies in Educational Evaluation*, 33(3): 197–212.

Sammons, P. (2009). The dynamics of educational effectiveness: a contribution to policy, practice and theory in contemporary schools. *School Effectiveness and School Improvement*, 20(1): 123–9.

Seashore Louis, K., Leithwood, K., Wahlstrom, K.L. & Anderson, S. (2010). *Learning from Leadership: Investigating the Links to Improved Student Learning: Final Report of Research to the Wallace Foundation*. Minneapolis, MN: University of Minnesota.

Stronge, J.H., Ward, T.J., Tucker, P.D. & Hindman, J.L. (2007). What is the relationship between teacher quality and student achievement? An exploratory study. *Journal of Personnel Evaluation in Education*, 20(3–4): 165–84.

Sullivan, S. & Glanz, J. (2009). *Supervision that Improves Teaching and Learning: Strategies and Techniques*, 3rd edn. New York: Corwin Press.

Thoonen, E.E.J., Sleegers, P.J.C., Oort, F.J., Peetsma, T.T.D. & Geijsel, F.P. (2011). How to improve teaching practices, the role of teacher motivation, organizational factors, and leadership practices. *Educational Administration Quarterly*, 47(3): 496–536.

Warwas, J. (2009): Berufliches Selbstverständnis und Beanspruchung in der Schulleitung. *Zeitschrift für Erziehungswissenschaft*, 12, S. 475–98.

Woessmann, L., Lüdemann, E., Schütz, G. & West, M.R. (2007). School accountability, accountability, autonomy, choice, and the level of student achievement: international evidence from PISA 2003. OECD Education Working Paper 13.

Woessmann, L., Luedemann, E., Schütz, G. & West, M. (2009). *School Accountability, Autonomy and Choice Around the World*. Cheltenham: Edward Elgar.

Chapter 14

Brauckmann, S. & Schwarz, A. (2014). Autonomous leadership and a centralised school system – an odd couple? Empirical insights from Cyprus. *International Journal of Educational Management*, 28(7): 823–41.

Brauckmann, S. & Pashiardis, P. (2011). A validation study of the leadership styles of a holistic leadership theoretical framework. *International Journal of Educational Management*, 25(1): 11–32.

Bredeson, P.V. & Johansson, O. (2000). The school principal's role in teacher professional development. *Journal of In-Service Education*, 26(2): 385–401.

Bredeson, P.V., Klar, H.W. & Johansson, O. (2011). Context-responsive leadership: examining superintendent leadership in context. *Education Policy Analysis Archives*, 19(18). Retrieved 29 March 2015 from http://epaa.asu.edu/ojs/article/view/739.

Cheng, Y.C. (1994). Principals' leadership as a critical indicator of school performance: evidence from multi-levels of primary schools. *School Effectiveness and School Improvement*, 5(3): 299–317.

Edmonds, R. (1979). Effective schools for urban poor. *Educational Leadership*, 37(1): 15–24.

Fuller, B. (1987). School effects in the Third World. *Review of Educational Research*, 57: 255–92.

Heck, R. & Hallinger, P. (2014). Modeling the longitudinal effects of school leadership on teaching and learning. *Journal of Educational Administration*, 52(5): 653–81.

Kythreotis, A., Pashiardis, P. & Kyriakides, L. (2010). The influence of school leadership styles and school culture on students' achievement in Cyprus primary schools. *Journal of Educational Administration*, 48(2): 218–40.

Leithwood, K., Patten, S. & Jantzi, D. (2010). Testing a conception of how school leadership influences student learning. *Educational Administration Quarterly*, 46(5): 671–706.

Levine, D.U. & Lezotte, L.W. (1990). *Unusually Effective Schools*. Madison, WI: The National Center for Effective Schools Research and Development.

Mortimore, P., Sammons, P., Ecob, R. & Stoll, L. (1988). *School Matters: The Junior Years*. Salisbury: Open Books.

Mulford, B. & Silins, H. (2011). Revised models and conceptualization of successful school principalship for improved student outcomes. *International Journal of Educational Management*, 25(1): 61–82.

Pashiardis, P. (1995). Cyprus principals and the universalities of effective leadership. *International Studies in Educational Administration*, 23(1): 16–26.

Pashiardis, P. (1998). Researching the characteristics of effective primary school principals in Cyprus. A qualitative approach. *Educational Management & Administration*, 26(2): 117–30.

Pashiardis, P. (2004). *Educational Leadership: From the Era of Benevolent Neglect to the Current Era*. Athens: Metaichmio Publications.

Pashiardis, P. (ed.) (2014). *Modeling School Leadership Across Europe: In Search of New Frontiers*. Dordrech: Springer.

Reynolds, D. & Cuttance, P. (1992). *School Effectiveness: Research, Policy and Practice*. London: Cassell.

Sammons, P., Day, C. & Ko, J. (2011). Exploring the impact of school leadership on pupil outcomes: results from a study of academically improved and effective schools in England. *International Journal of Educational Management*, 25(1): 83–101.

Schwarz, A. & Brauckmann, S. (2015). Between facts and perceptions: a multilevel approach to leadership in challenging school environments. Paper presented at the AERA conference, Chicago.

Seashore Louis, K., Leithwood, K., Wahlstrom, K.L. & Anderson, S. (2010). *Learning from Leadership: Investigating the Links to Improved Student Learning: Final Report of Research to the Wallace Foundation*. Minneapolis, MN: University of Minnesota.

Index